A SHORT HISTORY OF BATTLER BRITTON

You Yanks are a lucky lot.

Americans tend to look after their history a little better than the British, and the comics industry is no exception. Archive editions, masterworks, hardbacks and more, lovingly reproducing thousands of pages of classic American comics, are widely available and kept in print for future generations to enjoy. But what about us Brits?

Well, some *2000AD* stuff gets collected. The incomparable *Charley's War* is back in print at last, thank God. Otherwise you may try your luck on e-bay, because apart from the odd trade paperback or el cheapo magazine reprint, several decades' worth of wonderful British comics have been cast into publishing limbo.

One of the hundreds of characters lost in this way was WWII fighter pilot Robert Hereward Britton, known to friend and foe alike as "Battler." He first appeared in 1956 (in issue #361 of the weekly anthology *Sun*), created by writer Mike Butterworth and artist Geoff Campion. The stories were as simple and straightforward as the character: our plucky hero would shoot down half a dozen Messerchmitts, get shot down himself, thrash the Huns on the ground with the

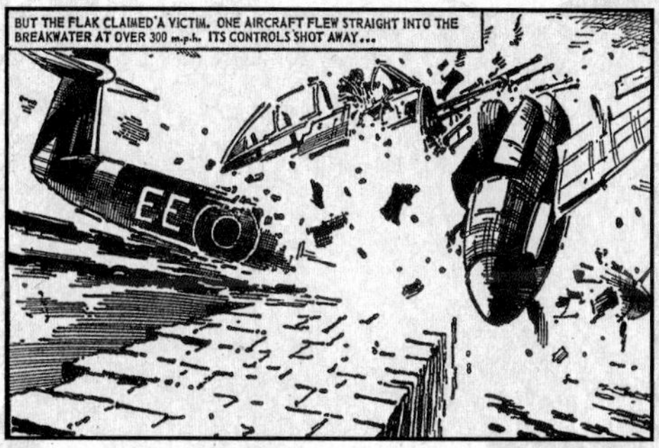
BUT THE FLAK CLAIMED A VICTIM. ONE AIRCRAFT FLEW STRAIGHT INTO THE BREAKWATER AT OVER 300 m.p.h. ITS CONTROLS SHOT AWAY...

Art by GRAHAM COTON

same cheerful enthusiasm as he had in the air, and escape back to Blighty in time for tea. And so he continued for around the next ten years, in various comics, under several creative teams.

Around the mid sixties, Battler found a new home in the highly successful *Air Ace Picture Library*. There were many *Picture Libraries*, little A5 size, 60-page black and white gems that any 30-plus British comics reader will remember. (I first encountered Battler in the *War* and *Battle* titles, reprinting his *Air Ace* appearances.) With no creator credits in the books, determining who wrote what is sometimes tricky, though Syd Bounds is known to have scripted several stories. Identifying artists is a little easier.

The great Francisco Solano Lopez drew Battler in his *Air Ace* days. So did Hugo Pratt, Victor Hugo Arias, Luis Bermejo, and many more. A young Carlos Pino handled some of the later stories. Best of all, to my mind, were British artists Ian Kennedy and Graham Coton. No one nailed the aircraft quite like Kennedy; no one captured the whirling, burning chaos of aerial combat in the manner Coton could.

The stories these men illustrated–the better ones, at any rate–seemed to have gotten just a little harsher. There was a certain darkness to them, a willingness to acknowledge the butcher's bill that comes with war. Battler's comrades could die quite suddenly, randomly, seemingly without meaning. Men might be driven to and past the breaking point. Battler himself continued much as he always had, though perhaps he smiled where once he laughed, cold calculation replacing out-and-out bravado. He might get tired, or even daunted; he would not throw his men's lives away against impossible odds. In the end, however, he remained indefatigable. Battler Britton always got the job done.

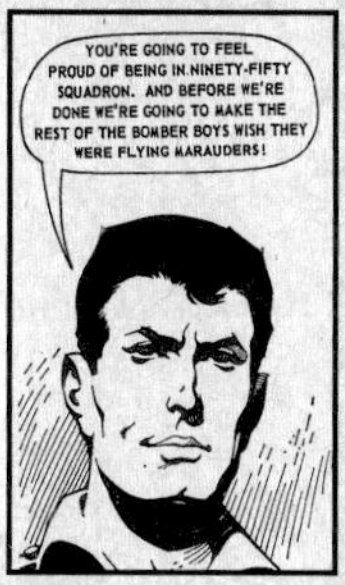
YOU'RE GOING TO FEEL PROUD OF BEING IN NINETY-FIFTY SQUADRON. AND BEFORE WE'RE DONE WE'RE GOING TO MAKE THE REST OF THE BOMBER BOYS WISH THEY WERE FLYING MARAUDERS!

Art by IAN KENNEDY

My own favourite amongst these tales is "False Glory" (*Air Ace #406*). Commanding a strike squadron engaged in sometimes lethal anti-shipping operations, Battler is assigned one Rupert Harding, a selfish, headstrong young pilot who seems to trade on his hero father's reputation. When the two are shot down into the freezing North Sea, Harding–believing neither man will last the night–reveals that his father won the Victoria Cross through deceit, having taken the credit for a dead man's actions. The pair survive, Battler with a new-found understanding of the troubled young man's personality. Harding is subsequently terribly wounded in a feat of incredible heroism, and when Battler visits him in hospital with a citation for the V.C., things come full circle. "Tear it up sir," says Harding. "Then that squares the family account. Do you understand?" And Battler does.

What you're now holding is–by my reckoning–the first all-new Battler Britton comic in well over 30 years, and I'm proud to play a part in bringing the character back from such a long retirement. It's a real pleasure to be working with Colin Wilson, whose superb draughtsmanship does so much to get "the old Battler" into the air once more. Maybe–just maybe, if enough of you come along for the ride–we might inspire enough interest for a collection of Battler's *Air Ace* adventures; with all those great stories, and all that fabulous art.

Be a damn shame to let them just rot.

- Garth Ennis, February 2006

(Thanks to David Roach, Andrew Sumner and Vic Whittle for their help in researching Battler's early appearances.)

CHAPTER 1

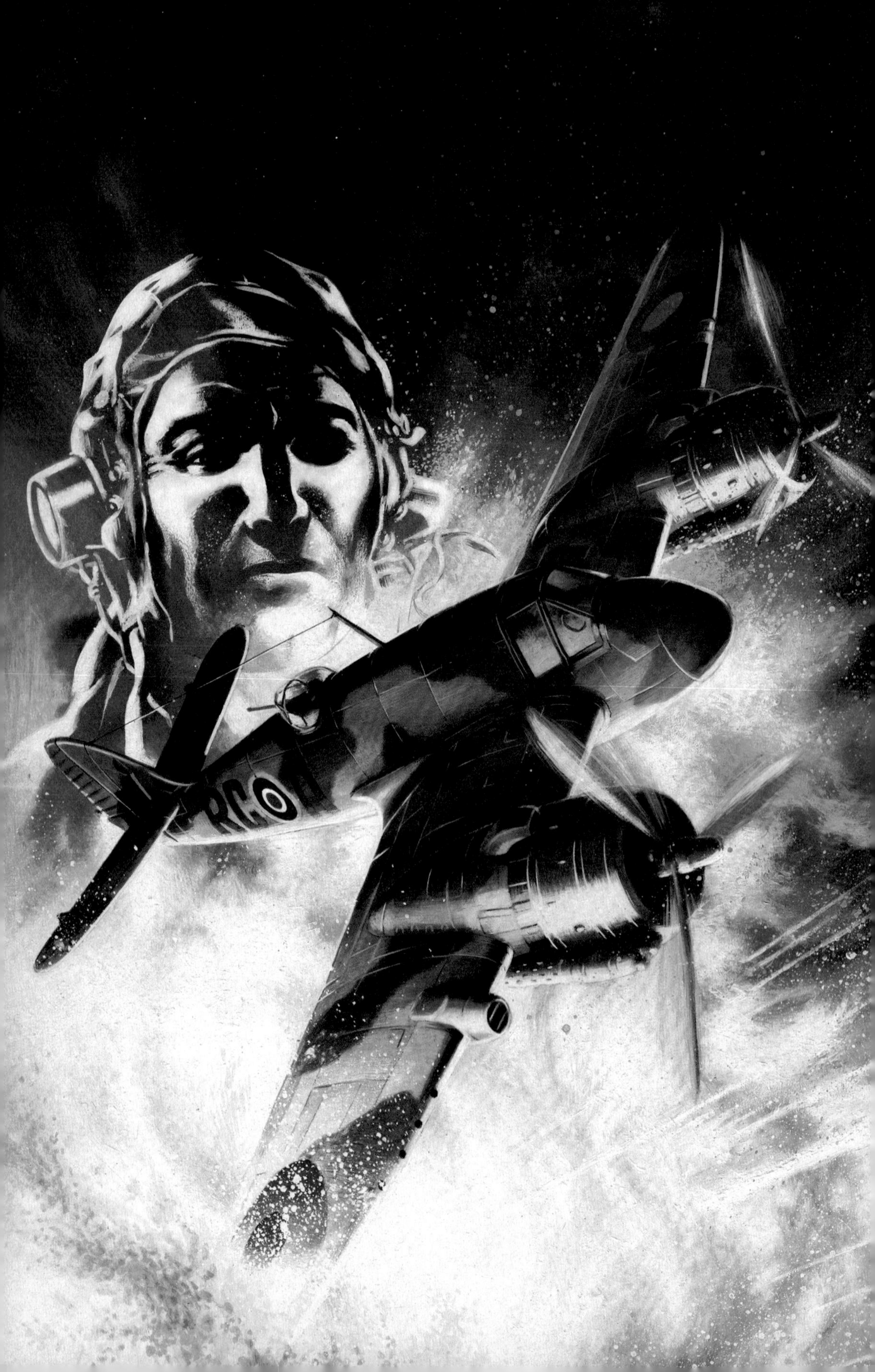

BATTLER BRITTON

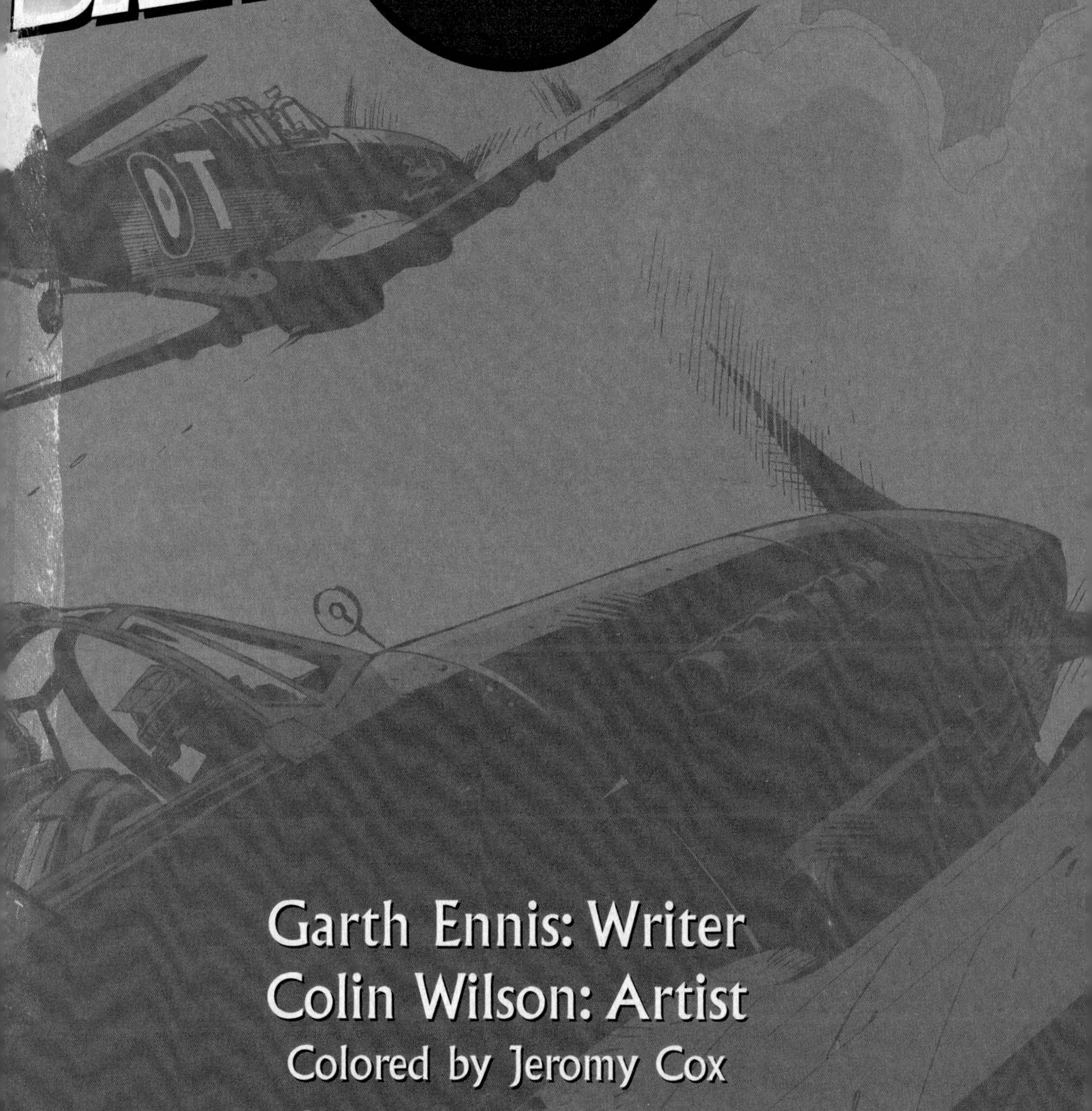

Garth Ennis: Writer

Colin Wilson: Artist

Colored by Jeromy Cox

Lettered by Rob Leigh

Original series covers by Garry Leach

Dedicated to Ian Kennedy and Graham Coton,
and to all the other artists and writers who made Battler fly.

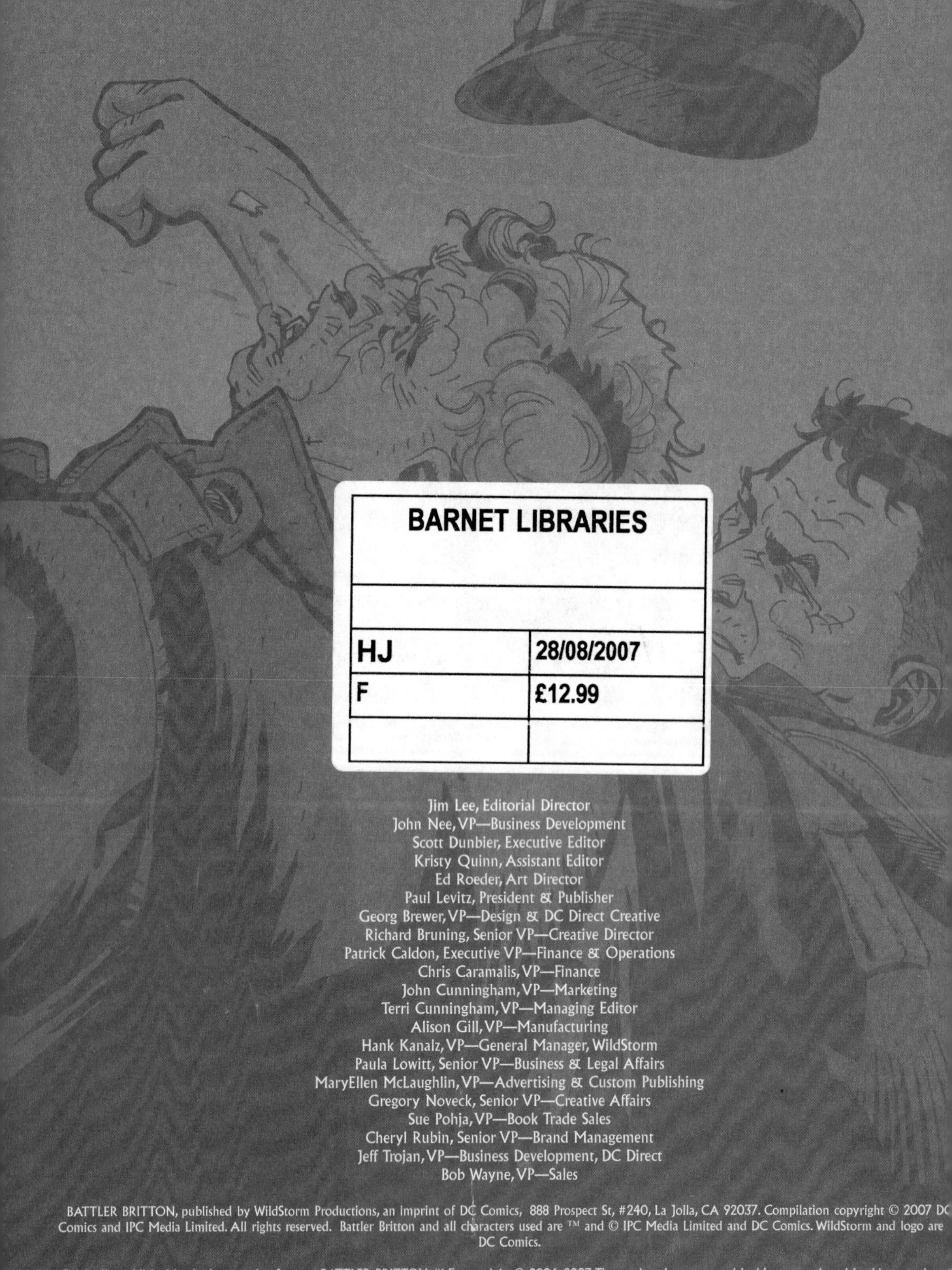

Jim Lee, Editorial Director
John Nee, VP—Business Development
Scott Dunbier, Executive Editor
Kristy Quinn, Assistant Editor
Ed Roeder, Art Director
Paul Levitz, President & Publisher
Georg Brewer, VP—Design & DC Direct Creative
Richard Bruning, Senior VP—Creative Director
Patrick Caldon, Executive VP—Finance & Operations
Chris Caramalis, VP—Finance
John Cunningham, VP—Marketing
Terri Cunningham, VP—Managing Editor
Alison Gill, VP—Manufacturing
Hank Kanalz, VP—General Manager, WildStorm
Paula Lowitt, Senior VP—Business & Legal Affairs
MaryEllen McLaughlin, VP—Advertising & Custom Publishing
Gregory Noveck, Senior VP—Creative Affairs
Sue Pohja, VP—Book Trade Sales
Cheryl Rubin, Senior VP—Brand Management
Jeff Trojan, VP—Business Development, DC Direct
Bob Wayne, VP—Sales

BATTLER BRITTON, published by WildStorm Productions, an imprint of DC Comics, 888 Prospect St, #240, La Jolla, CA 92037. Compilation copyright © 2007 DC Comics and IPC Media Limited. All rights reserved. Battler Britton and all characters used are ™ and © IPC Media Limited and DC Comics. WildStorm and logo are DC Comics.

Originally published in single magazine form as BATTLER BRITTON #1-5 copyright © 2006, 2007. The stories, characters and incidents mentioned in this magazine are entirely fictional. Printed on recyclable paper. WildStorm does not read or accept unsolicited submissions of ideas, stories or artwork. Printed in Canada.
DC Comics, a Warner Bros. Entertainment Company.

ISBN: 1-4012-1378-2
ISBN-13: 978-1-4012-1378-7

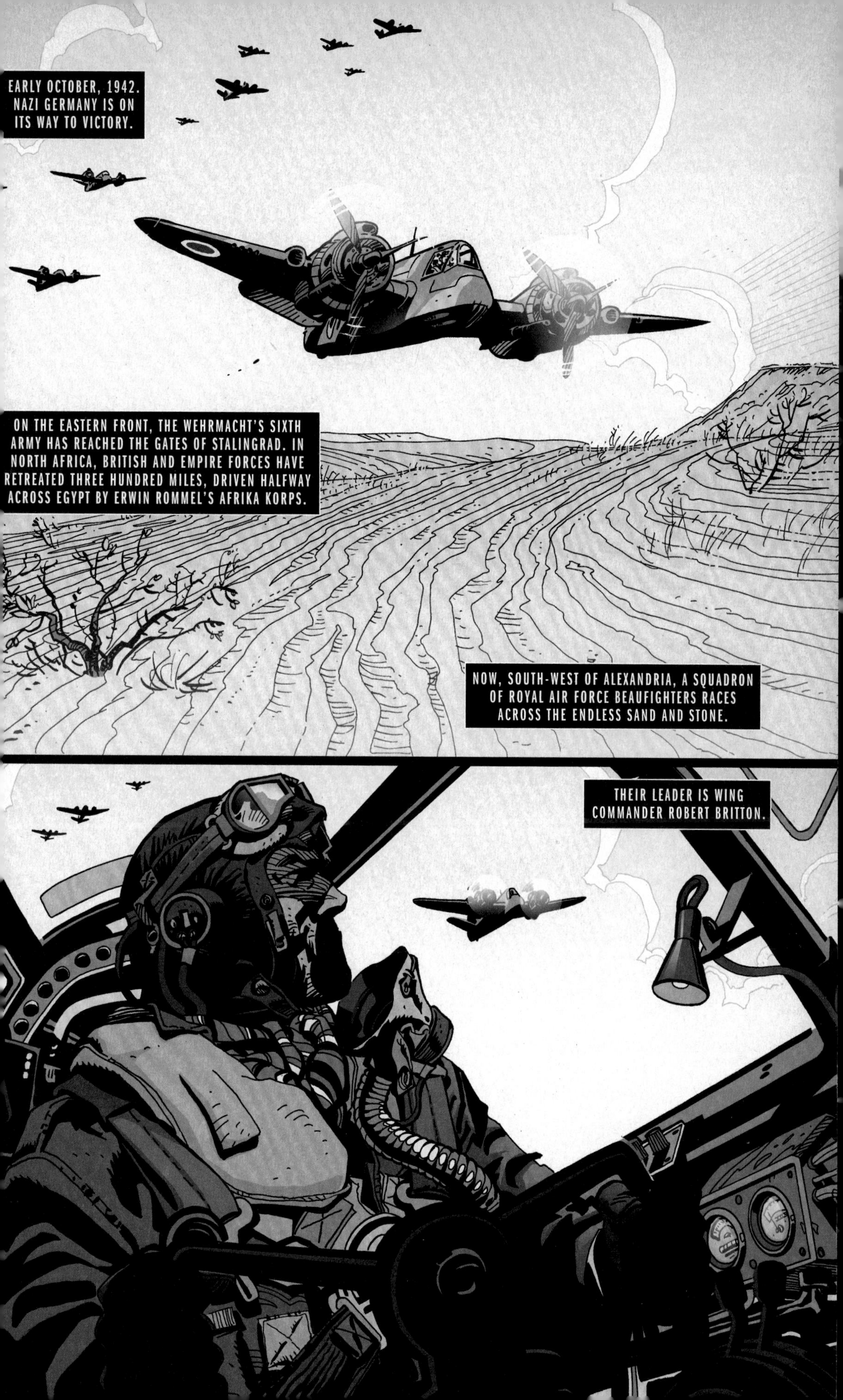
EARLY OCTOBER, 1942. NAZI GERMANY IS ON ITS WAY TO VICTORY.
ON THE EASTERN FRONT, THE WEHRMACHT'S SIXTH ARMY HAS REACHED THE GATES OF STALINGRAD. IN NORTH AFRICA, BRITISH AND EMPIRE FORCES HAVE RETREATED THREE HUNDRED MILES, DRIVEN HALFWAY ACROSS EGYPT BY ERWIN ROMMEL'S AFRIKA KORPS.
NOW, SOUTH-WEST OF ALEXANDRIA, A SQUADRON OF ROYAL AIR FORCE BEAUFIGHTERS RACES ACROSS THE ENDLESS SAND AND STONE.
THEIR LEADER IS WING COMMANDER ROBERT BRITTON.

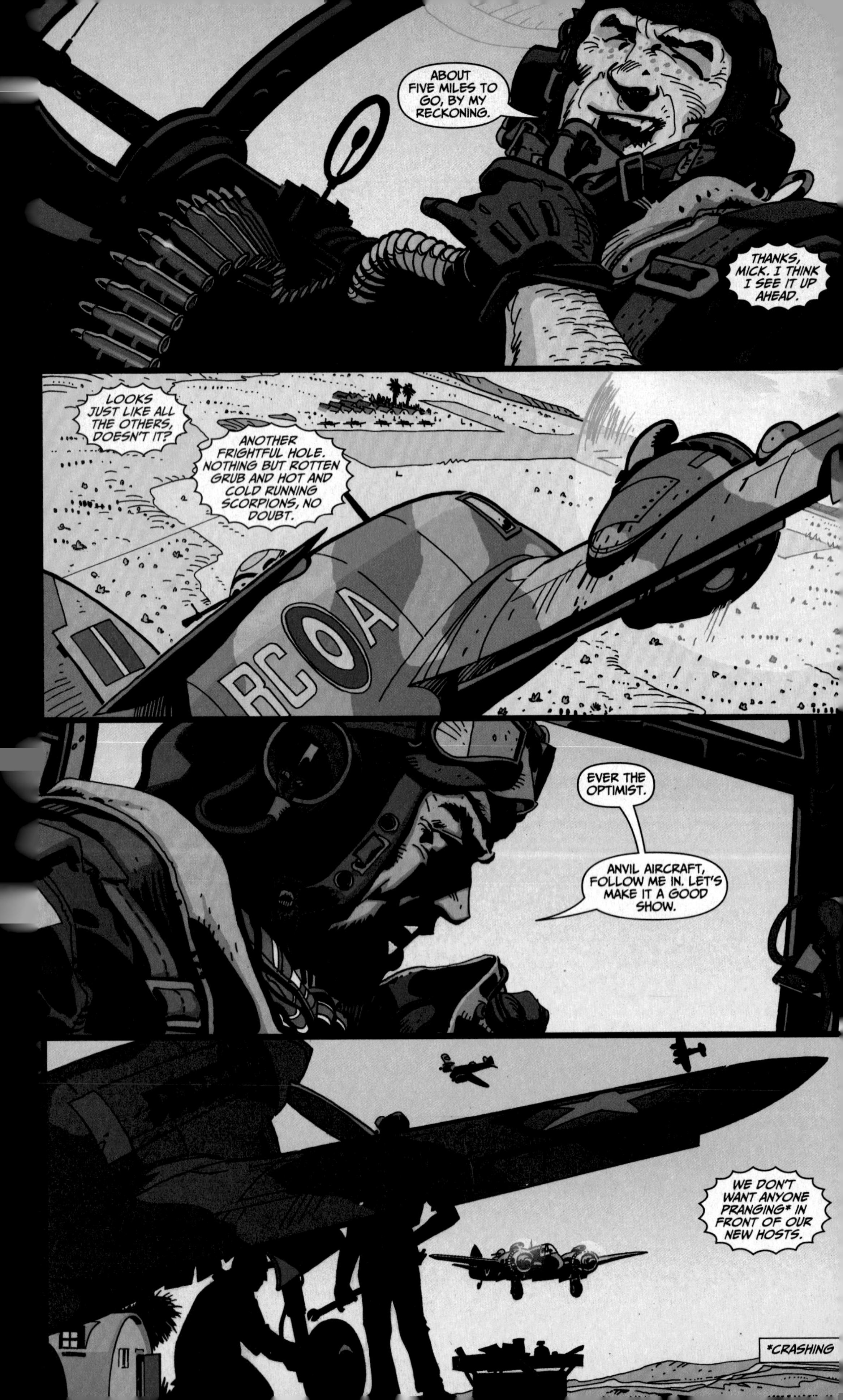
ABOUT FIVE MILES TO GO, BY MY RECKONING.
THANKS, MICK. I THINK I SEE IT UP AHEAD.
LOOKS JUST LIKE ALL THE OTHERS, DOESN'T IT?
ANOTHER FRIGHTFUL HOLE. NOTHING BUT ROTTEN GRUB AND HOT AND COLD RUNNING SCORPIONS, NO DOUBT.
RC A
EVER THE OPTIMIST.
ANVIL AIRCRAFT, FOLLOW ME IN. LET'S MAKE IT A GOOD SHOW.
WE DON'T WANT ANYONE PRANGING* IN FRONT OF OUR NEW HOSTS.
*CRASHING

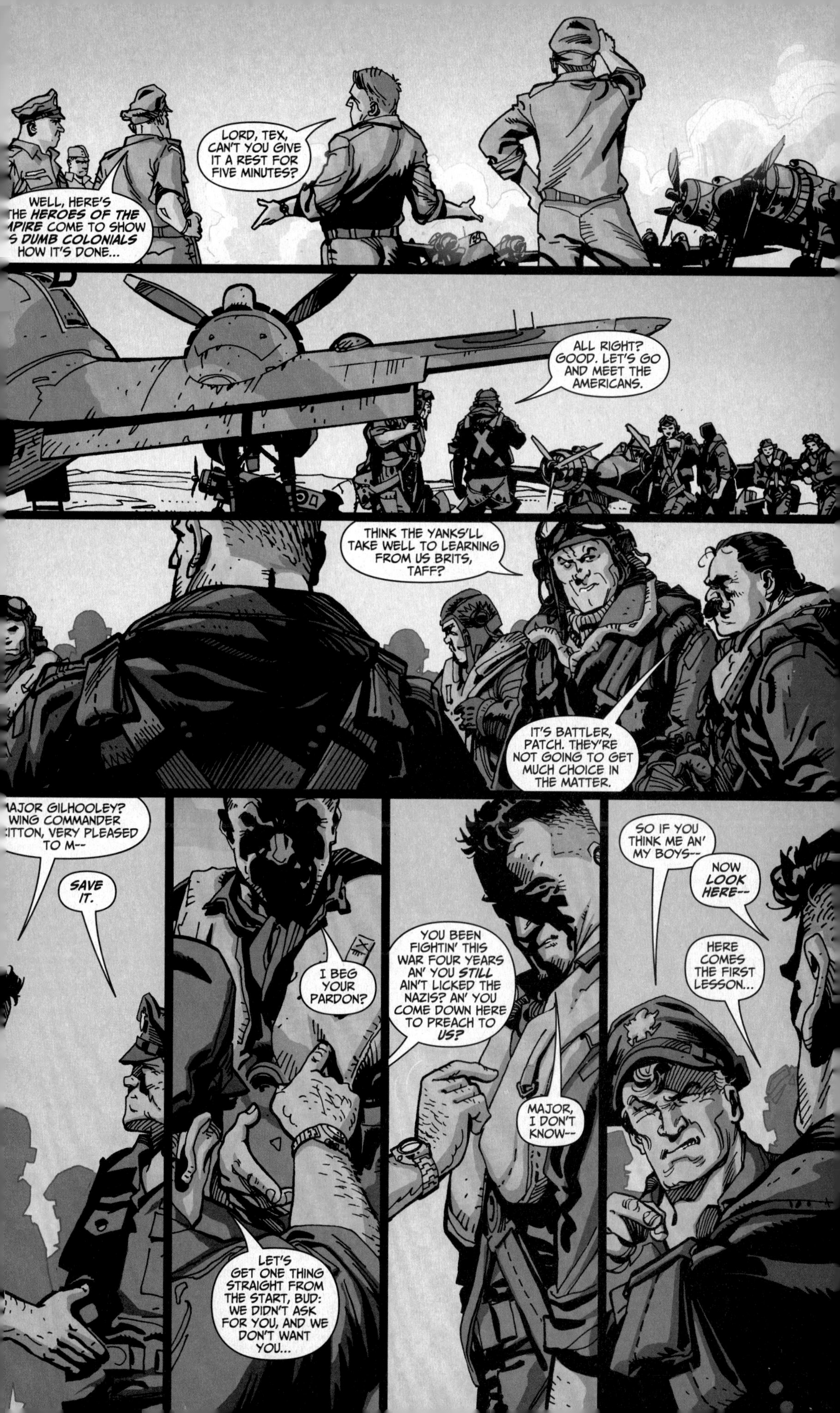

LORD, TEX, CAN'T YOU GIVE IT A REST FOR FIVE MINUTES?
WELL, HERE'S THE HEROES OF THE MPIRE COME TO SHOW S DUMB COLONIALS HOW IT'S DONE...
ALL RIGHT? GOOD. LET'S GO AND MEET THE AMERICANS.
THINK THE YANKS'LL TAKE WELL TO LEARNING FROM US BRITS, TAFF?
IT'S BATTLER, PATCH. THEY'RE NOT GOING TO GET MUCH CHOICE IN THE MATTER.
MAJOR GILHOOLEY? WING COMMANDER ITTON, VERY PLEASED TO M--
SAVE IT.
I BEG YOUR PARDON?
LET'S GET ONE THING STRAIGHT FROM THE START, BUD: WE DIDN'T ASK FOR YOU, AND WE DON'T WANT YOU...
YOU BEEN FIGHTIN' THIS WAR FOUR YEARS AN' YOU STILL AIN'T LICKED THE NAZIS? AN' YOU COME DOWN HERE TO PREACH TO US?
MAJOR, I DON'T KNOW--
SO IF YOU THINK ME AN' MY BOYS--
NOW LOOK HERE--
HERE COMES THE FIRST LESSON...

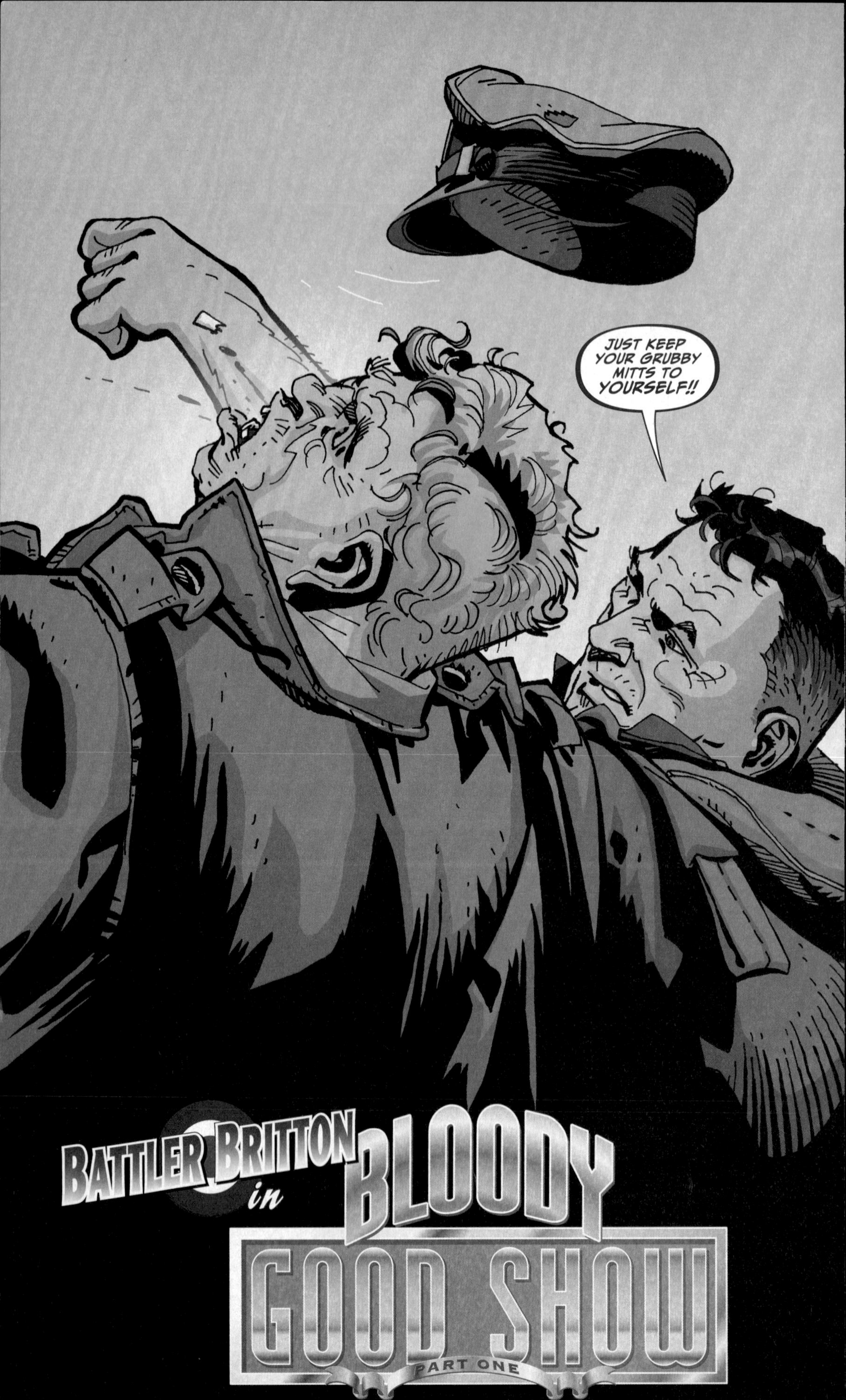
JUST KEEP YOUR GRUBBY MITTS TO YOURSELF!!
BATTLER BRITTON in
BLOODY GOOD SHOW
PART ONE

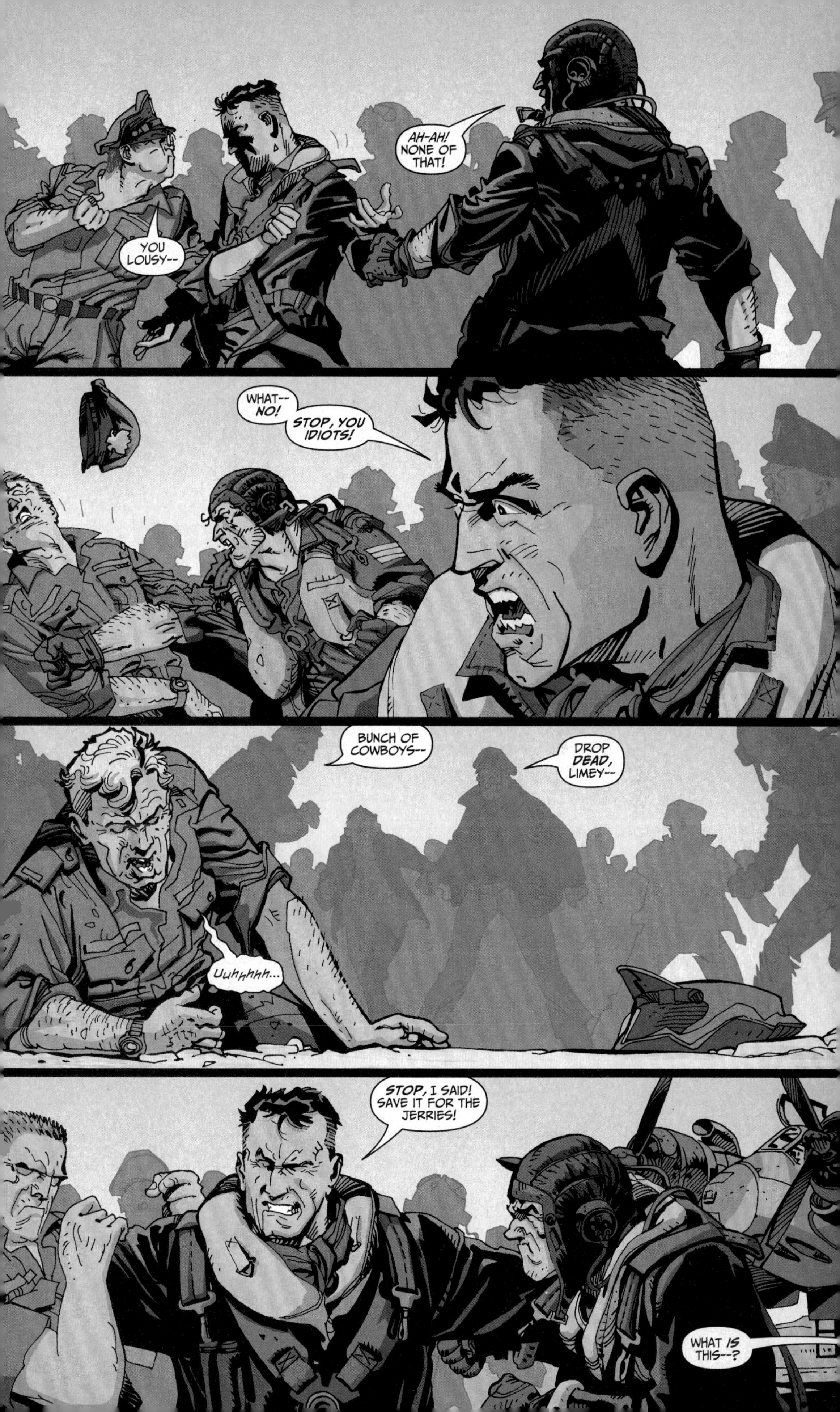
YOU LOUSY--
AH-AH! NONE OF THAT!
WHAT-- NO!
STOP, YOU IDIOTS!
BUNCH OF COWBOYS--
DROP DEAD, LIMEY--
Uuhhhhh...
STOP, I SAID! SAVE IT FOR THE JERRIES!
WHAT IS THIS--?

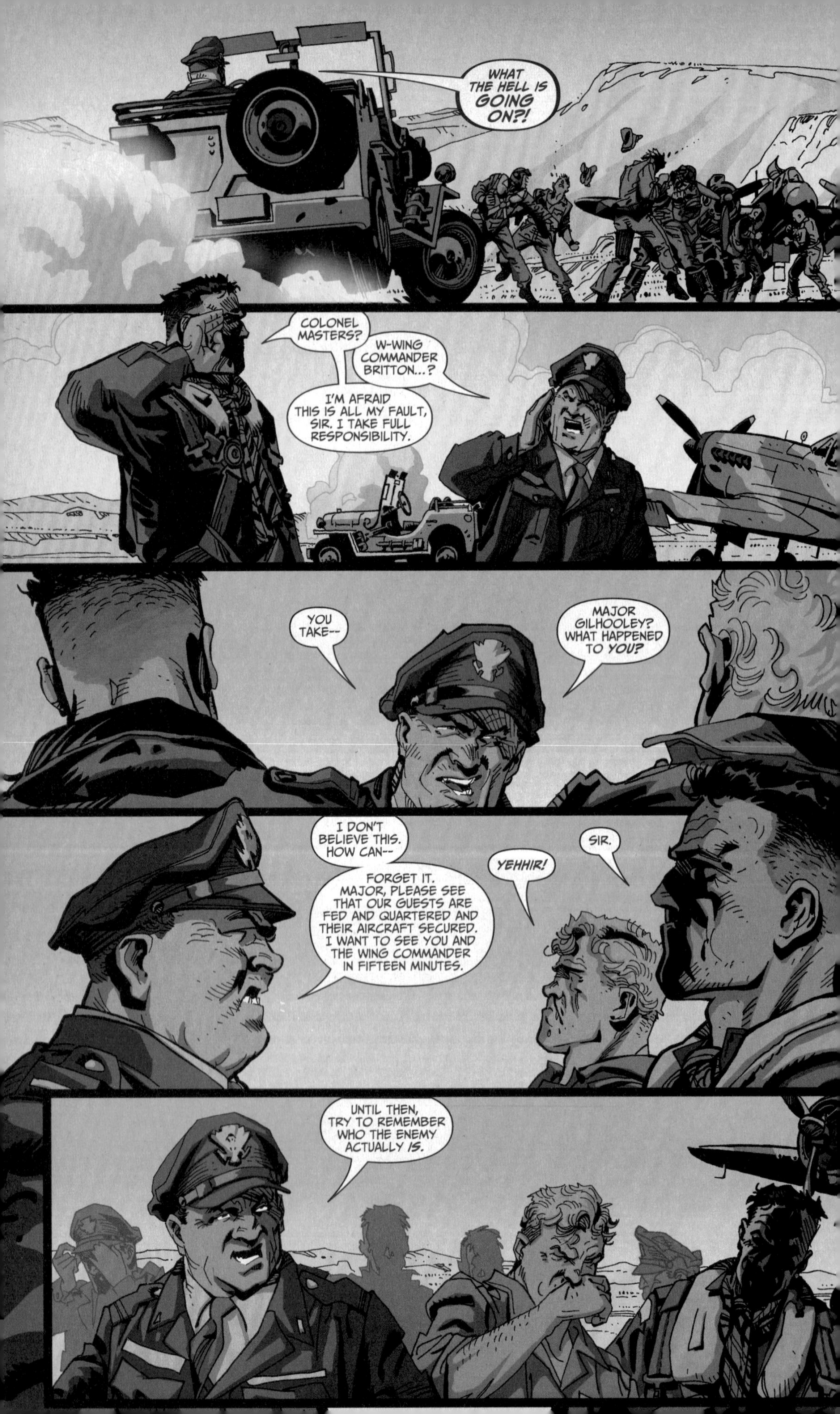
WHAT THE HELL IS GOING ON?!
COLONEL MASTERS?
W-WING COMMANDER BRITTON...?
I'M AFRAID THIS IS ALL MY FAULT, SIR. I TAKE FULL RESPONSIBILITY.
YOU TAKE--
MAJOR GILHOOLEY? WHAT HAPPENED TO YOU?
I DON'T BELIEVE THIS. HOW CAN--
FORGET IT. MAJOR, PLEASE SEE THAT OUR GUESTS ARE FED AND QUARTERED AND THEIR AIRCRAFT SECURED. I WANT TO SEE YOU AND THE WING COMMANDER IN FIFTEEN MINUTES.
YEHHIR!
SIR.
UNTIL THEN, TRY TO REMEMBER WHO THE ENEMY ACTUALLY IS.

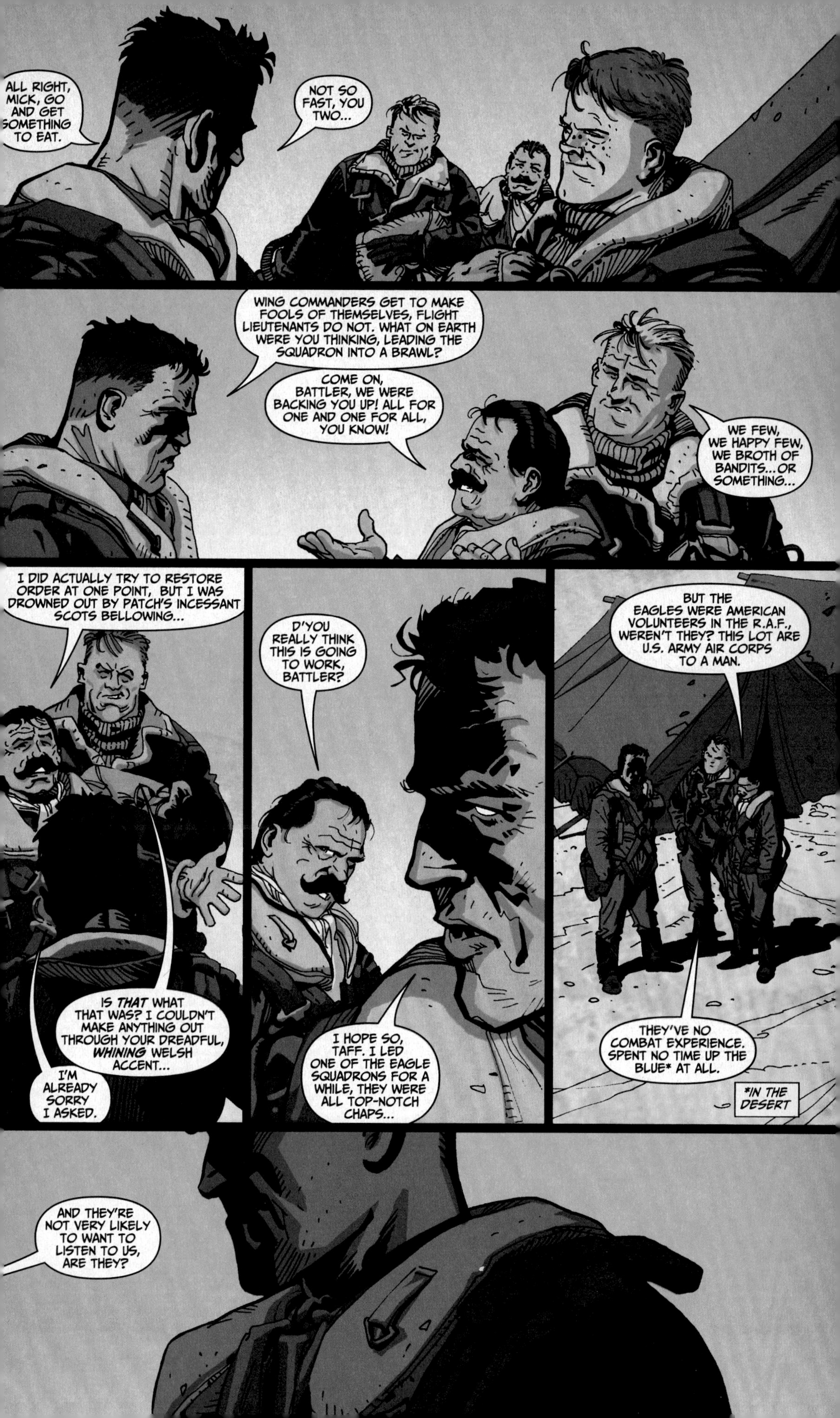
ALL RIGHT, MICK, GO AND GET SOMETHING TO EAT.
NOT SO FAST, YOU TWO...
WING COMMANDERS GET TO MAKE FOOLS OF THEMSELVES, FLIGHT LIEUTENANTS DO NOT. WHAT ON EARTH WERE YOU THINKING, LEADING THE SQUADRON INTO A BRAWL?
COME ON, BATTLER, WE WERE BACKING YOU UP! ALL FOR ONE AND ONE FOR ALL, YOU KNOW!
WE FEW, WE HAPPY FEW, WE BROTH OF BANDITS...OR SOMETHING...
I DID ACTUALLY TRY TO RESTORE ORDER AT ONE POINT, BUT I WAS DROWNED OUT BY PATCH'S INCESSANT SCOTS BELLOWING...
IS *THAT* WHAT THAT WAS? I COULDN'T MAKE ANYTHING OUT THROUGH YOUR DREADFUL, ***WHINING*** WELSH ACCENT...
I'M ALREADY SORRY I ASKED.
D'YOU REALLY THINK THIS IS GOING TO WORK, BATTLER?
I HOPE SO, TAFF. I LED ONE OF THE EAGLE SQUADRONS FOR A WHILE, THEY WERE ALL TOP-NOTCH CHAPS...
BUT THE EAGLES WERE AMERICAN VOLUNTEERS IN THE R.A.F., WEREN'T THEY? THIS LOT ARE U.S. ARMY AIR CORPS TO A MAN.
THEY'VE NO COMBAT EXPERIENCE. SPENT NO TIME UP THE BLUE* AT ALL.
*IN THE DESERT
AND THEY'RE NOT VERY LIKELY TO WANT TO LISTEN TO US, ARE THEY?

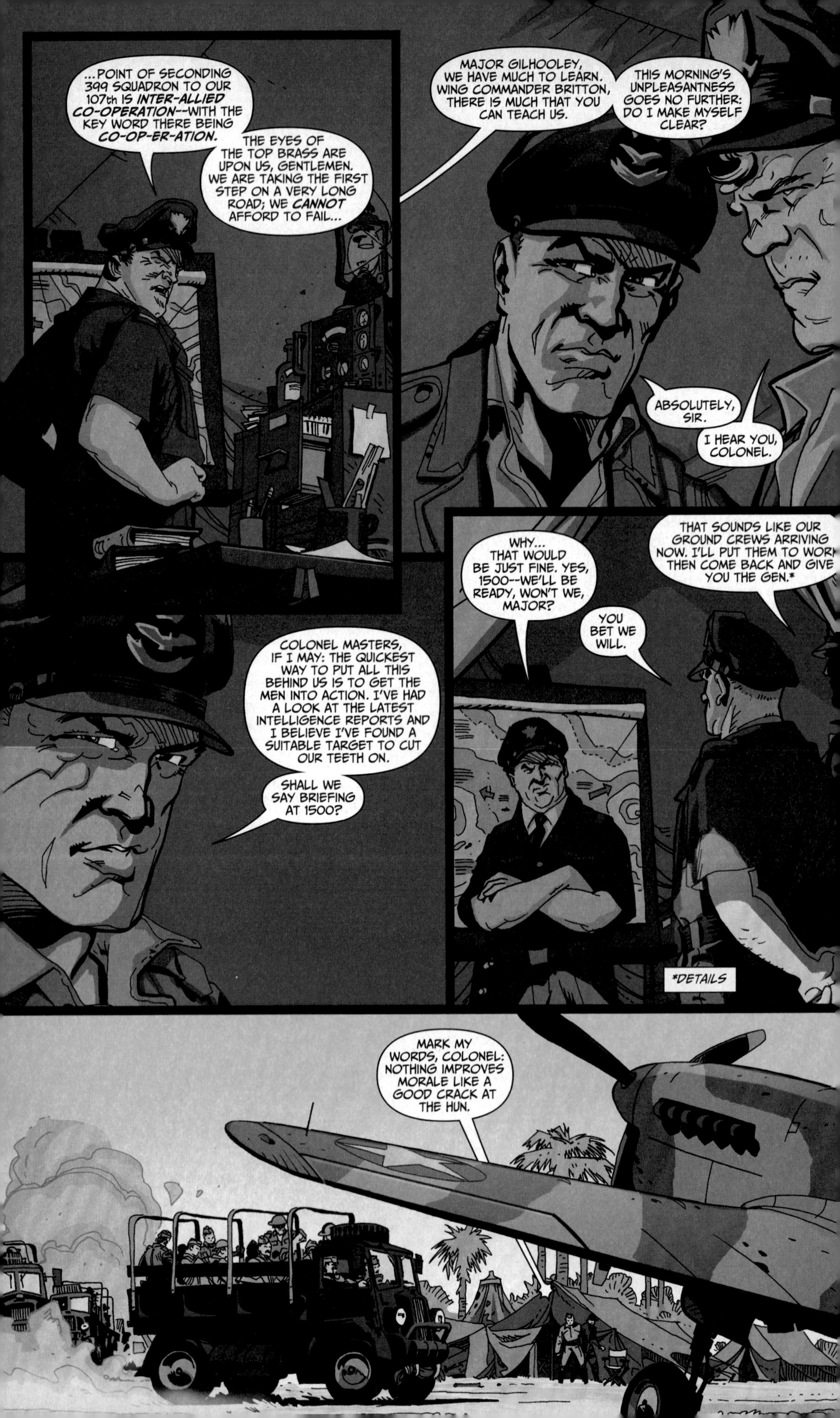
...POINT OF SECONDING 399 SQUADRON TO OUR 107th IS INTER-ALLIED CO-OPERATION--WITH THE KEY WORD THERE BEING CO-OP-ER-ATION.
THE EYES OF THE TOP BRASS ARE UPON US, GENTLEMEN. WE ARE TAKING THE FIRST STEP ON A VERY LONG ROAD; WE CANNOT AFFORD TO FAIL...
MAJOR GILHOOLEY, WE HAVE MUCH TO LEARN. WING COMMANDER BRITTON, THERE IS MUCH THAT YOU CAN TEACH US.
THIS MORNING'S UNPLEASANTNESS GOES NO FURTHER: DO I MAKE MYSELF CLEAR?
ABSOLUTELY, SIR.
I HEAR YOU, COLONEL.
COLONEL MASTERS, IF I MAY: THE QUICKEST WAY TO PUT ALL THIS BEHIND US IS TO GET THE MEN INTO ACTION. I'VE HAD A LOOK AT THE LATEST INTELLIGENCE REPORTS AND I BELIEVE I'VE FOUND A SUITABLE TARGET TO CUT OUR TEETH ON.
SHALL WE SAY BRIEFING AT 1500?
WHY... THAT WOULD BE JUST FINE. YES, 1500--WE'LL BE READY, WON'T WE, MAJOR?
YOU BET WE WILL.
THAT SOUNDS LIKE OUR GROUND CREWS ARRIVING NOW. I'LL PUT THEM TO WORK THEN COME BACK AND GIVE YOU THE GEN.*
*DETAILS
MARK MY WORDS, COLONEL: NOTHING IMPROVES MORALE LIKE A GOOD CRACK AT THE HUN.

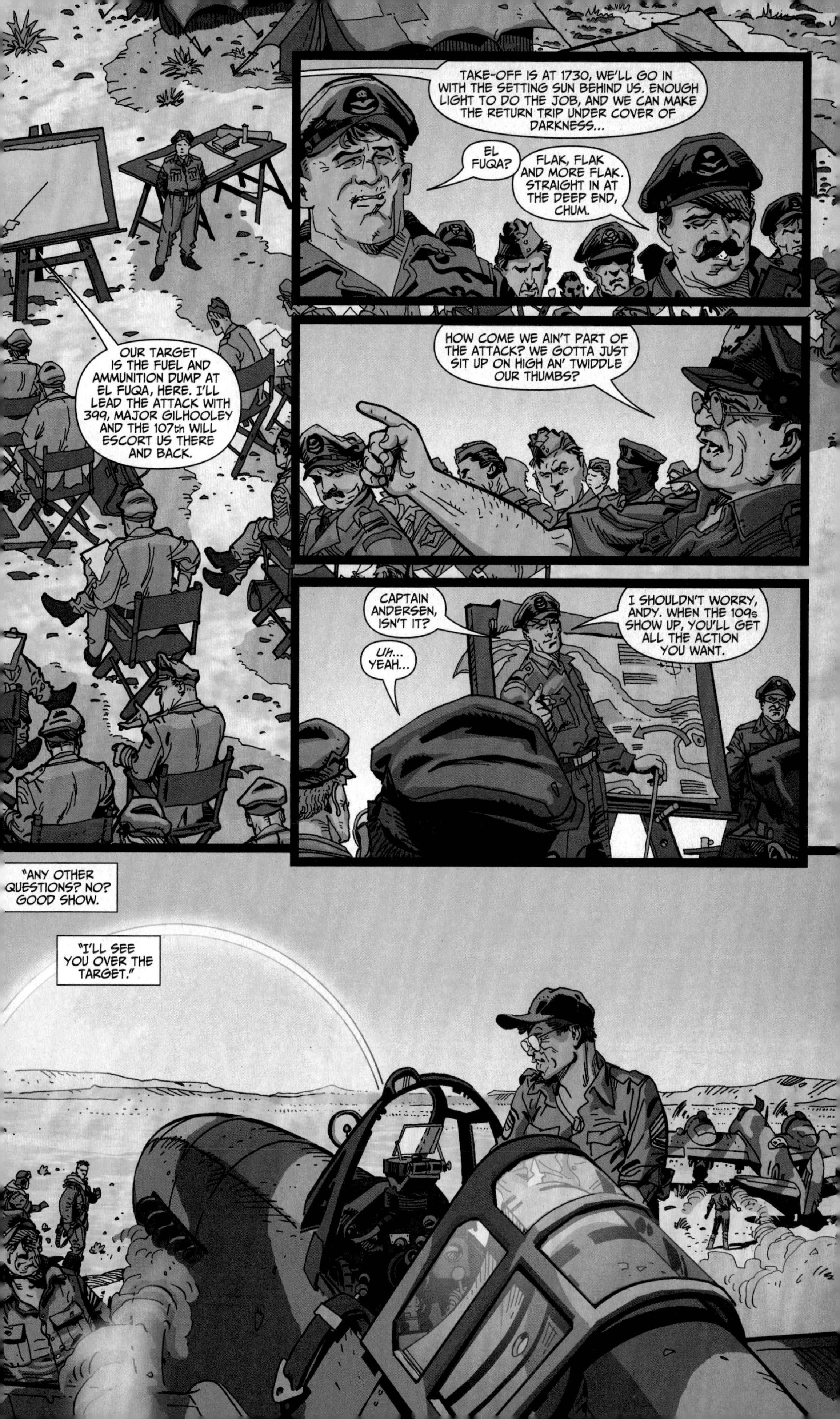
OUR TARGET IS THE FUEL AND AMMUNITION DUMP AT EL FUQA, HERE. I'LL LEAD THE ATTACK WITH 399, MAJOR GILHOOLEY AND THE 107th WILL ESCORT US THERE AND BACK.
TAKE-OFF IS AT 1730, WE'LL GO IN WITH THE SETTING SUN BEHIND US. ENOUGH LIGHT TO DO THE JOB, AND WE CAN MAKE THE RETURN TRIP UNDER COVER OF DARKNESS...
EL FUQA?
FLAK, FLAK AND MORE FLAK. STRAIGHT IN AT THE DEEP END, CHUM.
HOW COME WE AIN'T PART OF THE ATTACK? WE GOTTA JUST SIT UP ON HIGH AN' TWIDDLE OUR THUMBS?
CAPTAIN ANDERSEN, ISN'T IT?
UH... YEAH...
I SHOULDN'T WORRY, ANDY. WHEN THE 109s SHOW UP, YOU'LL GET ALL THE ACTION YOU WANT.
"ANY OTHER QUESTIONS? NO? GOOD SHOW.
"I'LL SEE YOU OVER THE TARGET."

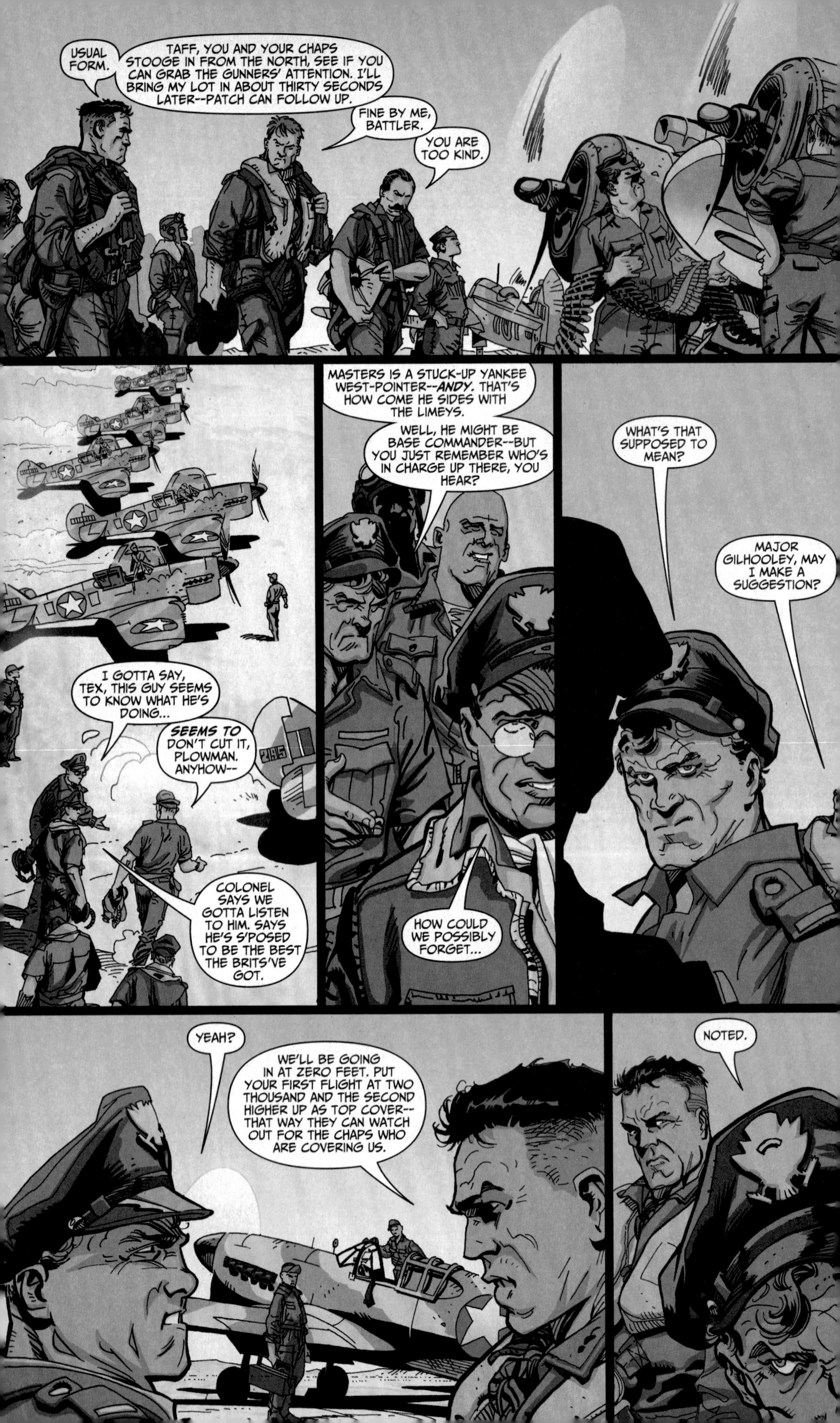
USUAL FORM.
TAFF, YOU AND YOUR CHAPS STOOGE IN FROM THE NORTH, SEE IF YOU CAN GRAB THE GUNNERS' ATTENTION. I'LL BRING MY LOT IN ABOUT THIRTY SECONDS LATER--PATCH CAN FOLLOW UP.
FINE BY ME, BATTLER.
YOU ARE TOO KIND.
I GOTTA SAY, TEX, THIS GUY SEEMS TO KNOW WHAT HE'S DOING...
SEEMS TO DON'T CUT IT, PLOWMAN. ANYHOW--
COLONEL SAYS WE GOTTA LISTEN TO HIM. SAYS HE'S S'POSED TO BE THE BEST THE BRITS'VE GOT.
MASTERS IS A STUCK-UP YANKEE WEST-POINTER--ANDY. THAT'S HOW COME HE SIDES WITH THE LIMEYS.
WELL, HE MIGHT BE BASE COMMANDER--BUT YOU JUST REMEMBER WHO'S IN CHARGE UP THERE, YOU HEAR?
HOW COULD WE POSSIBLY FORGET...
WHAT'S THAT SUPPOSED TO MEAN?
MAJOR GILHOOLEY, MAY I MAKE A SUGGESTION?
YEAH?
WE'LL BE GOING IN AT ZERO FEET. PUT YOUR FIRST FLIGHT AT TWO THOUSAND AND THE SECOND HIGHER UP AS TOP COVER--THAT WAY THEY CAN WATCH OUT FOR THE CHAPS WHO ARE COVERING US.
NOTED.

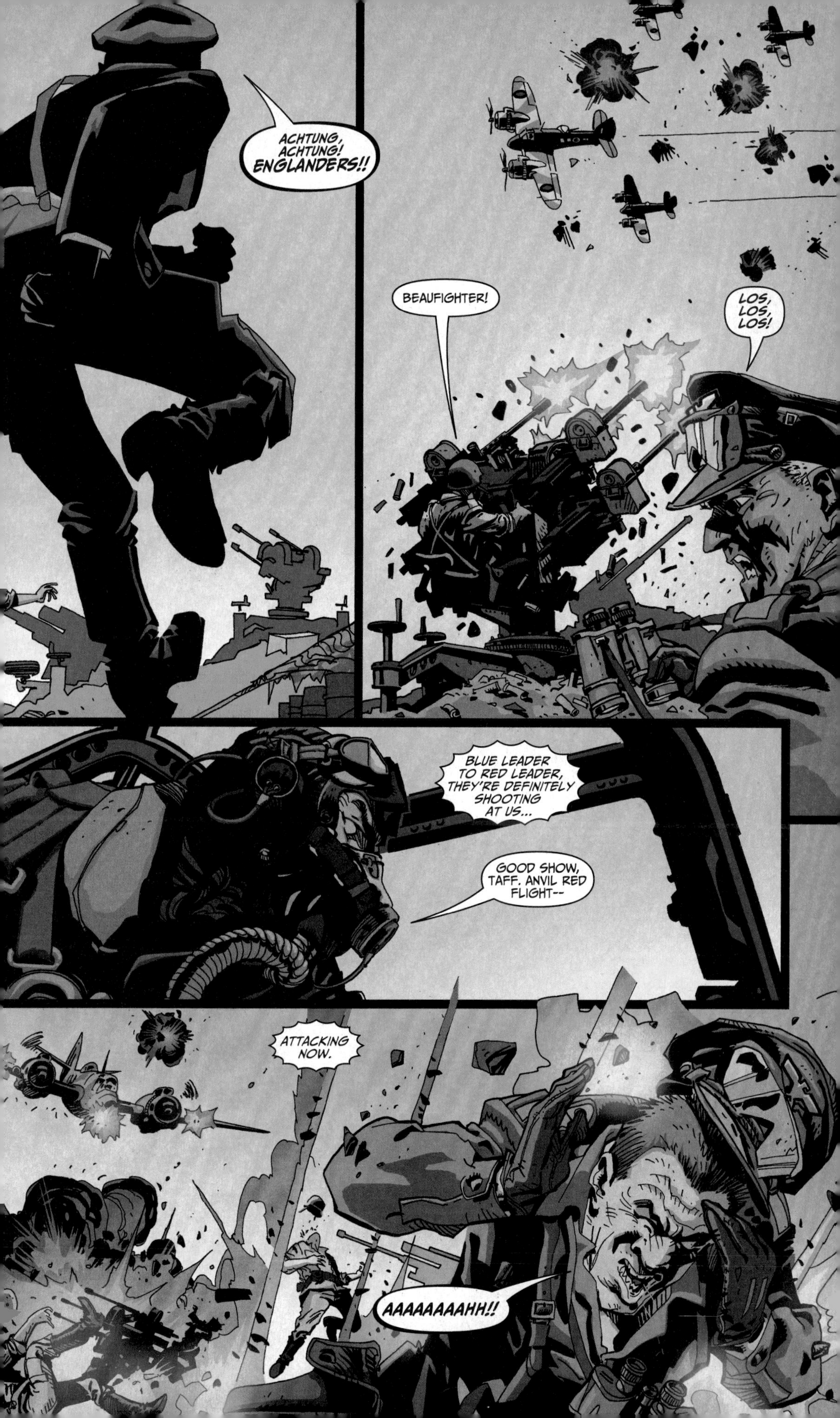
ACHTUNG, ACHTUNG! ENGLANDERS!!
BEAUFIGHTER!
LOS, LOS, LOS!
BLUE LEADER TO RED LEADER, THEY'RE DEFINITELY SHOOTING AT US...
GOOD SHOW, TAFF. ANVIL RED FLIGHT--
ATTACKING NOW.
AAAAAAAAHH!!

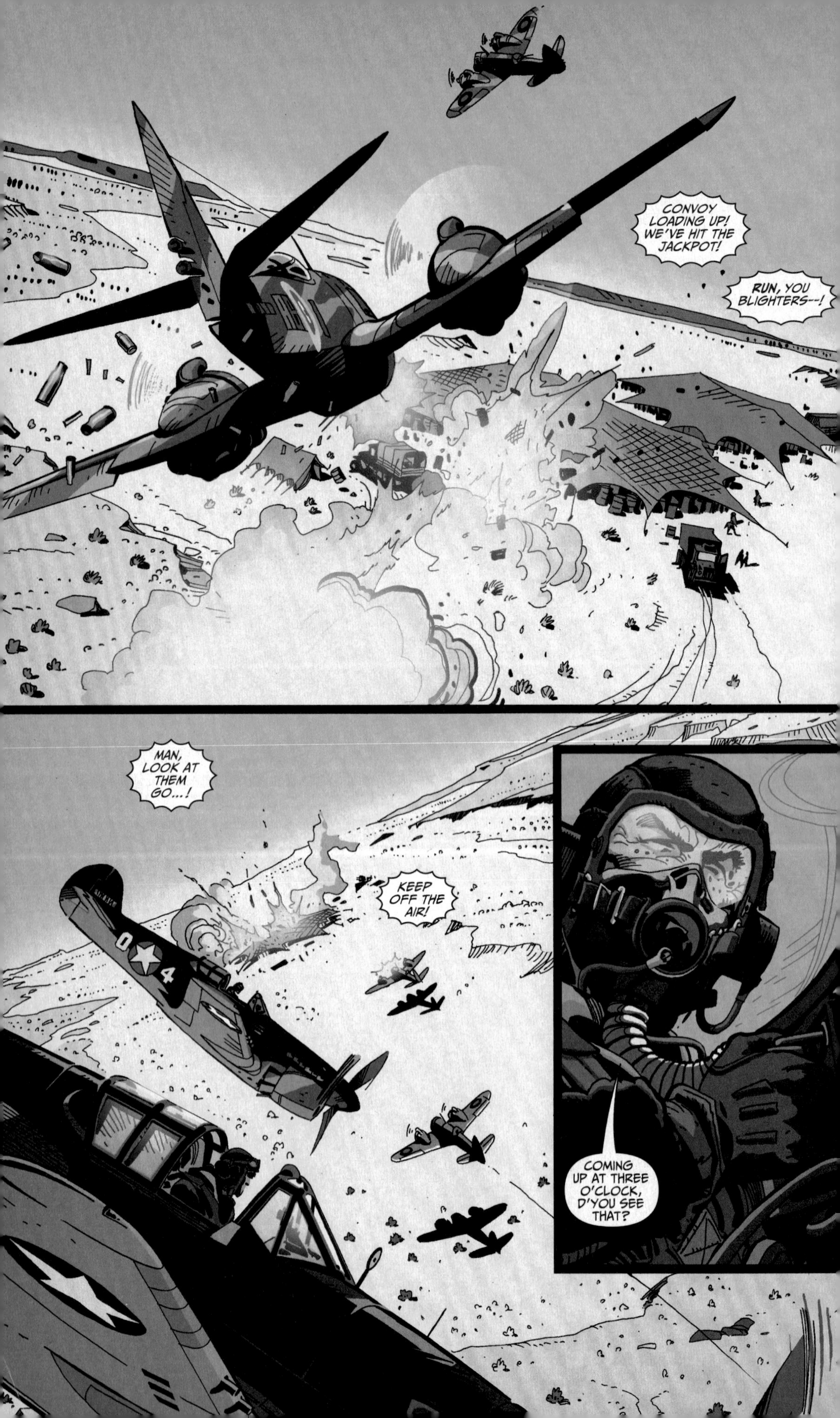
CONVOY LOADING UP! WE'VE HIT THE JACKPOT!
RUN, YOU BLIGHTERS--!
MAN, LOOK AT THEM GO...!
KEEP OFF THE AIR!
COMING UP AT THREE O'CLOCK, D'YOU SEE THAT?

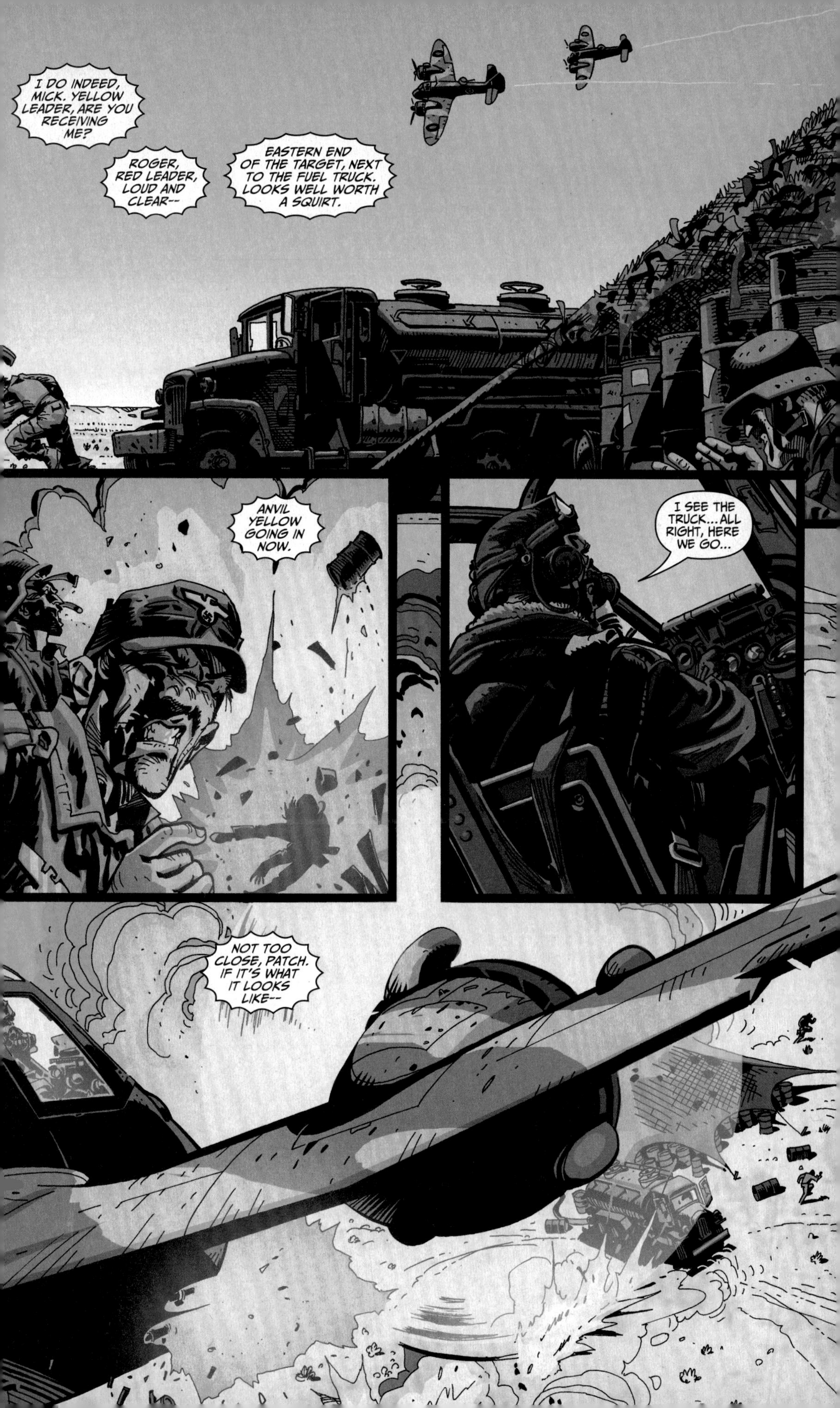

I DO INDEED, MICK. YELLOW LEADER, ARE YOU RECEIVING ME?
ROGER, RED LEADER, LOUD AND CLEAR--
EASTERN END OF THE TARGET, NEXT TO THE FUEL TRUCK. LOOKS WELL WORTH A SQUIRT.
ANVIL YELLOW GOING IN NOW.
I SEE THE TRUCK...ALL RIGHT, HERE WE GO...
NOT TOO CLOSE, PATCH. IF IT'S WHAT IT LOOKS LIKE--

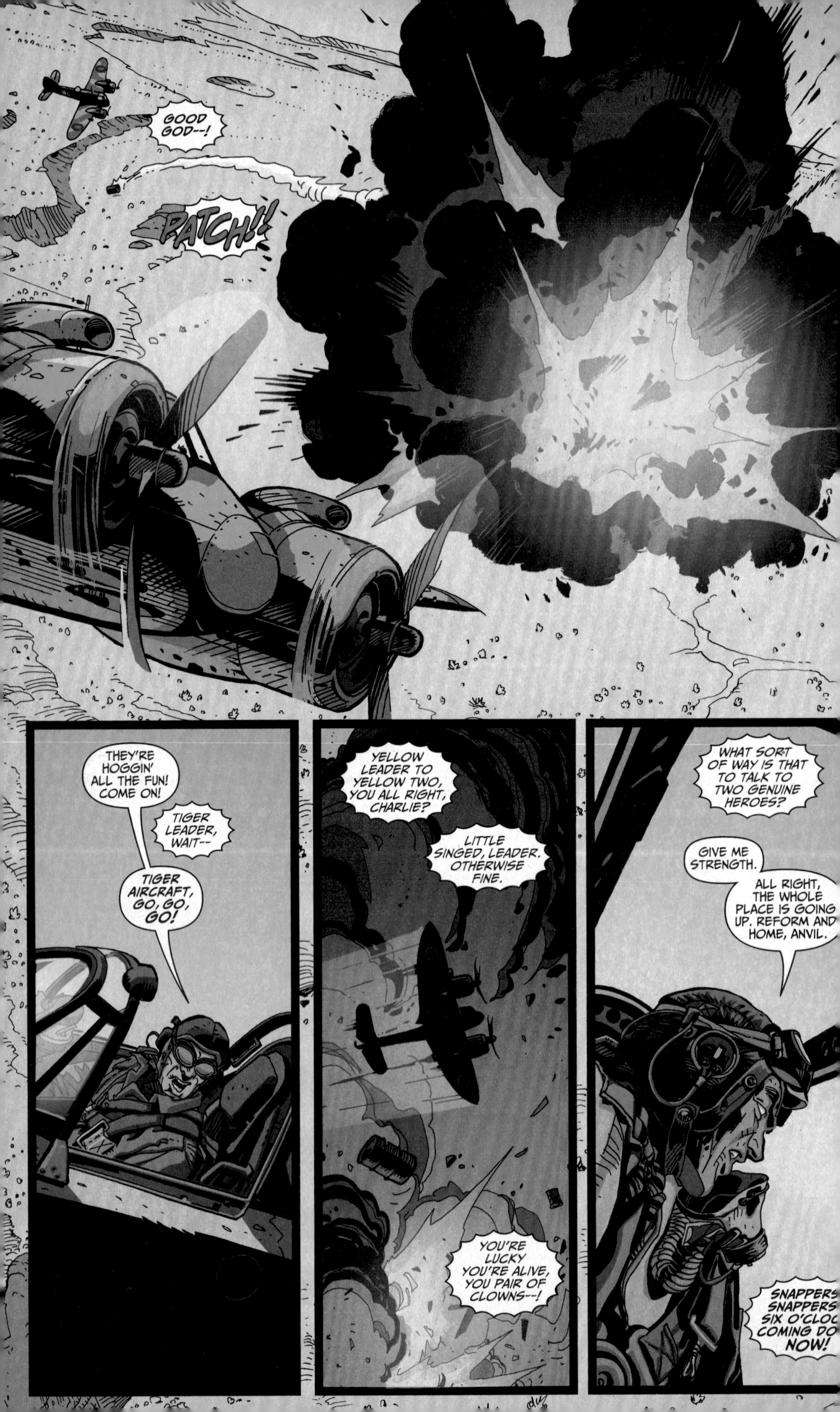
GOOD GOD--!
PATCH!!
THEY'RE HOGGIN' ALL THE FUN! COME ON!
TIGER LEADER, WAIT--
TIGER AIRCRAFT, GO, GO, GO!
YELLOW LEADER TO YELLOW TWO, YOU ALL RIGHT, CHARLIE?
LITTLE SINGED, LEADER. OTHERWISE FINE.
YOU'RE LUCKY YOU'RE ALIVE, YOU PAIR OF CLOWNS--!
WHAT SORT OF WAY IS THAT TO TALK TO TWO GENUINE HEROES?
GIVE ME STRENGTH.
ALL RIGHT, THE WHOLE PLACE IS GOING UP. REFORM AND HOME, ANVIL.
SNAPPERS
SNAPPERS
SIX O'CLOC
COMING DO
NOW!

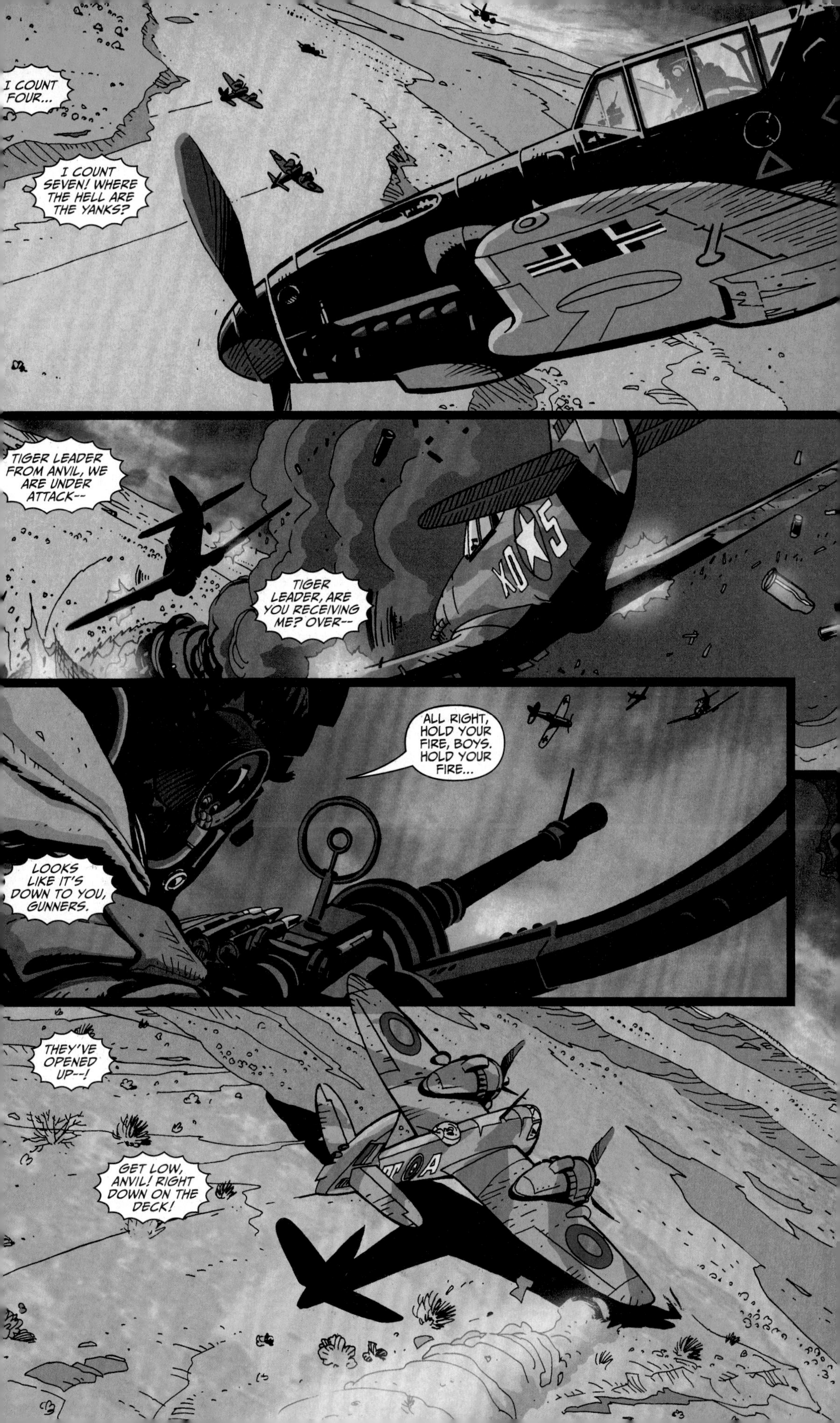
I COUNT FOUR...
I COUNT SEVEN! WHERE THE HELL ARE THE YANKS?
TIGER LEADER FROM ANVIL, WE ARE UNDER ATTACK--
TIGER LEADER, ARE YOU RECEIVING ME? OVER--
XO 5
ALL RIGHT, HOLD YOUR FIRE, BOYS. HOLD YOUR FIRE...
LOOKS LIKE IT'S DOWN TO YOU, GUNNERS.
THEY'VE OPENED UP--!
GET LOW, ANVIL! RIGHT DOWN ON THE DECK!

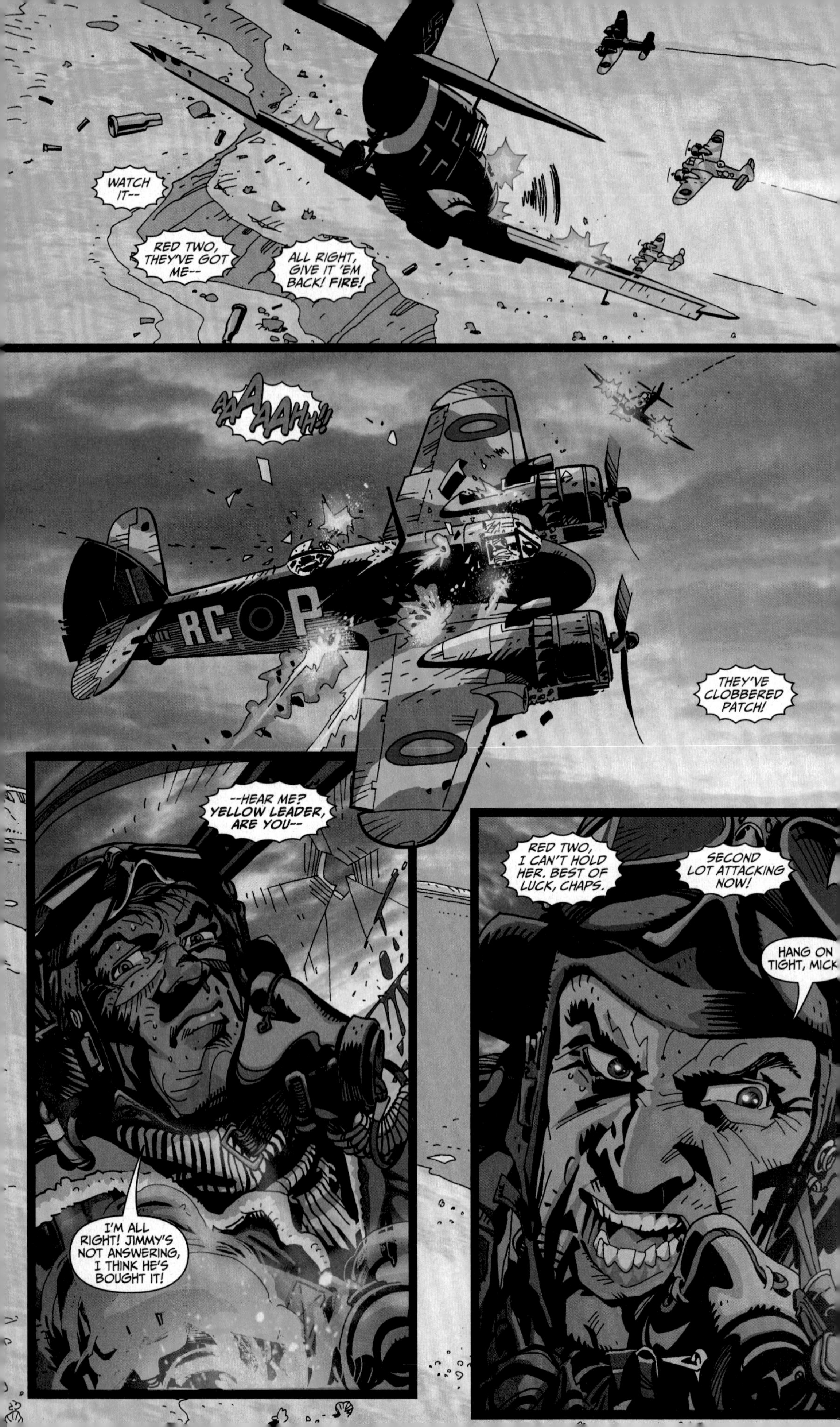

WATCH IT--
RED TWO, THEY'VE GOT ME--
ALL RIGHT, GIVE IT 'EM BACK! FIRE!
AAAAHH!!
THEY'VE CLOBBERED PATCH!
--HEAR ME? YELLOW LEADER, ARE YOU--
I'M ALL RIGHT! JIMMY'S NOT ANSWERING, I THINK HE'S BOUGHT IT!
RED TWO, I CAN'T HOLD HER. BEST OF LUCK, CHAPS.
SECOND LOT ATTACKING NOW!
HANG ON TIGHT, MICK

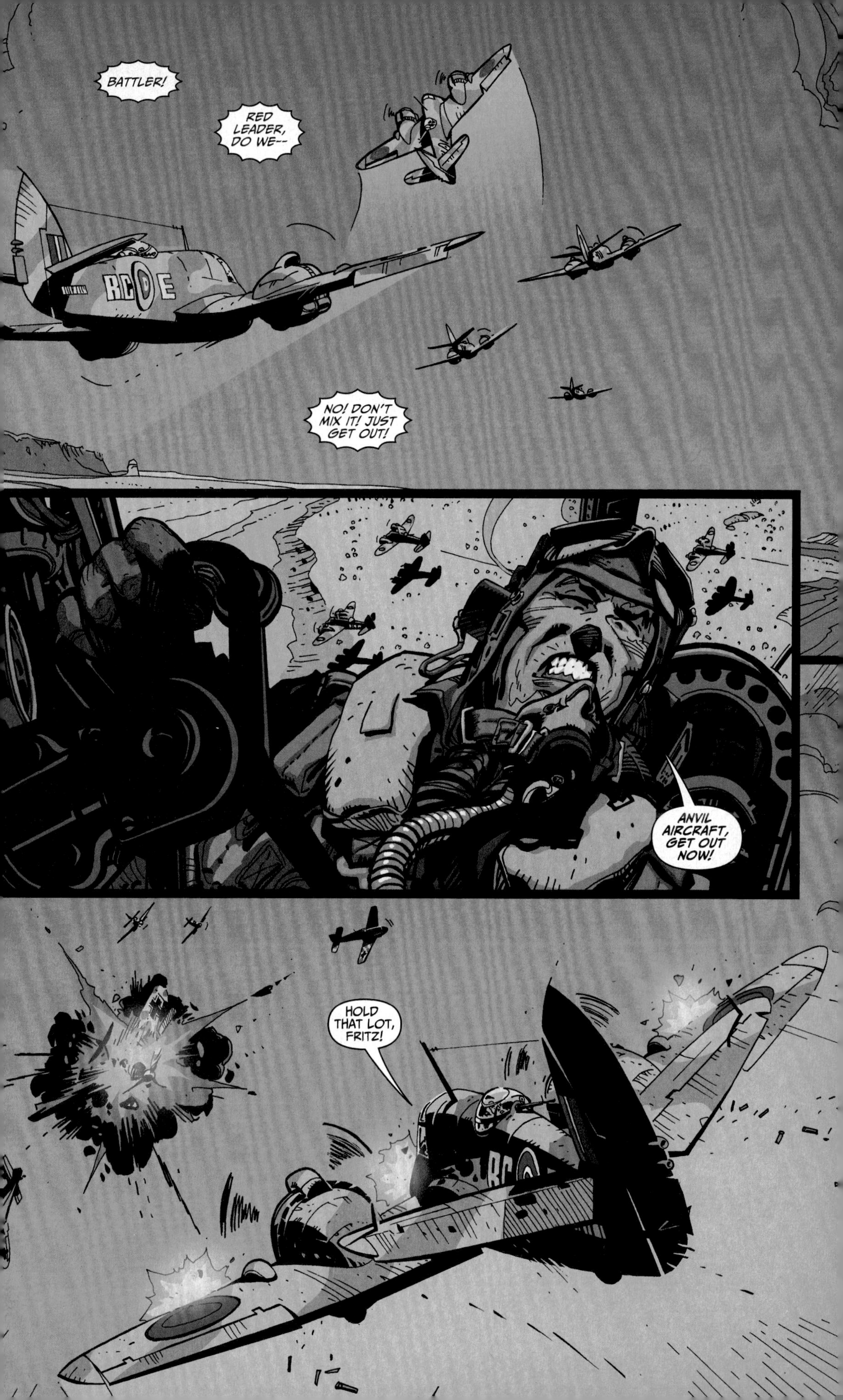
BATTLER!
RED LEADER, DO WE--
NO! DON'T MIX IT! JUST GET OUT!
ANVIL AIRCRAFT, GET OUT NOW!
HOLD THAT LOT, FRITZ!

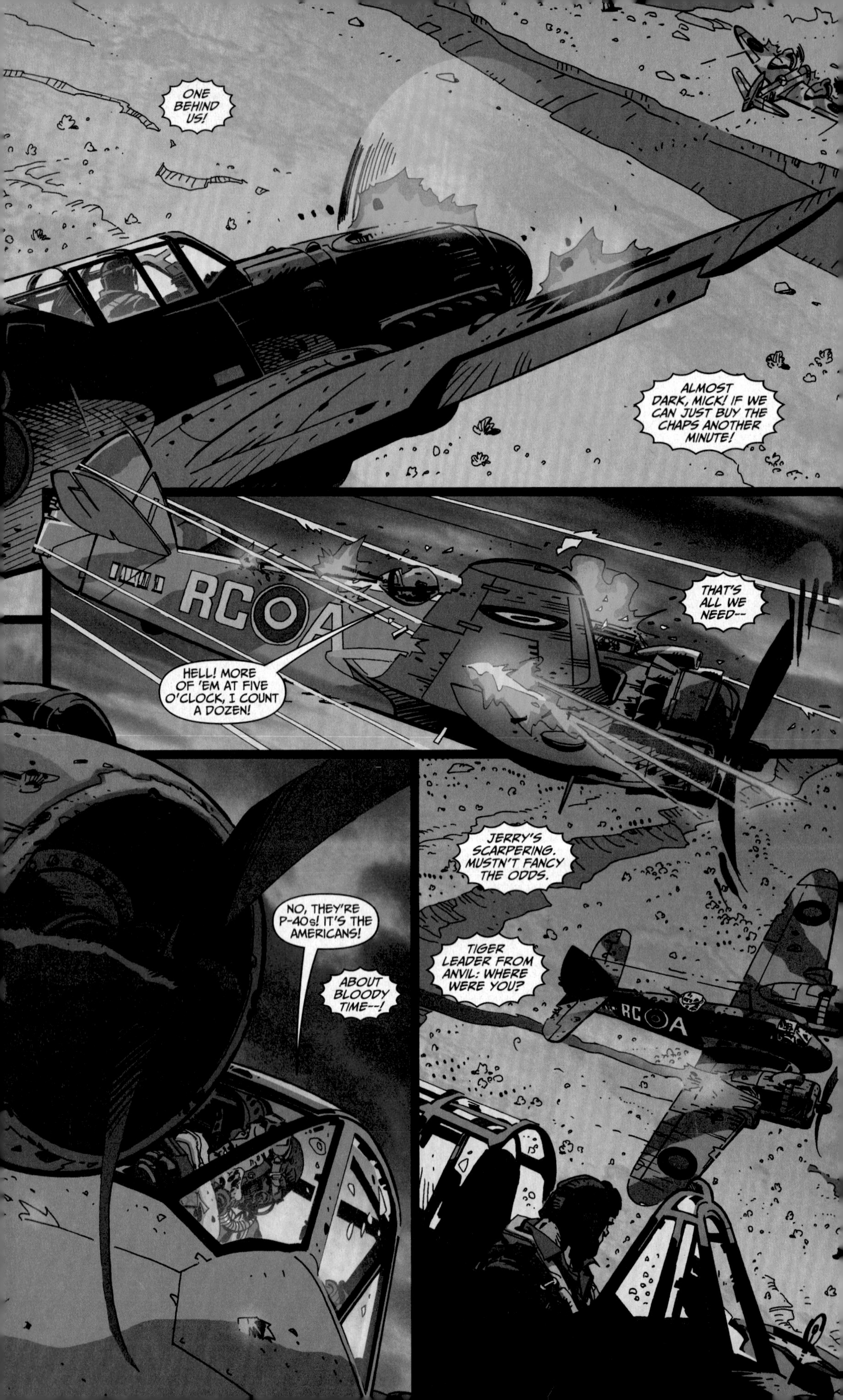
ONE BEHIND US!
ALMOST DARK, MICK! IF WE CAN JUST BUY THE CHAPS ANOTHER MINUTE!
THAT'S ALL WE NEED--
HELL! MORE OF 'EM AT FIVE O'CLOCK, I COUNT A DOZEN!
RC A
NO, THEY'RE P-40s! IT'S THE AMERICANS!
ABOUT BLOODY TIME--!
JERRY'S SCARPERING. MUSTN'T FANCY THE ODDS.
TIGER LEADER FROM ANVIL: WHERE WERE YOU?
RC A

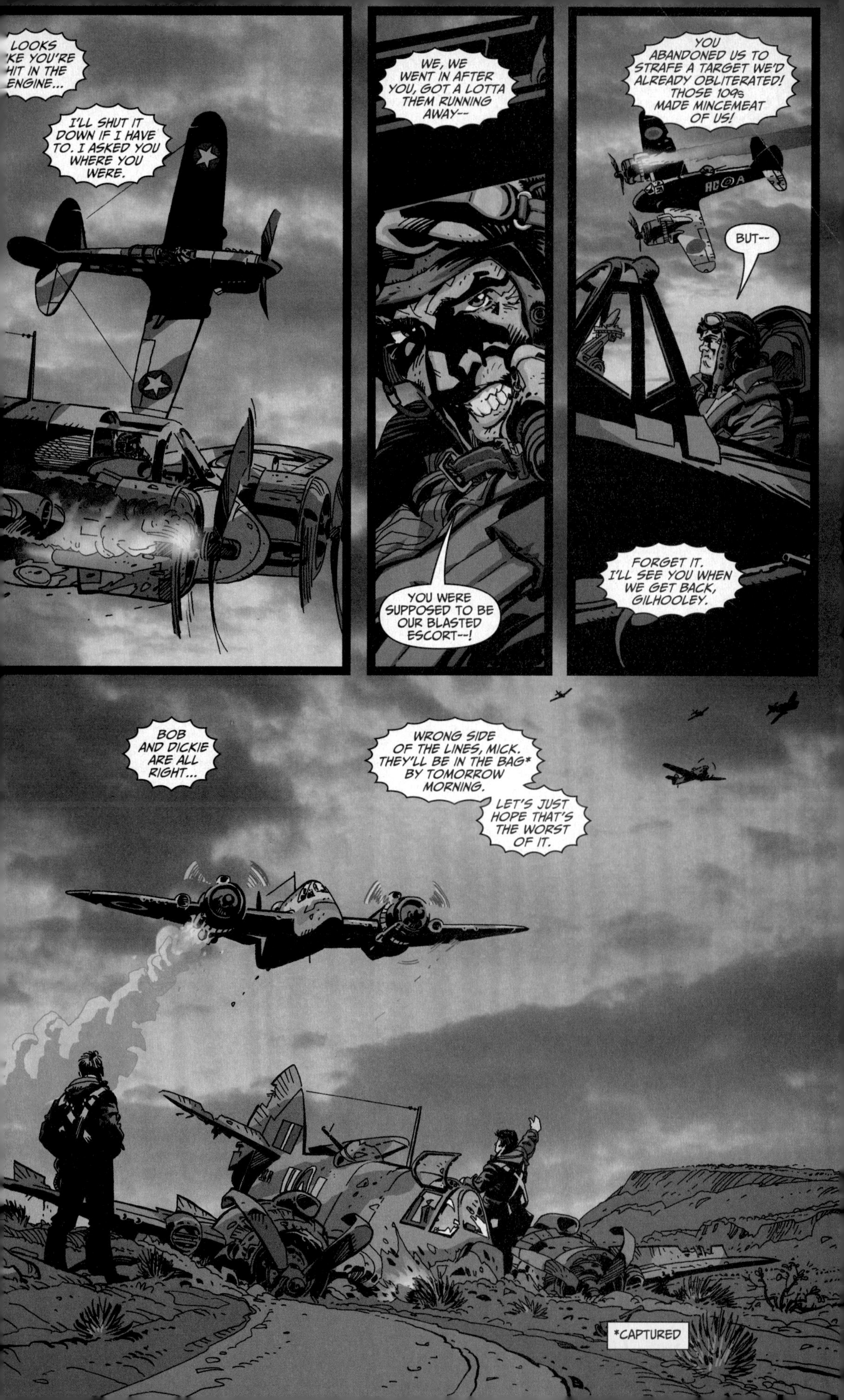

LOOKS 'KE YOU'RE HIT IN THE ENGINE...
I'LL SHUT IT DOWN IF I HAVE TO. I ASKED YOU WHERE YOU WERE.
WE, WE WENT IN AFTER YOU, GOT A LOTTA THEM RUNNING AWAY--
YOU WERE SUPPOSED TO BE OUR BLASTED ESCORT--!
YOU ABANDONED US TO STRAFE A TARGET WE'D ALREADY OBLITERATED! THOSE 109s MADE MINCEMEAT OF US!
BUT--
FORGET IT. I'LL SEE YOU WHEN WE GET BACK, GILHOOLEY.
BOB AND DICKIE ARE ALL RIGHT...
WRONG SIDE OF THE LINES, MICK. THEY'LL BE IN THE BAG* BY TOMORROW MORNING.
LET'S JUST HOPE THAT'S THE WORST OF IT.
*CAPTURED

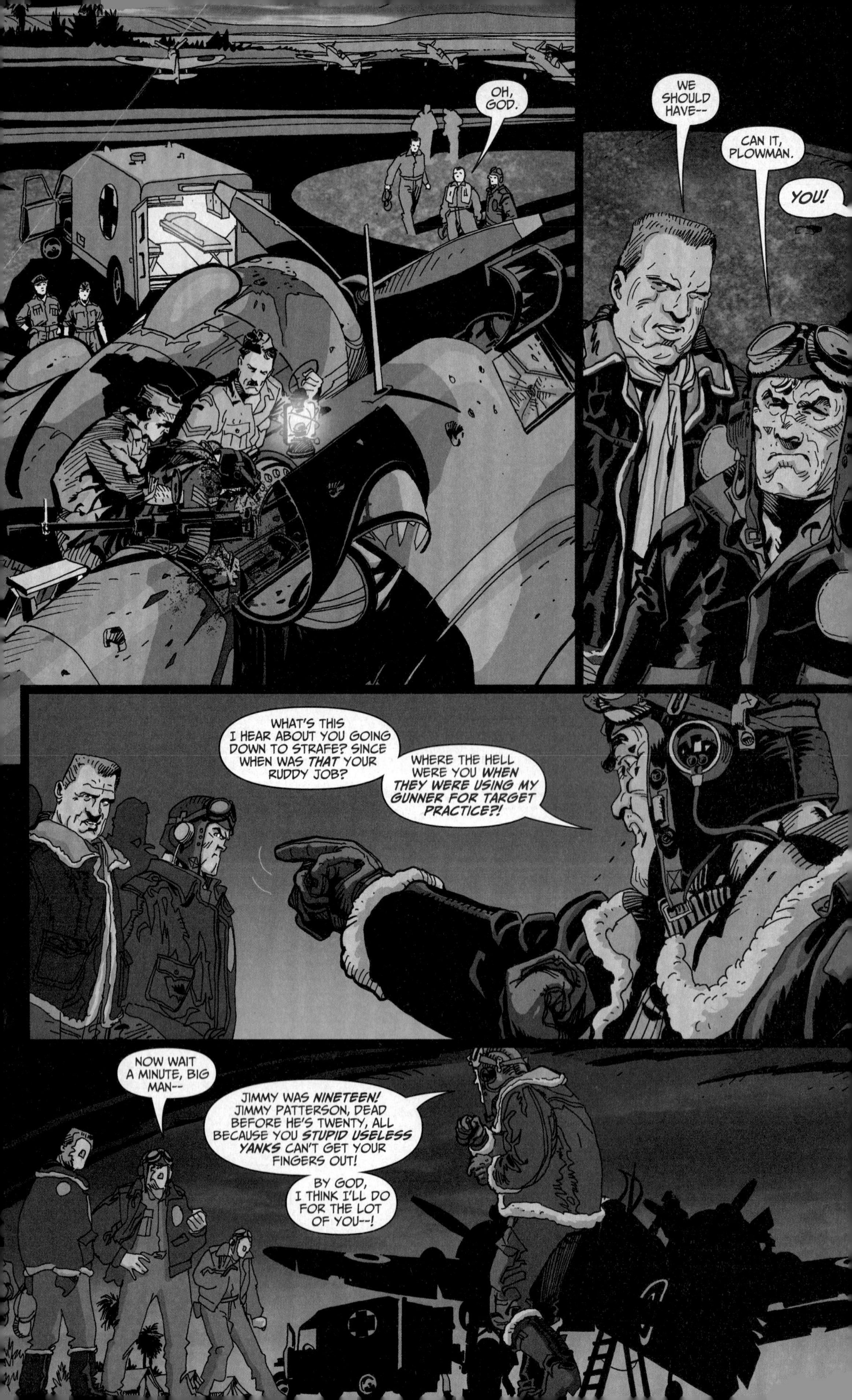
OH, GOD.
WE SHOULD HAVE--
CAN IT, PLOWMAN.
YOU!
WHAT'S THIS I HEAR ABOUT YOU GOING DOWN TO STRAFE? SINCE WHEN WAS THAT YOUR RUDDY JOB?
WHERE THE HELL WERE YOU WHEN THEY WERE USING MY GUNNER FOR TARGET PRACTICE?!
NOW WAIT A MINUTE, BIG MAN--
JIMMY WAS NINETEEN! JIMMY PATTERSON, DEAD BEFORE HE'S TWENTY, ALL BECAUSE YOU STUPID USELESS YANKS CAN'T GET YOUR FINGERS OUT!
BY GOD, I THINK I'LL DO FOR THE LOT OF YOU--!

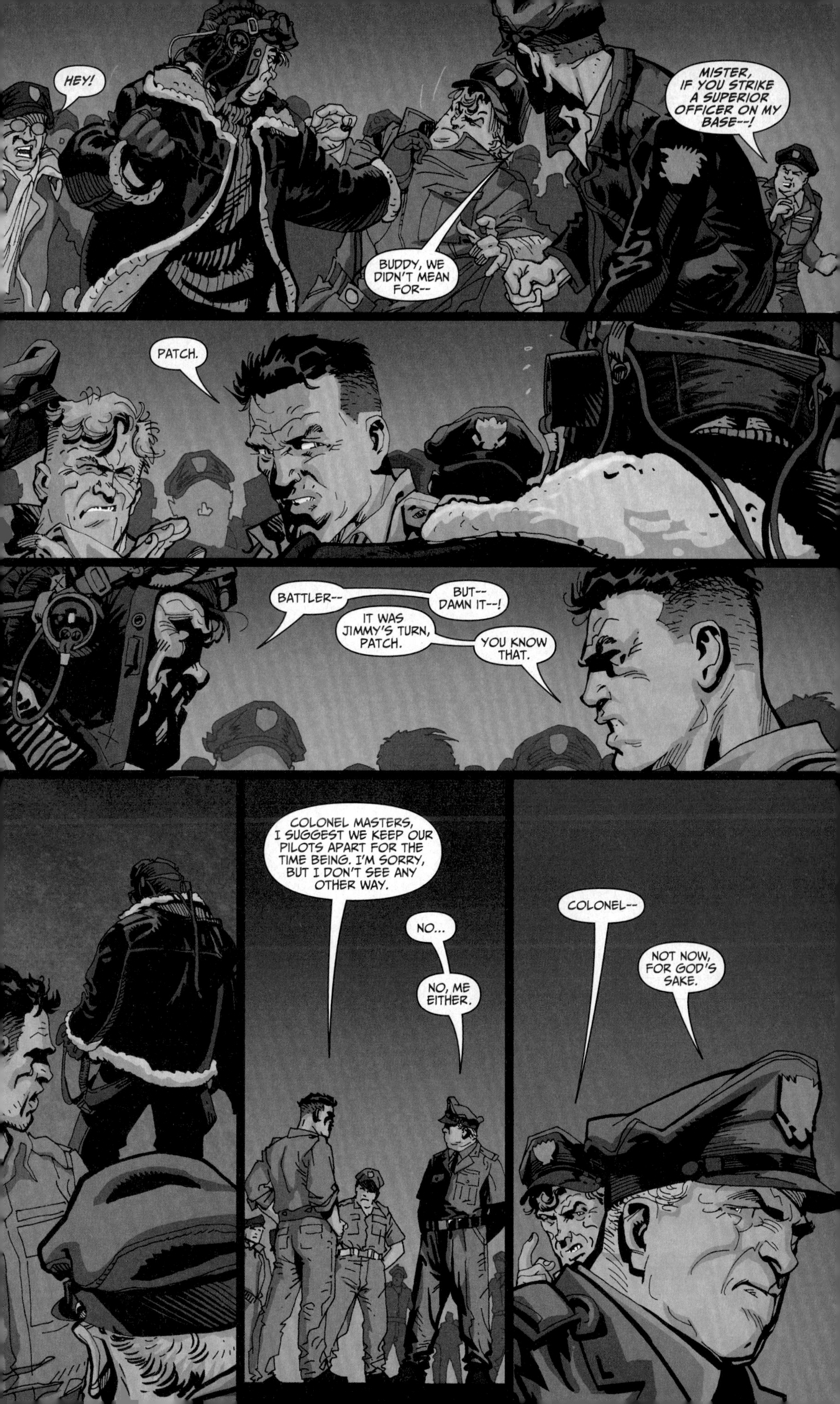
HEY!
MISTER, IF YOU STRIKE A SUPERIOR OFFICER ON MY BASE--!
BUDDY, WE DIDN'T MEAN FOR--
PATCH.
BATTLER--
BUT-- DAMN IT--!
IT WAS JIMMY'S TURN, PATCH.
YOU KNOW THAT.
COLONEL MASTERS, I SUGGEST WE KEEP OUR PILOTS APART FOR THE TIME BEING. I'M SORRY, BUT I DON'T SEE ANY OTHER WAY.
NO...
NO, ME EITHER.
COLONEL--
NOT NOW, FOR GOD'S SAKE.

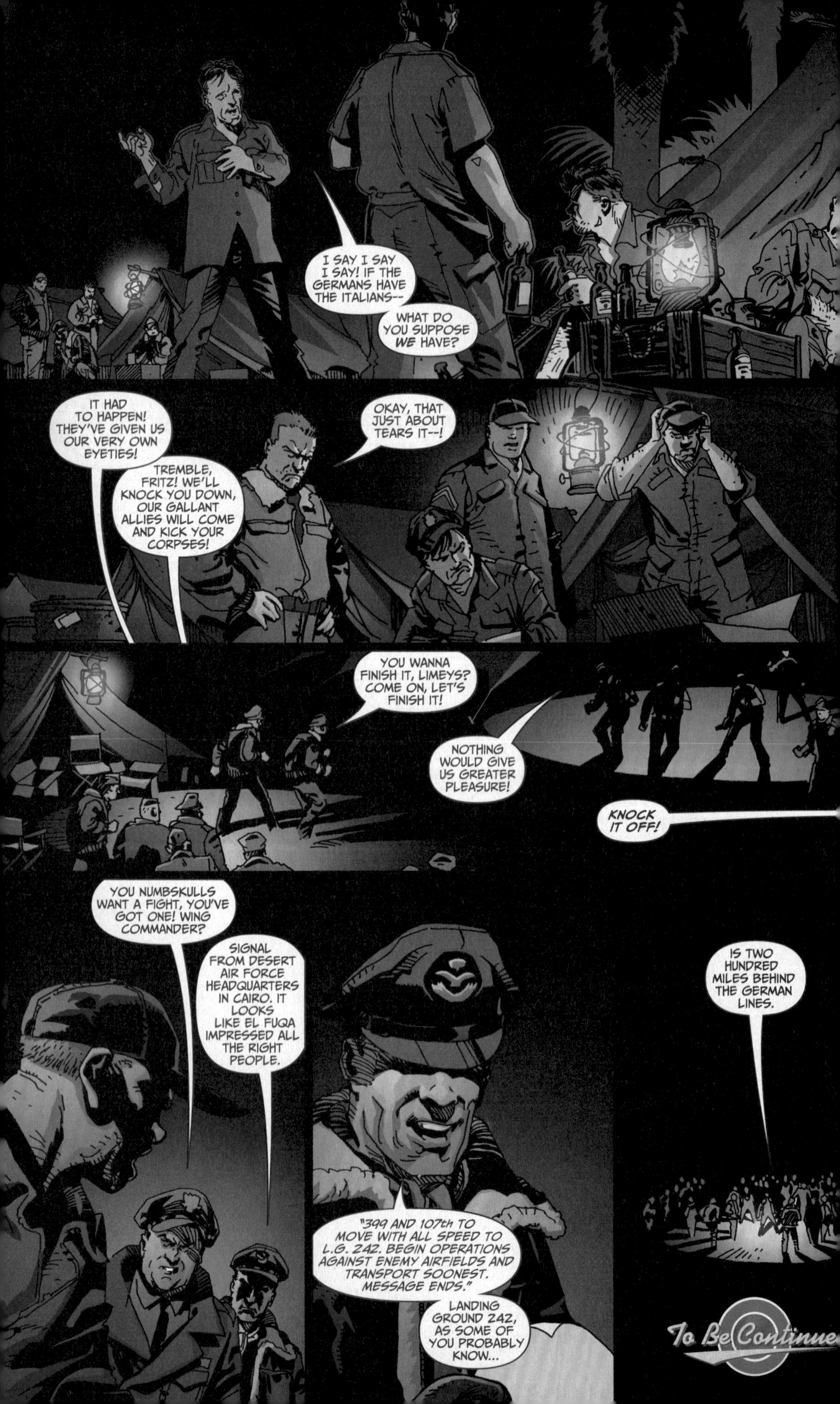
I SAY I SAY I SAY! IF THE GERMANS HAVE THE ITALIANS--
WHAT DO YOU SUPPOSE *WE* HAVE?
IT HAD TO HAPPEN! THEY'VE GIVEN US OUR VERY OWN EYETIES!
TREMBLE, FRITZ! WE'LL KNOCK YOU DOWN, OUR GALLANT ALLIES WILL COME AND KICK YOUR CORPSES!
OKAY, THAT JUST ABOUT TEARS IT--!
YOU WANNA FINISH IT, LIMEYS? COME ON, LET'S FINISH IT!
NOTHING WOULD GIVE US GREATER PLEASURE!
KNOCK IT OFF!
YOU NUMBSKULLS WANT A FIGHT, YOU'VE GOT ONE! WING COMMANDER?
SIGNAL FROM DESERT AIR FORCE HEADQUARTERS IN CAIRO. IT LOOKS LIKE EL FUQA IMPRESSED ALL THE RIGHT PEOPLE.
"399 AND 107th TO MOVE WITH ALL SPEED TO L.G. 242. BEGIN OPERATIONS AGAINST ENEMY AIRFIELDS AND TRANSPORT SOONEST. MESSAGE ENDS."
LANDING GROUND 242, AS SOME OF YOU PROBABLY KNOW...
IS TWO HUNDRED MILES BEHIND THE GERMAN LINES.
To Be Continue

CHAPTER 2

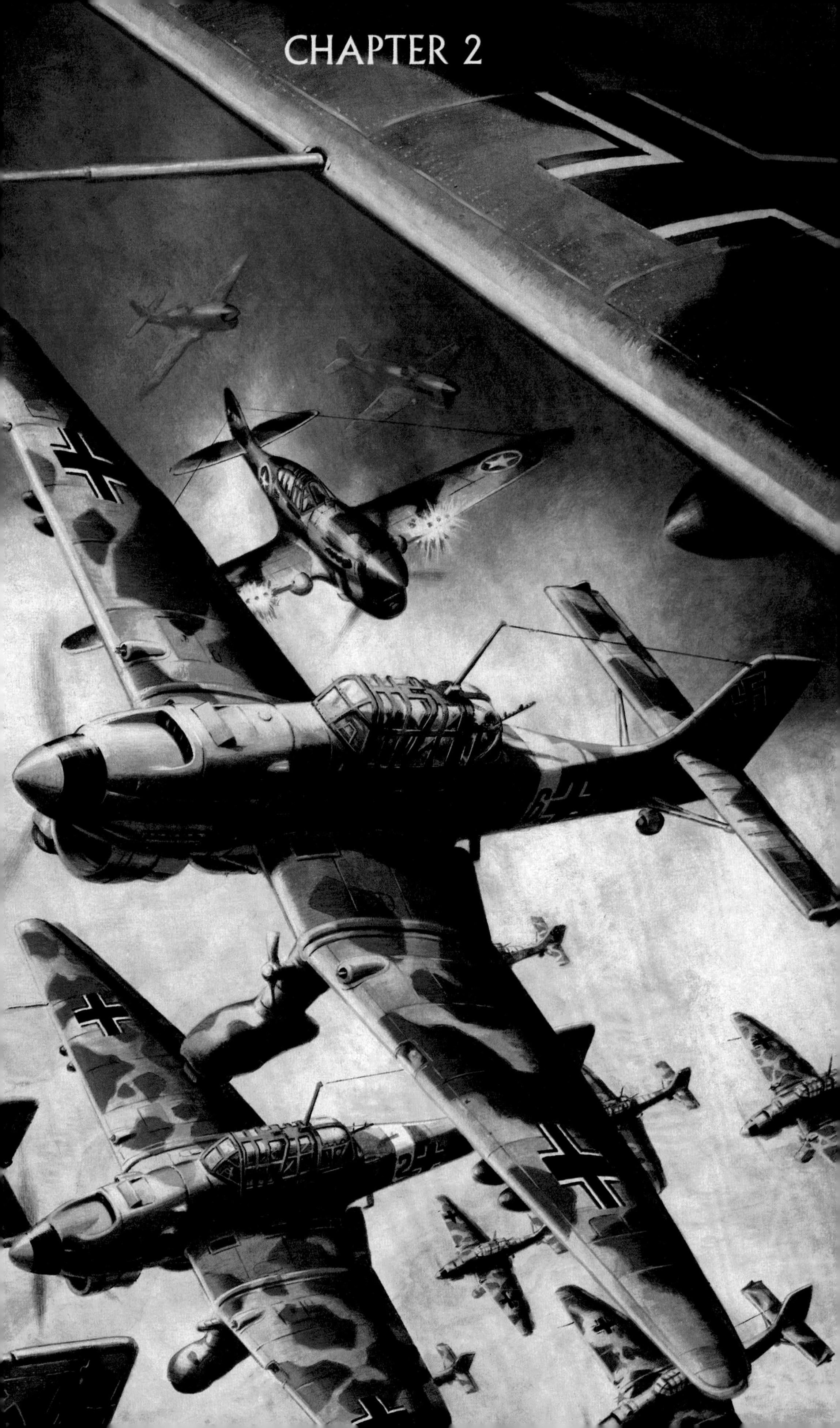

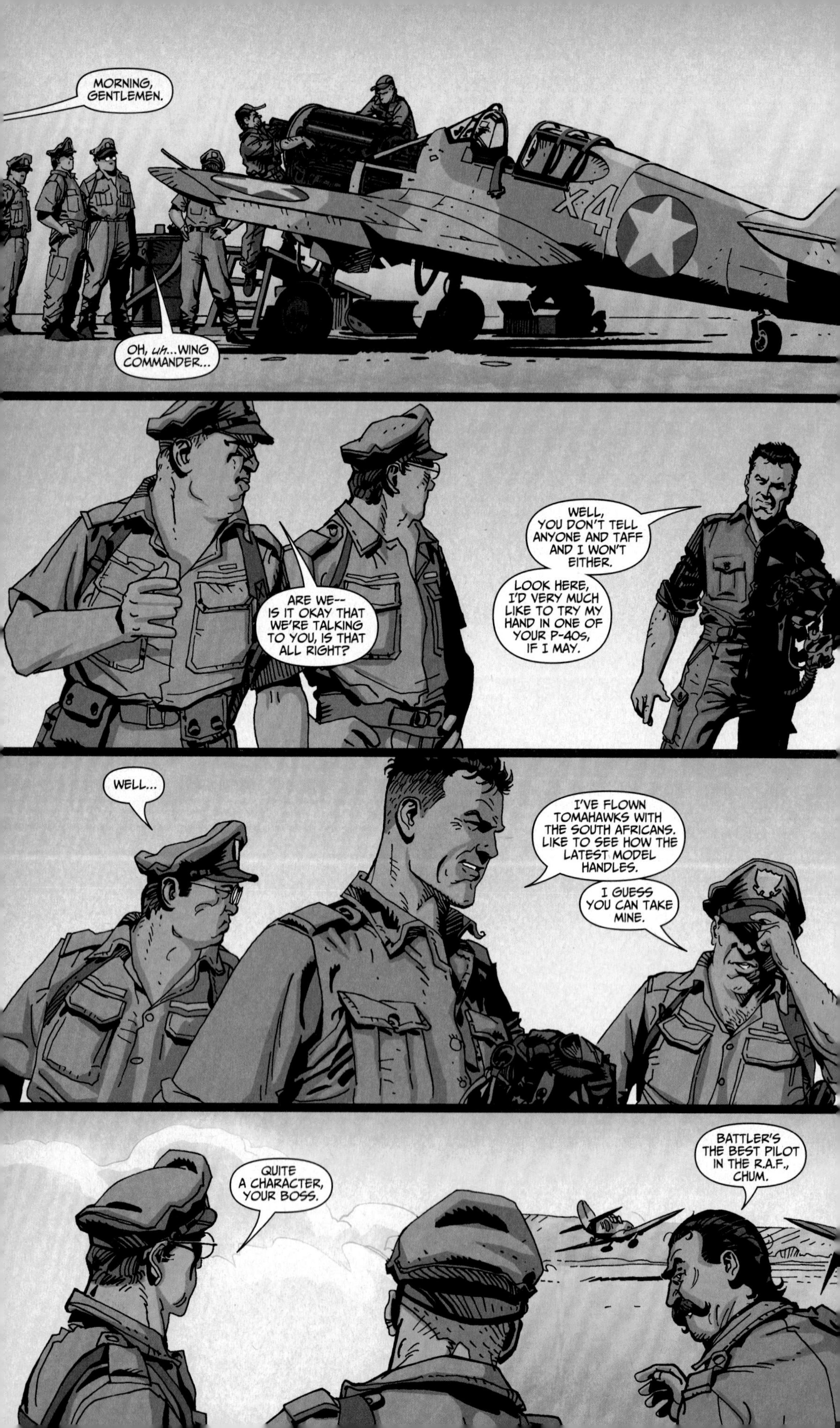
MORNING, GENTLEMEN.
OH, *uh*...WING COMMANDER...
ARE WE-- IS IT OKAY THAT WE'RE TALKING TO YOU, IS THAT ALL RIGHT?
WELL, YOU DON'T TELL ANYONE AND TAFF AND I WON'T EITHER.
LOOK HERE, I'D VERY MUCH LIKE TO TRY MY HAND IN ONE OF YOUR P-40s, IF I MAY.
WELL...
I'VE FLOWN TOMAHAWKS WITH THE SOUTH AFRICANS. LIKE TO SEE HOW THE LATEST MODEL HANDLES.
I GUESS YOU CAN TAKE MINE.
QUITE A CHARACTER, YOUR BOSS.
BATTLER'S THE BEST PILOT IN THE R.A.F., CHUM.

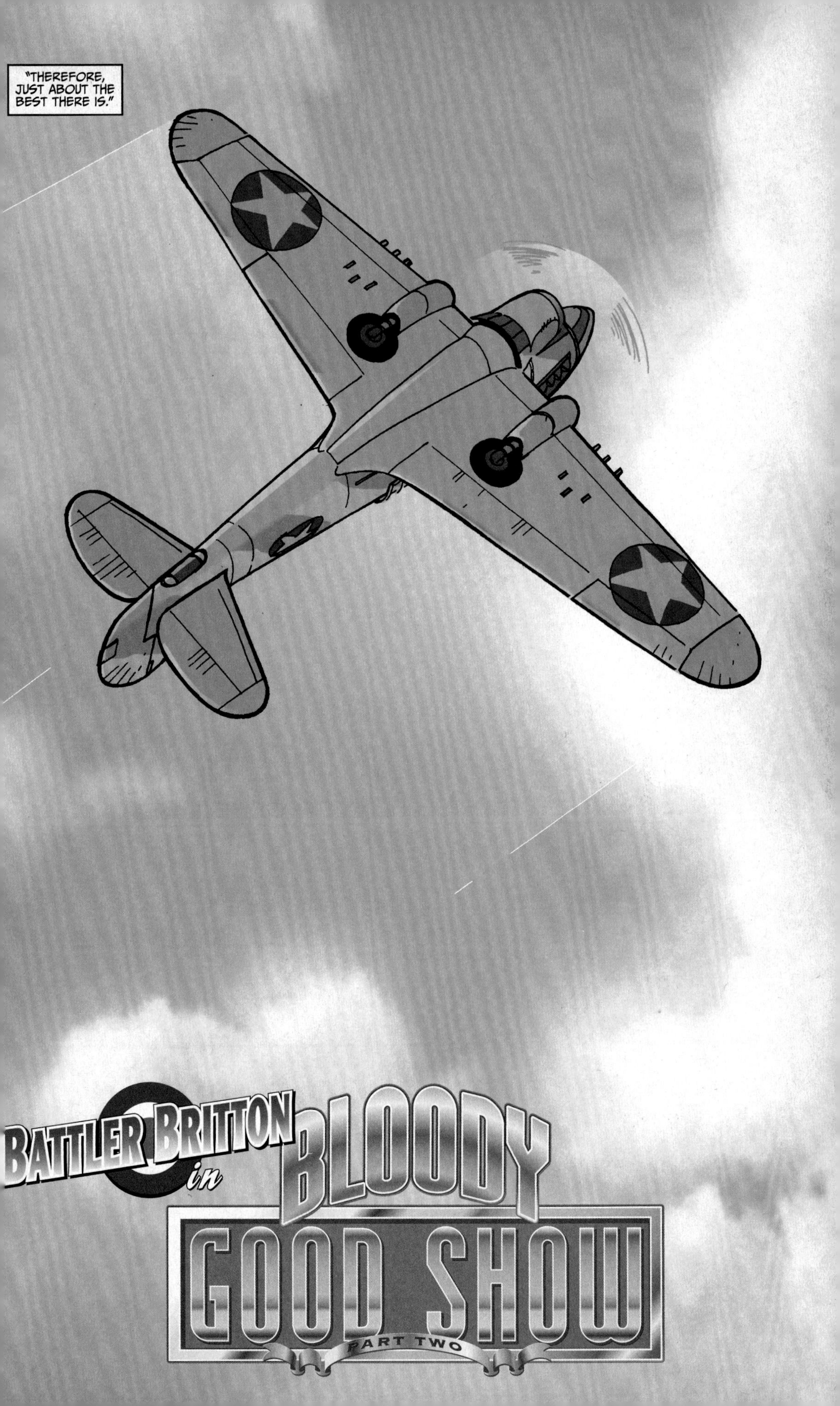

"THEREFORE, JUST ABOUT THE BEST THERE IS."
BATTLER BRITTON in
BLOODY GOOD SHOW
PART TWO

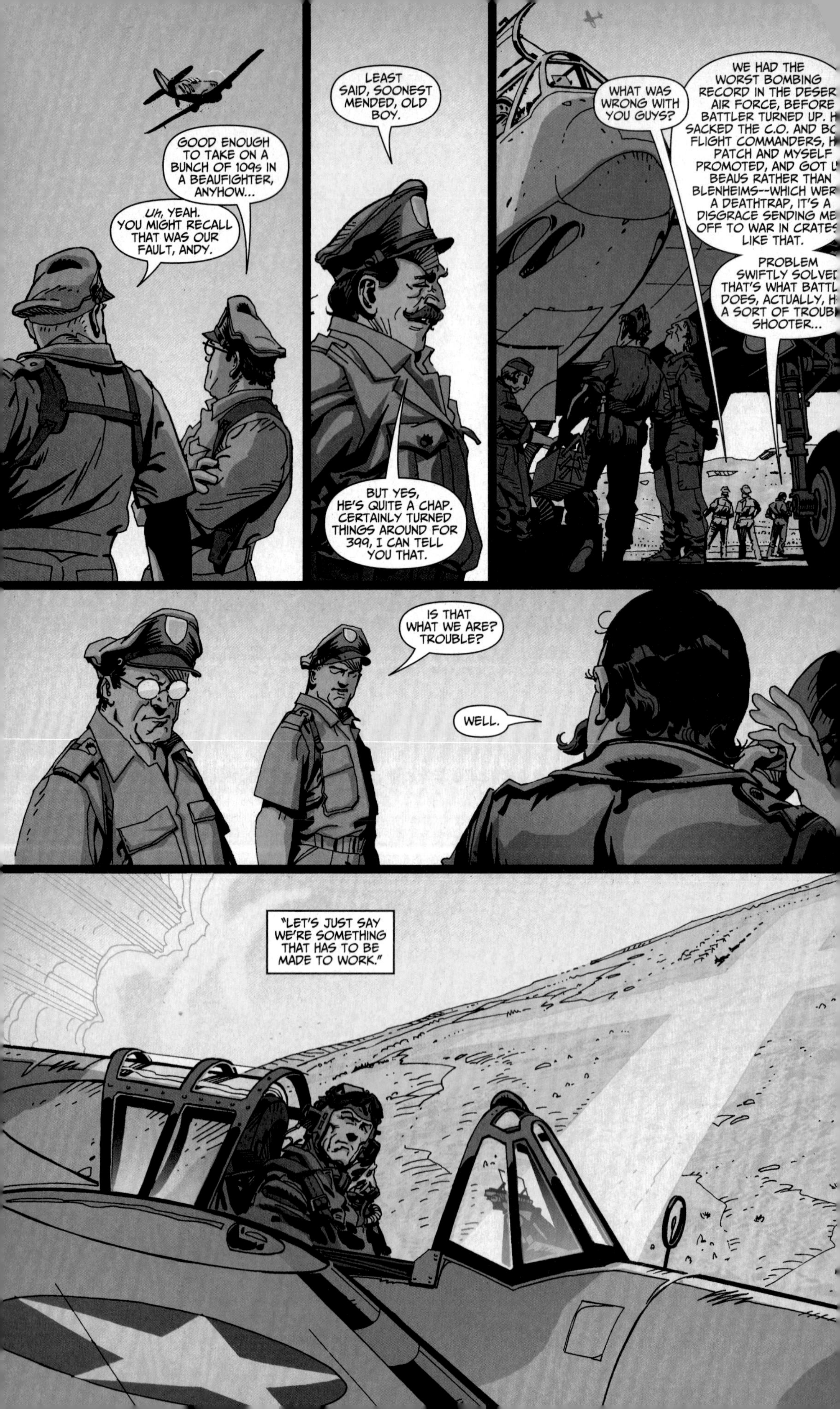

GOOD ENOUGH TO TAKE ON A BUNCH OF 109s IN A BEAUFIGHTER, ANYHOW...
Uh, YEAH. YOU MIGHT RECALL THAT WAS OUR FAULT, ANDY.
LEAST SAID, SOONEST MENDED, OLD BOY.
BUT YES, HE'S QUITE A CHAP. CERTAINLY TURNED THINGS AROUND FOR 399, I CAN TELL YOU THAT.
WHAT WAS WRONG WITH YOU GUYS?
WE HAD THE WORST BOMBING RECORD IN THE DESER AIR FORCE, BEFORE BATTLER TURNED UP. H SACKED THE C.O. AND BO FLIGHT COMMANDERS, H PATCH AND MYSELF PROMOTED, AND GOT U BEAUS RATHER THAN BLENHEIMS--WHICH WER A DEATHTRAP, IT'S A DISGRACE SENDING ME OFF TO WAR IN CRATES LIKE THAT.
PROBLEM SWIFTLY SOLVED THAT'S WHAT BATTL DOES, ACTUALLY, H A SORT OF TROUB SHOOTER...
IS THAT WHAT WE ARE? TROUBLE?
WELL.
"LET'S JUST SAY WE'RE SOMETHING THAT HAS TO BE MADE TO WORK."

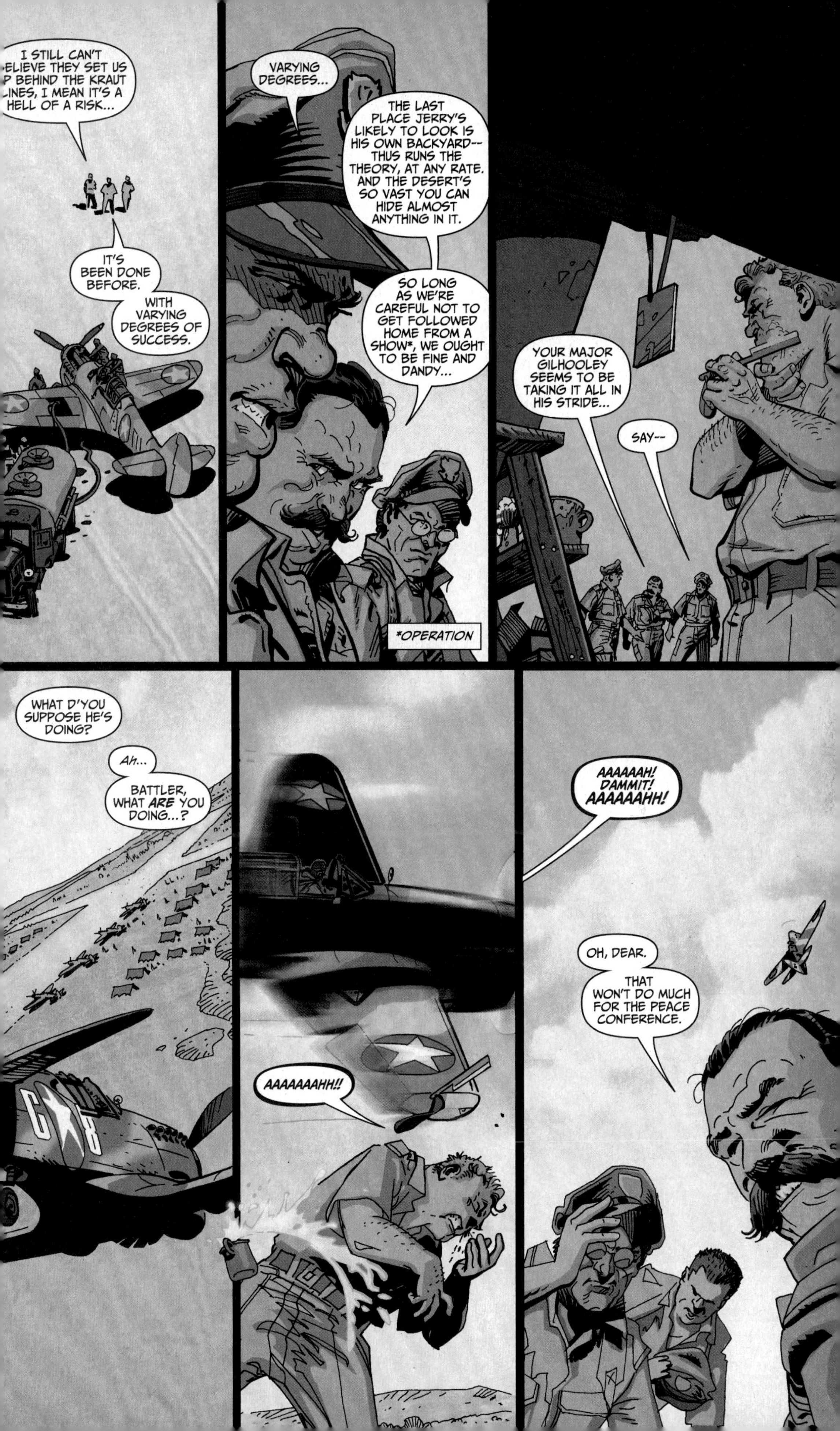
I STILL CAN'T
ELIEVE THEY SET US
P BEHIND THE KRAUT
LINES, I MEAN IT'S A
HELL OF A RISK...
IT'S BEEN DONE BEFORE.
WITH VARYING DEGREES OF SUCCESS.
VARYING DEGREES...
THE LAST PLACE JERRY'S LIKELY TO LOOK IS HIS OWN BACKYARD-- THUS RUNS THE THEORY, AT ANY RATE. AND THE DESERT'S SO VAST YOU CAN HIDE ALMOST ANYTHING IN IT.
SO LONG AS WE'RE CAREFUL NOT TO GET FOLLOWED HOME FROM A SHOW*, WE OUGHT TO BE FINE AND DANDY...
*OPERATION
YOUR MAJOR GILHOOLEY SEEMS TO BE TAKING IT ALL IN HIS STRIDE...
SAY--
WHAT D'YOU SUPPOSE HE'S DOING?
Ah...
BATTLER, WHAT ARE YOU DOING...?
AAAAAAAHH!!
AAAAAAH! DAMMIT! AAAAAAAHH!
OH, DEAR.
THAT WON'T DO MUCH FOR THE PEACE CONFERENCE.

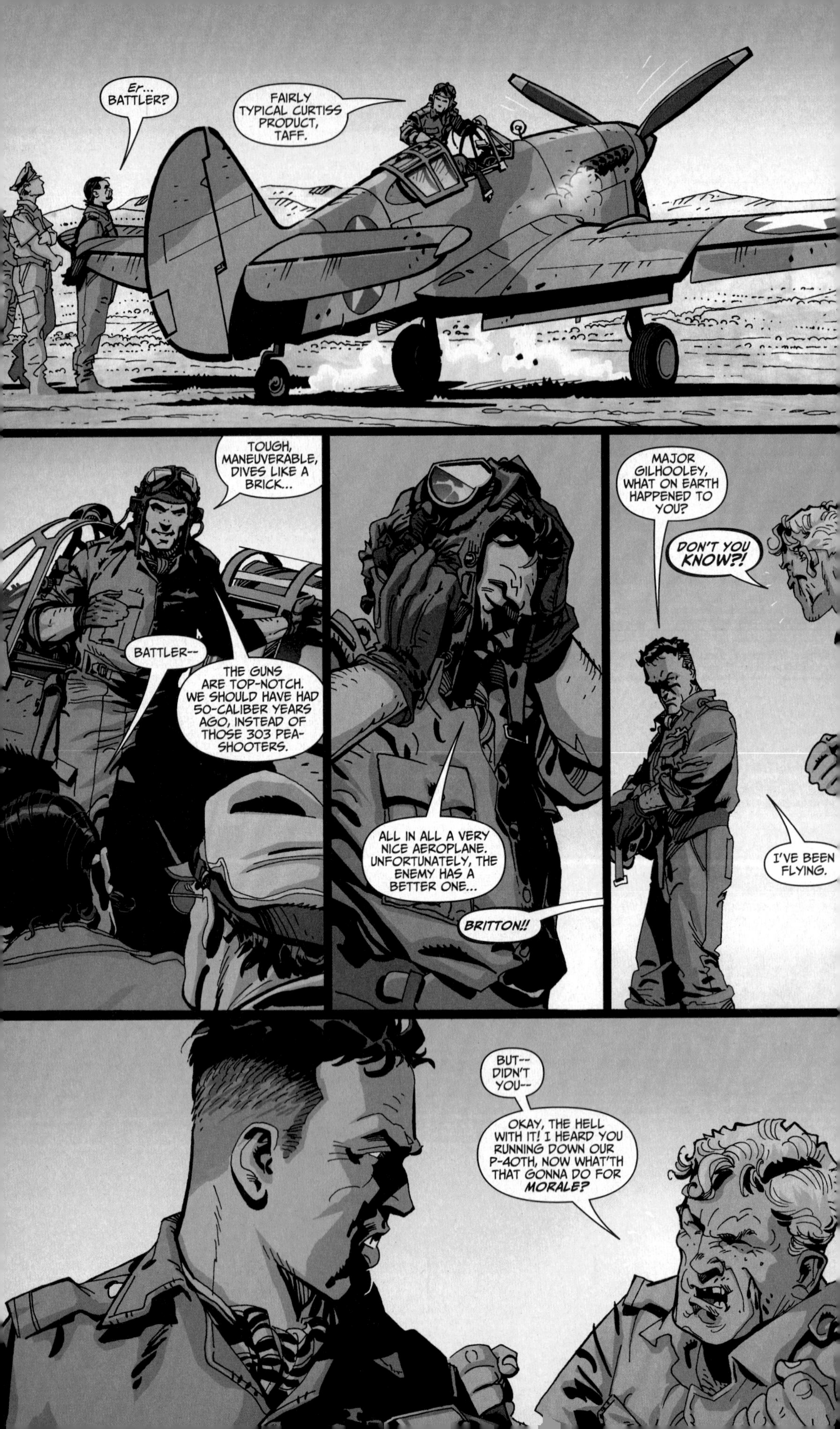
Er... BATTLER?
FAIRLY TYPICAL CURTISS PRODUCT, TAFF.
TOUGH, MANEUVERABLE, DIVES LIKE A BRICK...
BATTLER--
THE GUNS ARE TOP-NOTCH. WE SHOULD HAVE HAD 50-CALIBER YEARS AGO, INSTEAD OF THOSE 303 PEA-SHOOTERS.
ALL IN ALL A VERY NICE AEROPLANE. UNFORTUNATELY, THE ENEMY HAS A BETTER ONE...
BRITTON!!
MAJOR GILHOOLEY, WHAT ON EARTH HAPPENED TO YOU?
DON'T YOU KNOW?!
I'VE BEEN FLYING.
BUT-- DIDN'T YOU--
OKAY, THE HELL WITH IT! I HEARD YOU RUNNING DOWN OUR P-40TH, NOW WHAT'TH THAT GONNA DO FOR MORALE?

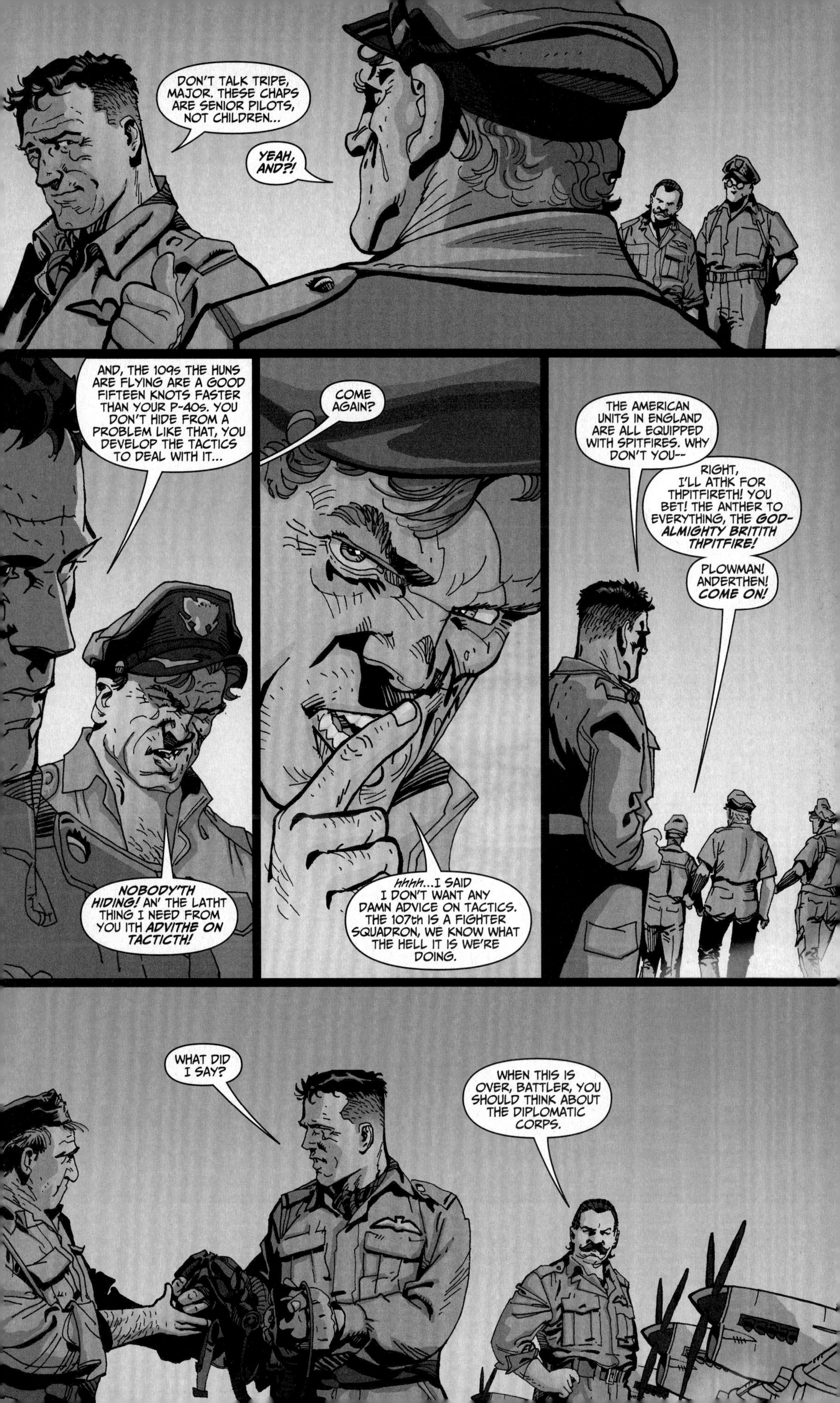

DON'T TALK TRIPE, MAJOR. THESE CHAPS ARE SENIOR PILOTS, NOT CHILDREN...
YEAH, AND?!
AND, THE 109s THE HUNS ARE FLYING ARE A GOOD FIFTEEN KNOTS FASTER THAN YOUR P-40s. YOU DON'T HIDE FROM A PROBLEM LIKE THAT, YOU DEVELOP THE TACTICS TO DEAL WITH IT...
NOBODY'TH HIDING! AN' THE LATHT THING I NEED FROM YOU ITH ADVITHE ON TACTICTH!
COME AGAIN?
hhhh...I SAID I DON'T WANT ANY DAMN ADVICE ON TACTICS. THE 107th IS A FIGHTER SQUADRON, WE KNOW WHAT THE HELL IT IS WE'RE DOING.
THE AMERICAN UNITS IN ENGLAND ARE ALL EQUIPPED WITH SPITFIRES. WHY DON'T YOU--
RIGHT, I'LL ATHK FOR THPITFIRETH! YOU BET! THE ANTHER TO EVERYTHING, THE GOD-ALMIGHTY BRITITH THPITFIRE!
PLOWMAN! ANDERTHEN! COME ON!
WHAT DID I SAY?
WHEN THIS IS OVER, BATTLER, YOU SHOULD THINK ABOUT THE DIPLOMATIC CORPS.

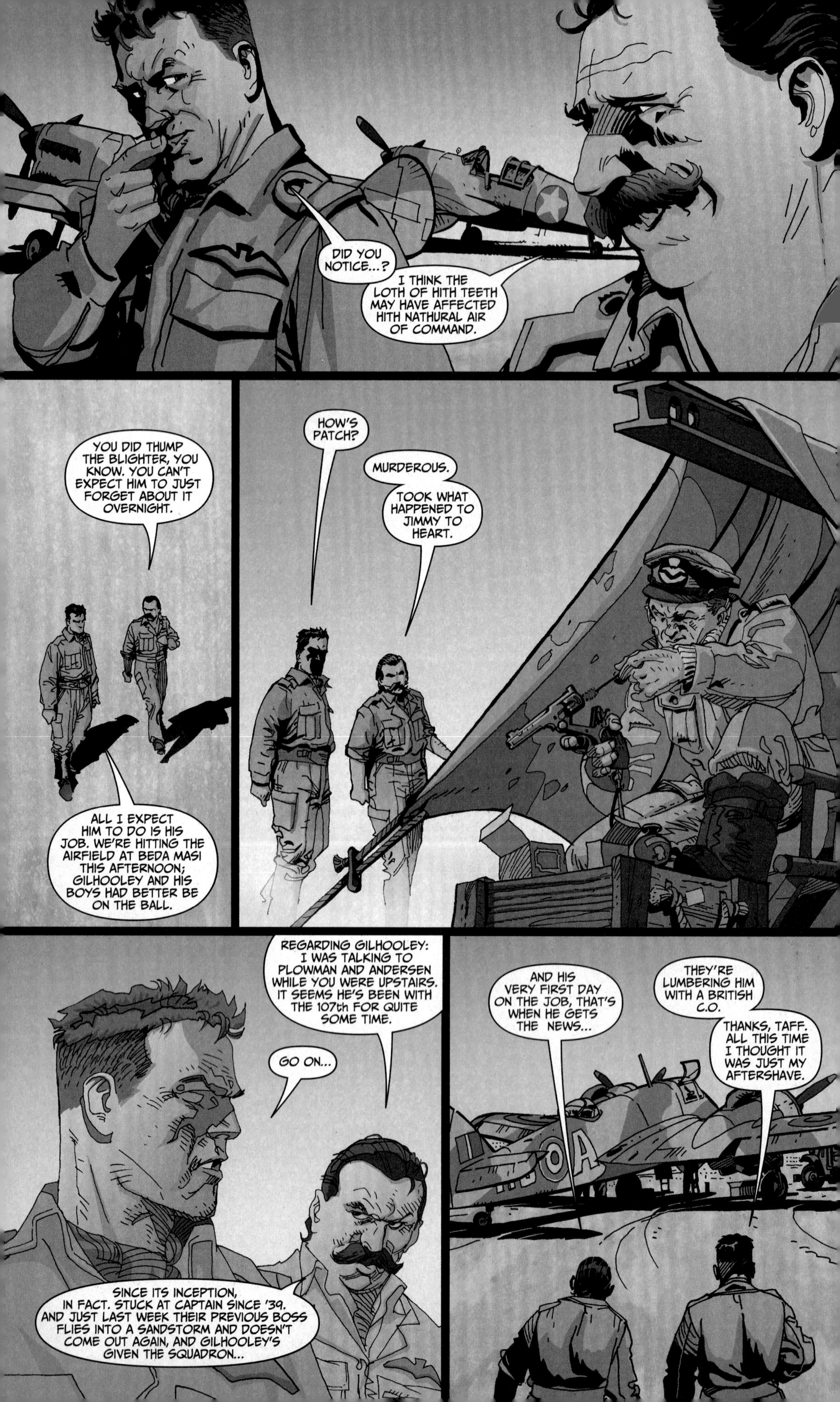

DID YOU NOTICE...?
I THINK THE LOTH OF HITH TEETH MAY HAVE AFFECTED HITH NATHURAL AIR OF COMMAND.
YOU DID THUMP THE BLIGHTER, YOU KNOW. YOU CAN'T EXPECT HIM TO JUST FORGET ABOUT IT OVERNIGHT.
ALL I EXPECT HIM TO DO IS HIS JOB. WE'RE HITTING THE AIRFIELD AT BEDA MASI THIS AFTERNOON; GILHOOLEY AND HIS BOYS HAD BETTER BE ON THE BALL.
HOW'S PATCH?
MURDEROUS.
TOOK WHAT HAPPENED TO JIMMY TO HEART.
REGARDING GILHOOLEY: I WAS TALKING TO PLOWMAN AND ANDERSEN WHILE YOU WERE UPSTAIRS. IT SEEMS HE'S BEEN WITH THE 107th FOR QUITE SOME TIME.
GO ON...
SINCE ITS INCEPTION, IN FACT. STUCK AT CAPTAIN SINCE '39. AND JUST LAST WEEK THEIR PREVIOUS BOSS FLIES INTO A SANDSTORM AND DOESN'T COME OUT AGAIN, AND GILHOOLEY'S GIVEN THE SQUADRON...
AND HIS VERY FIRST DAY ON THE JOB, THAT'S WHEN HE GETS THE NEWS...
THEY'RE LUMBERING HIM WITH A BRITISH C.O.
THANKS, TAFF. ALL THIS TIME I THOUGHT IT WAS JUST MY AFTERSHAVE.

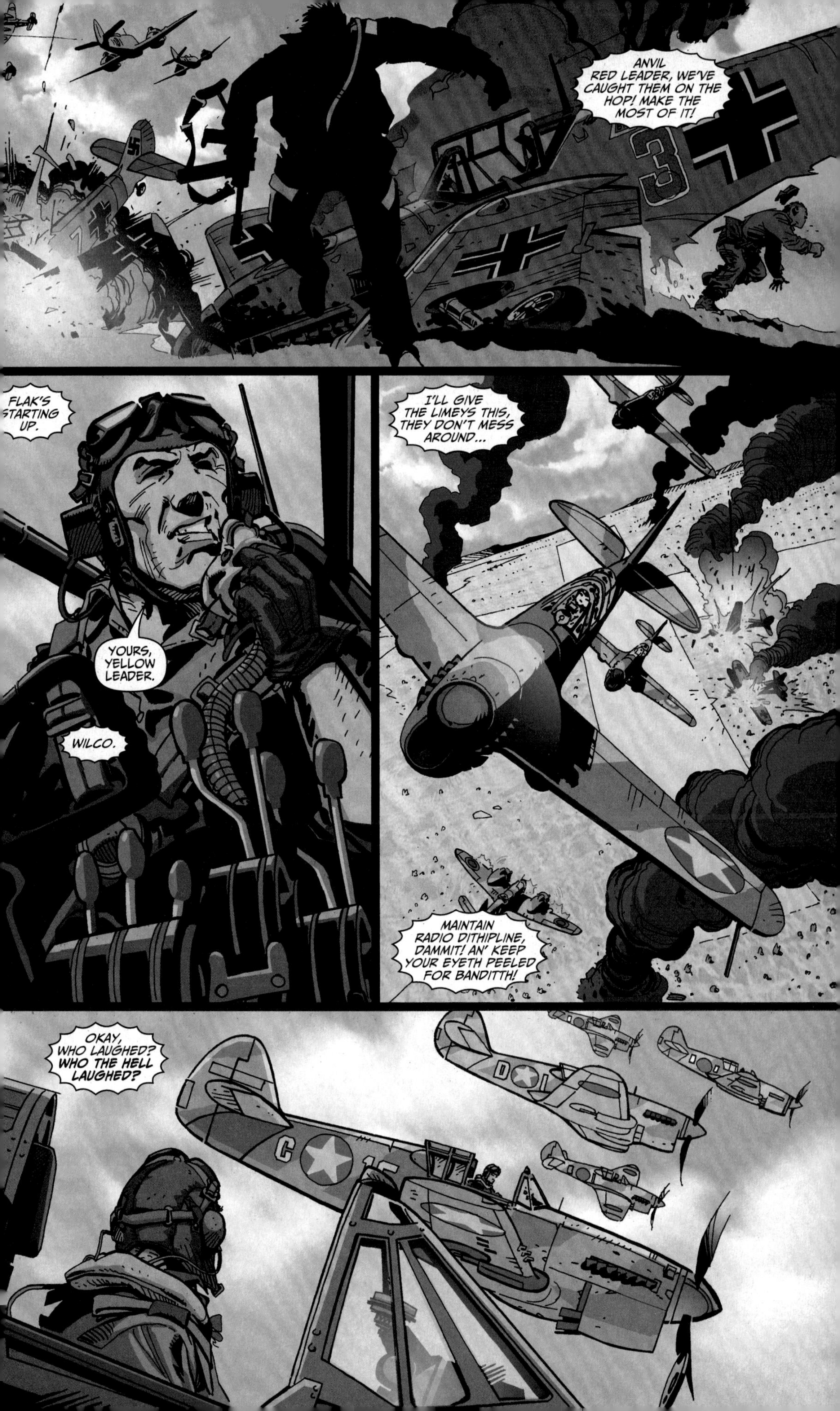

ANVIL RED LEADER, WE'VE CAUGHT THEM ON THE HOP! MAKE THE MOST OF IT!
FLAK'S STARTING UP.
YOURS, YELLOW LEADER.
WILCO.
I'LL GIVE THE LIMEYS THIS, THEY DON'T MESS AROUND...
MAINTAIN RADIO DITHIPLINE, DAMMIT! AN' KEEP YOUR EYETH PEELED FOR BANDITTH!
OKAY, WHO LAUGHED? WHO THE HELL LAUGHED?

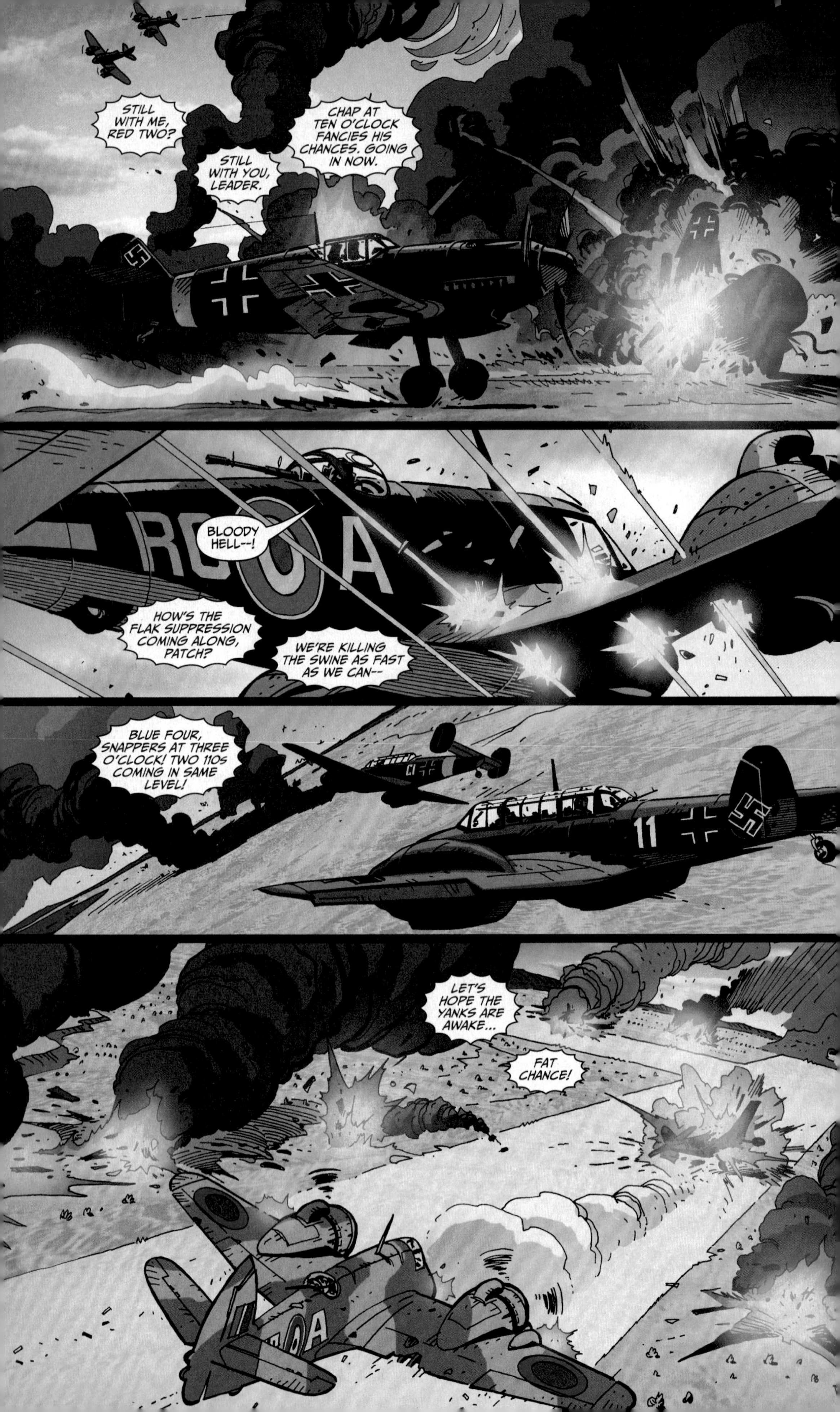
STILL WITH ME, RED TWO?
STILL WITH YOU, LEADER.
CHAP AT TEN O'CLOCK FANCIES HIS CHANCES. GOING IN NOW.
BLOODY HELL--!
HOW'S THE FLAK SUPPRESSION COMING ALONG, PATCH?
WE'RE KILLING THE SWINE AS FAST AS WE CAN--
BLUE FOUR, SNAPPERS AT THREE O'CLOCK! TWO 110S COMING IN SAME LEVEL!
LET'S HOPE THE YANKS ARE AWAKE...
FAT CHANCE!

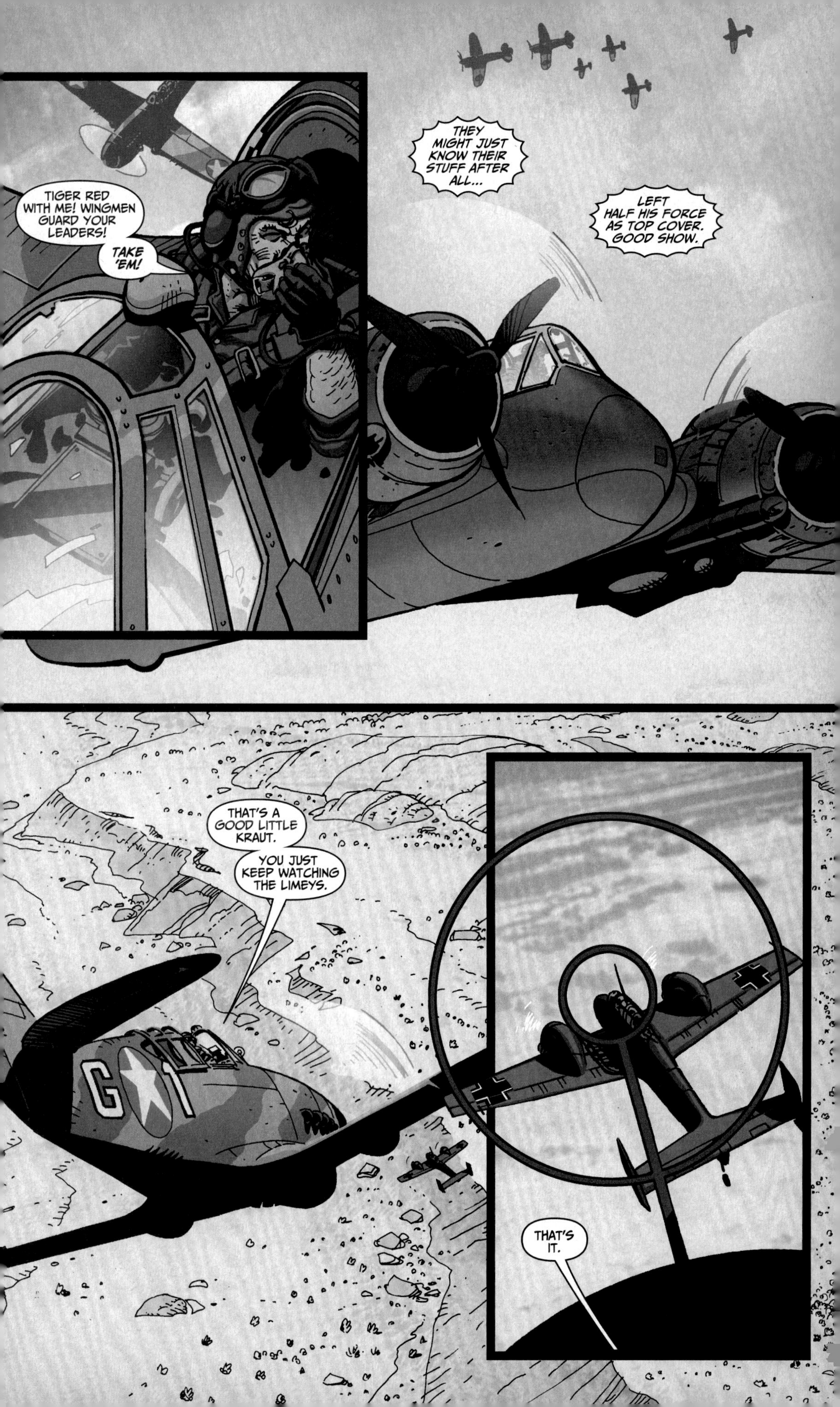

TIGER RED WITH ME! WINGMEN GUARD YOUR LEADERS!
TAKE 'EM!
THEY MIGHT JUST KNOW THEIR STUFF AFTER ALL...
LEFT HALF HIS FORCE AS TOP COVER. GOOD SHOW.
THAT'S A GOOD LITTLE KRAUT.
YOU JUST KEEP WATCHING THE LIMEYS.
THAT'S IT.

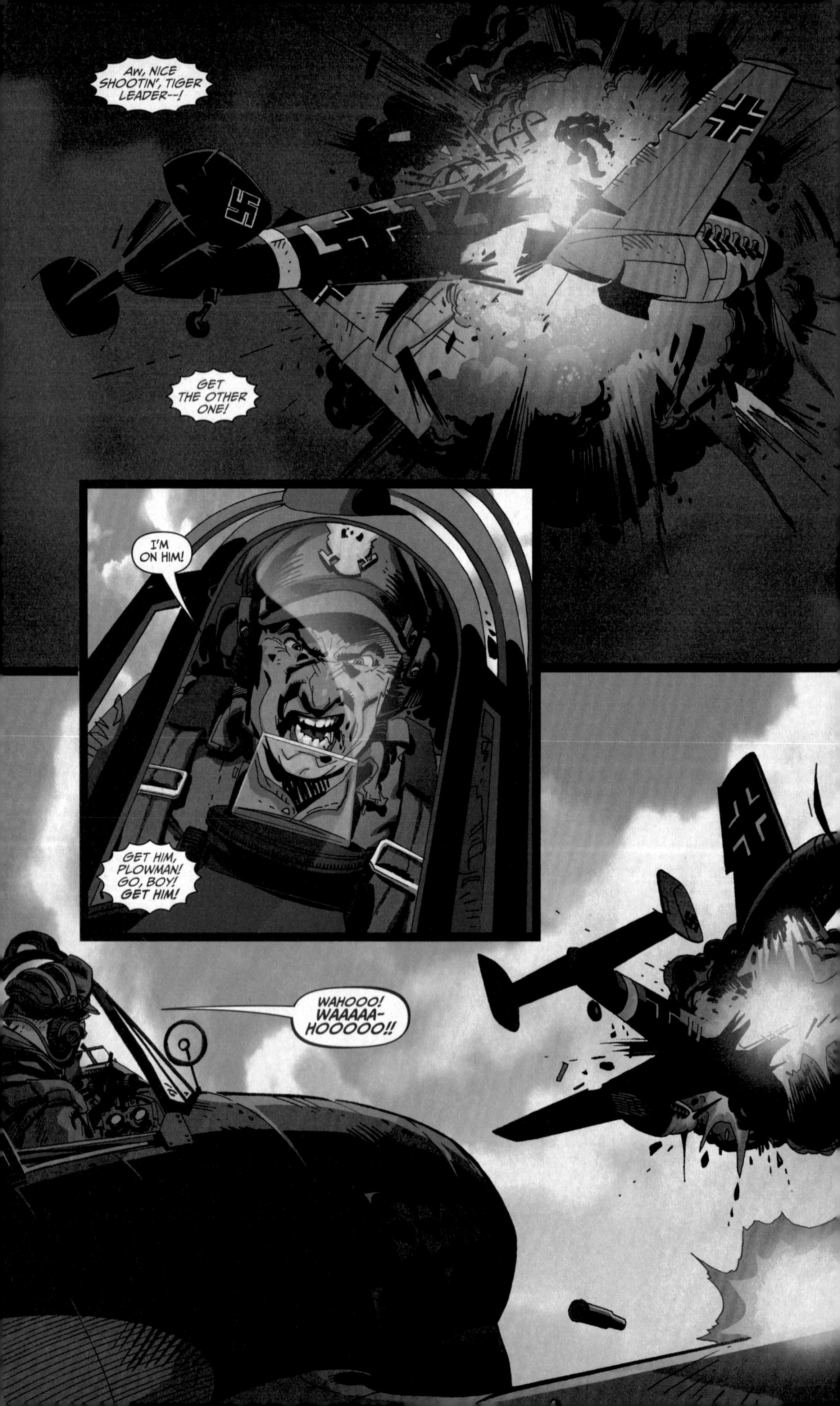
AW, NICE SHOOTIN', TIGER LEADER--!
GET THE OTHER ONE!
I'M ON HIM!
GET HIM, PLOWMAN! GO, BOY! GET HIM!
WAHOOO! WAAAAA-HOOOOO!!

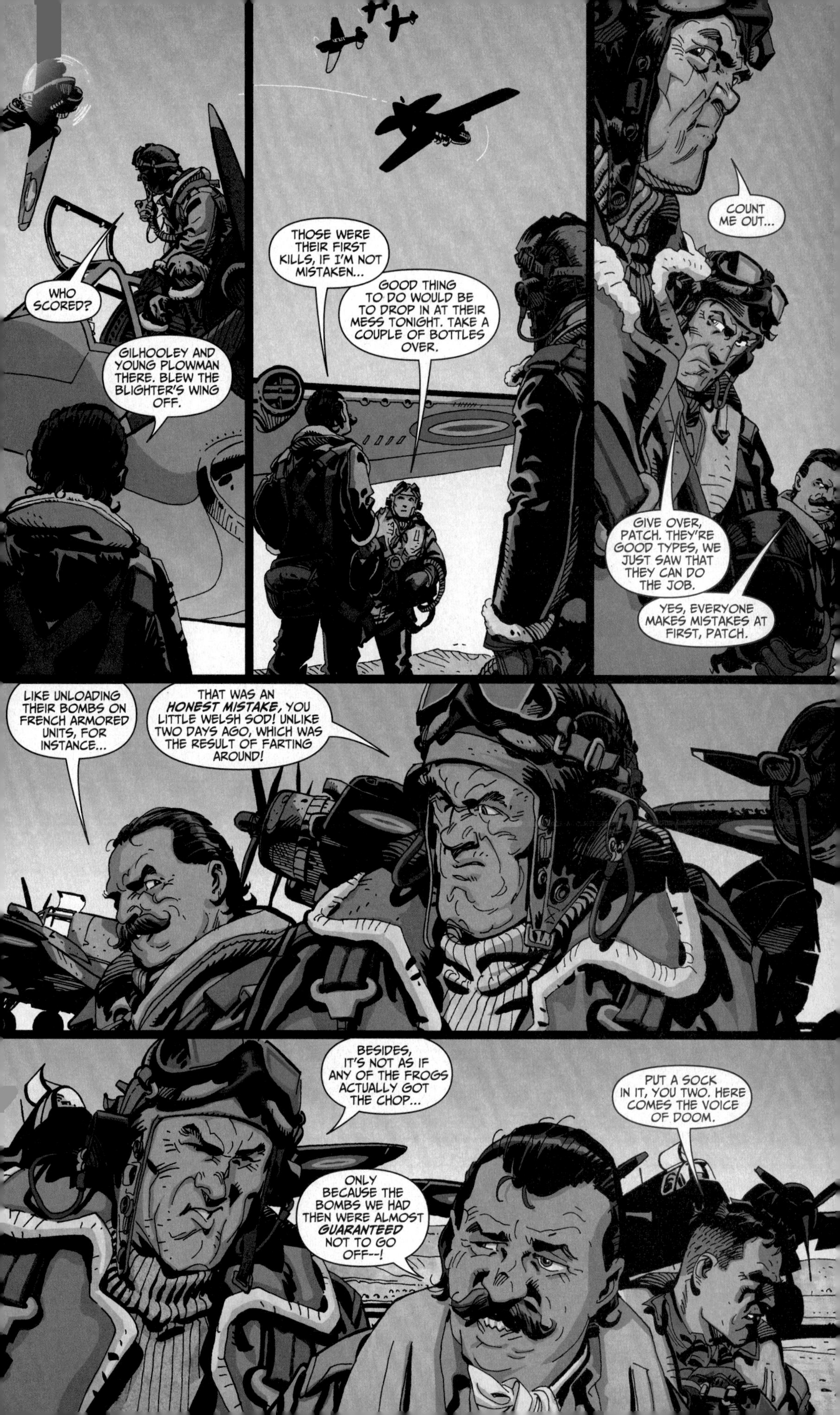
WHO SCORED?
GILHOOLEY AND YOUNG PLOWMAN THERE. BLEW THE BLIGHTER'S WING OFF.
THOSE WERE THEIR FIRST KILLS, IF I'M NOT MISTAKEN...
GOOD THING TO DO WOULD BE TO DROP IN AT THEIR MESS TONIGHT. TAKE A COUPLE OF BOTTLES OVER.
COUNT ME OUT...
GIVE OVER, PATCH. THEY'RE GOOD TYPES, WE JUST SAW THAT THEY CAN DO THE JOB.
YES, EVERYONE MAKES MISTAKES AT FIRST, PATCH.
LIKE UNLOADING THEIR BOMBS ON FRENCH ARMORED UNITS, FOR INSTANCE...
THAT WAS AN ***HONEST MISTAKE,*** YOU LITTLE WELSH SOD! UNLIKE TWO DAYS AGO, WHICH WAS THE RESULT OF FARTING AROUND!
BESIDES, IT'S NOT AS IF ANY OF THE FROGS ACTUALLY GOT THE CHOP...
ONLY BECAUSE THE BOMBS WE HAD THEN WERE ALMOST ***GUARANTEED*** NOT TO GO OFF--!
PUT A SOCK IN IT, YOU TWO. HERE COMES THE VOICE OF DOOM.

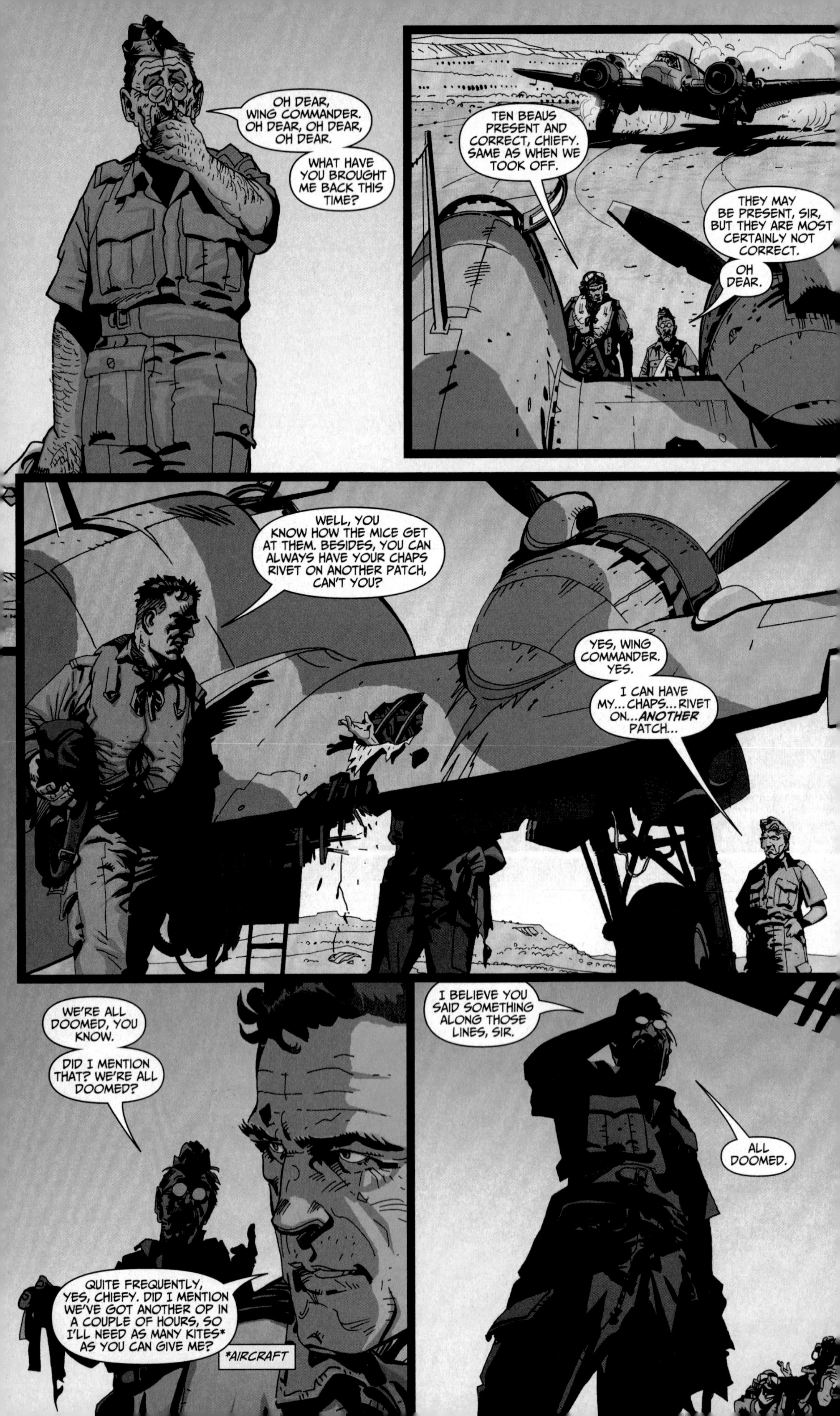
OH DEAR, WING COMMANDER. OH DEAR, OH DEAR, OH DEAR.
WHAT HAVE YOU BROUGHT ME BACK THIS TIME?
TEN BEAUS PRESENT AND CORRECT, CHIEFY. SAME AS WHEN WE TOOK OFF.
THEY MAY BE PRESENT, SIR, BUT THEY ARE MOST CERTAINLY NOT CORRECT.
OH DEAR.
WELL, YOU KNOW HOW THE MICE GET AT THEM. BESIDES, YOU CAN ALWAYS HAVE YOUR CHAPS RIVET ON ANOTHER PATCH, CAN'T YOU?
YES, WING COMMANDER. YES.
I CAN HAVE MY...CHAPS...RIVET ON...*ANOTHER* PATCH...
WE'RE ALL DOOMED, YOU KNOW.
DID I MENTION THAT? WE'RE ALL DOOMED?
QUITE FREQUENTLY, YES, CHIEFY. DID I MENTION WE'VE GOT ANOTHER OP IN A COUPLE OF HOURS, SO I'LL NEED AS MANY KITES* AS YOU CAN GIVE ME?
*AIRCRAFT
I BELIEVE YOU SAID SOMETHING ALONG THOSE LINES, SIR.
ALL DOOMED.

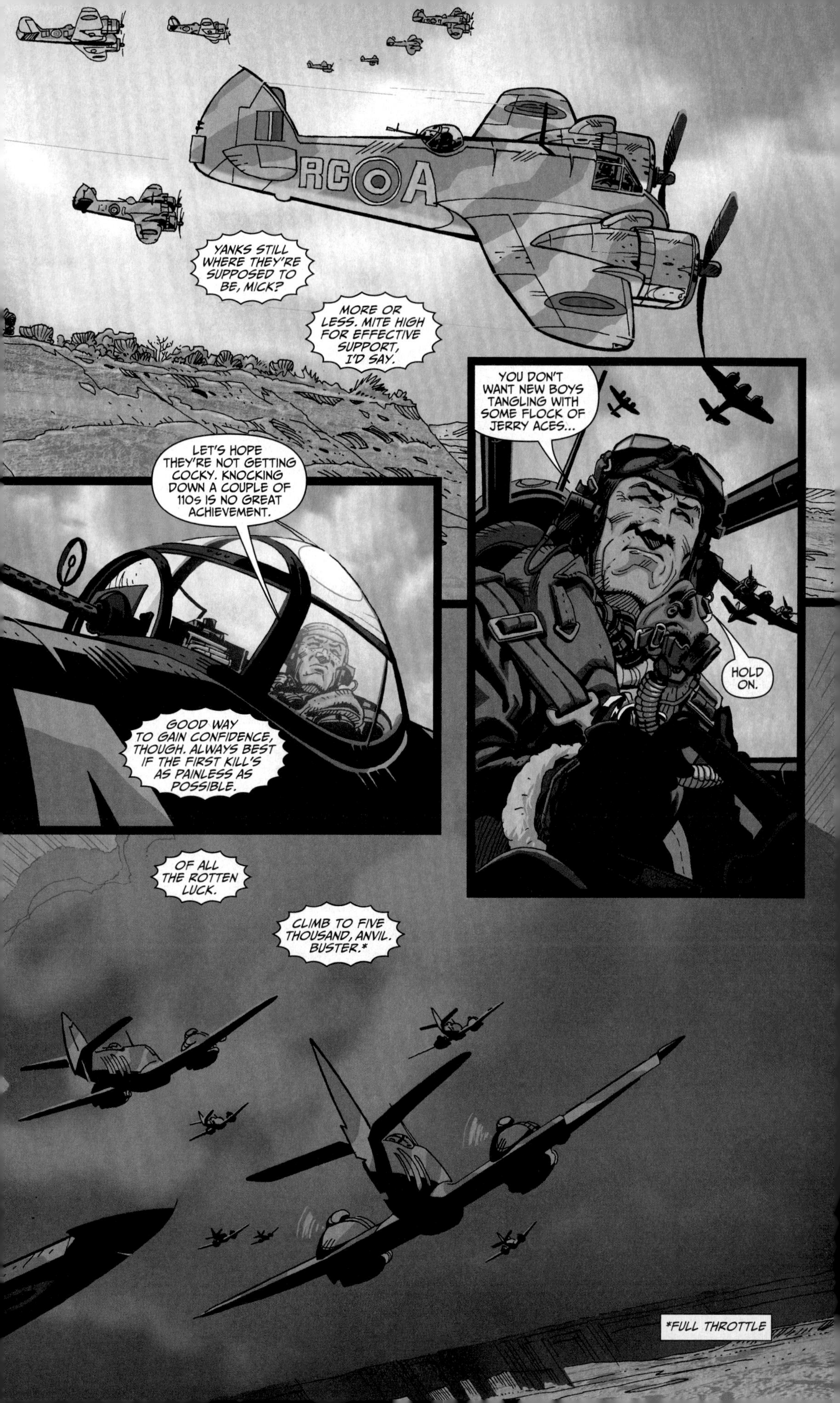
YANKS STILL WHERE THEY'RE SUPPOSED TO BE, MICK?
MORE OR LESS. MITE HIGH FOR EFFECTIVE SUPPORT, I'D SAY.
YOU DON'T WANT NEW BOYS TANGLING WITH SOME FLOCK OF JERRY ACES...
LET'S HOPE THEY'RE NOT GETTING COCKY. KNOCKING DOWN A COUPLE OF 110S IS NO GREAT ACHIEVEMENT.
GOOD WAY TO GAIN CONFIDENCE, THOUGH. ALWAYS BEST IF THE FIRST KILL'S AS PAINLESS AS POSSIBLE.
HOLD ON.
OF ALL THE ROTTEN LUCK.
CLIMB TO FIVE THOUSAND, ANVIL. BUSTER.*
*FULL THROTTLE

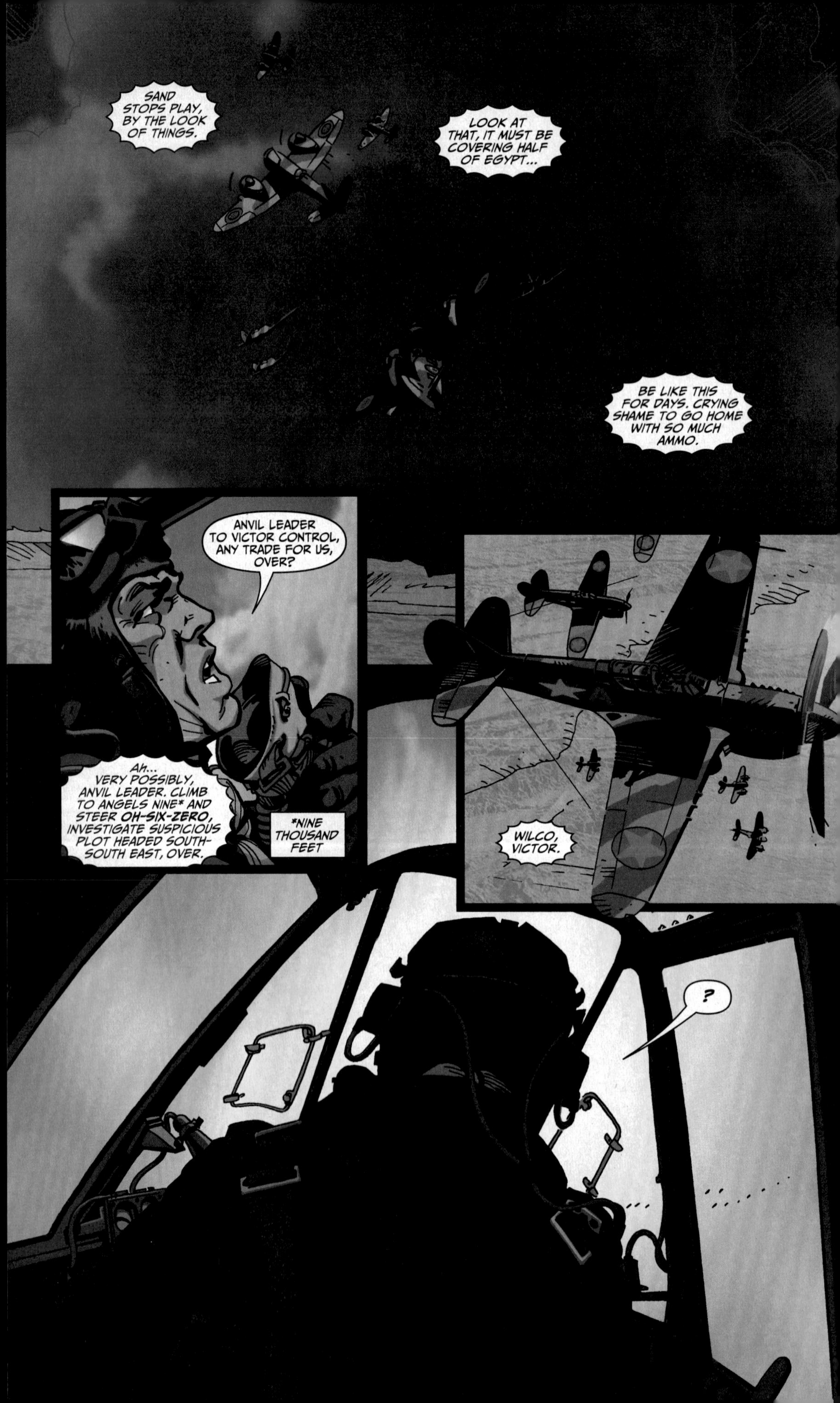
SAND STOPS PLAY, BY THE LOOK OF THINGS.
LOOK AT THAT, IT MUST BE COVERING HALF OF EGYPT...
BE LIKE THIS FOR DAYS. CRYING SHAME TO GO HOME WITH SO MUCH AMMO.
ANVIL LEADER TO VICTOR CONTROL, ANY TRADE FOR US, OVER?
AH... VERY POSSIBLY, ANVIL LEADER. CLIMB TO ANGELS NINE* AND STEER OH-SIX-ZERO, INVESTIGATE SUSPICIOUS PLOT HEADED SOUTH-SOUTH EAST, OVER.
*NINE THOUSAND FEET
WILCO, VICTOR.
?

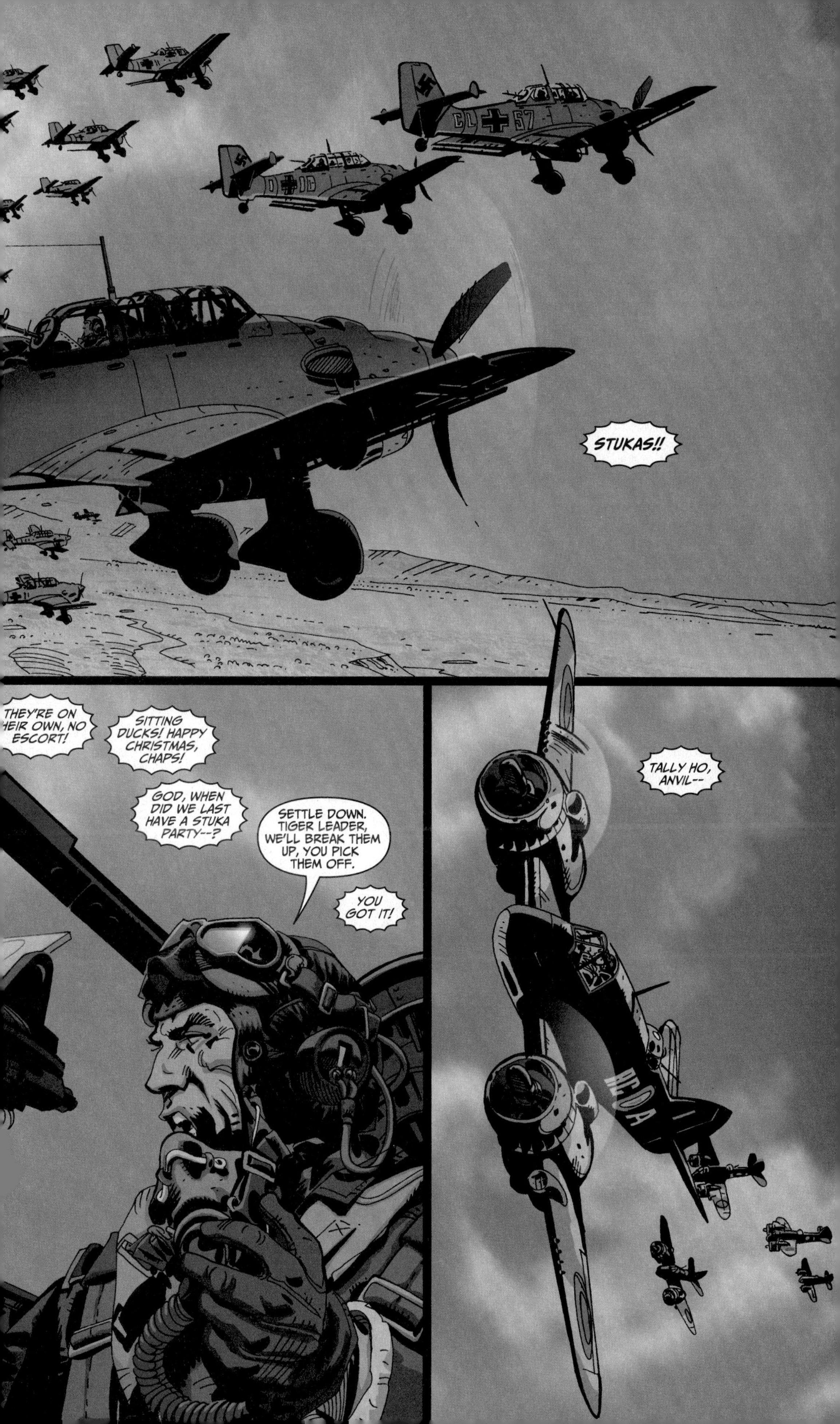

STUKAS!!
THEY'RE ON HEIR OWN, NO ESCORT!
SITTING DUCKS! HAPPY CHRISTMAS, CHAPS!
GOD, WHEN DID WE LAST HAVE A STUKA PARTY--?
SETTLE DOWN. TIGER LEADER, WE'LL BREAK THEM UP, YOU PICK THEM OFF.
YOU GOT IT!
TALLY HO, ANVIL--

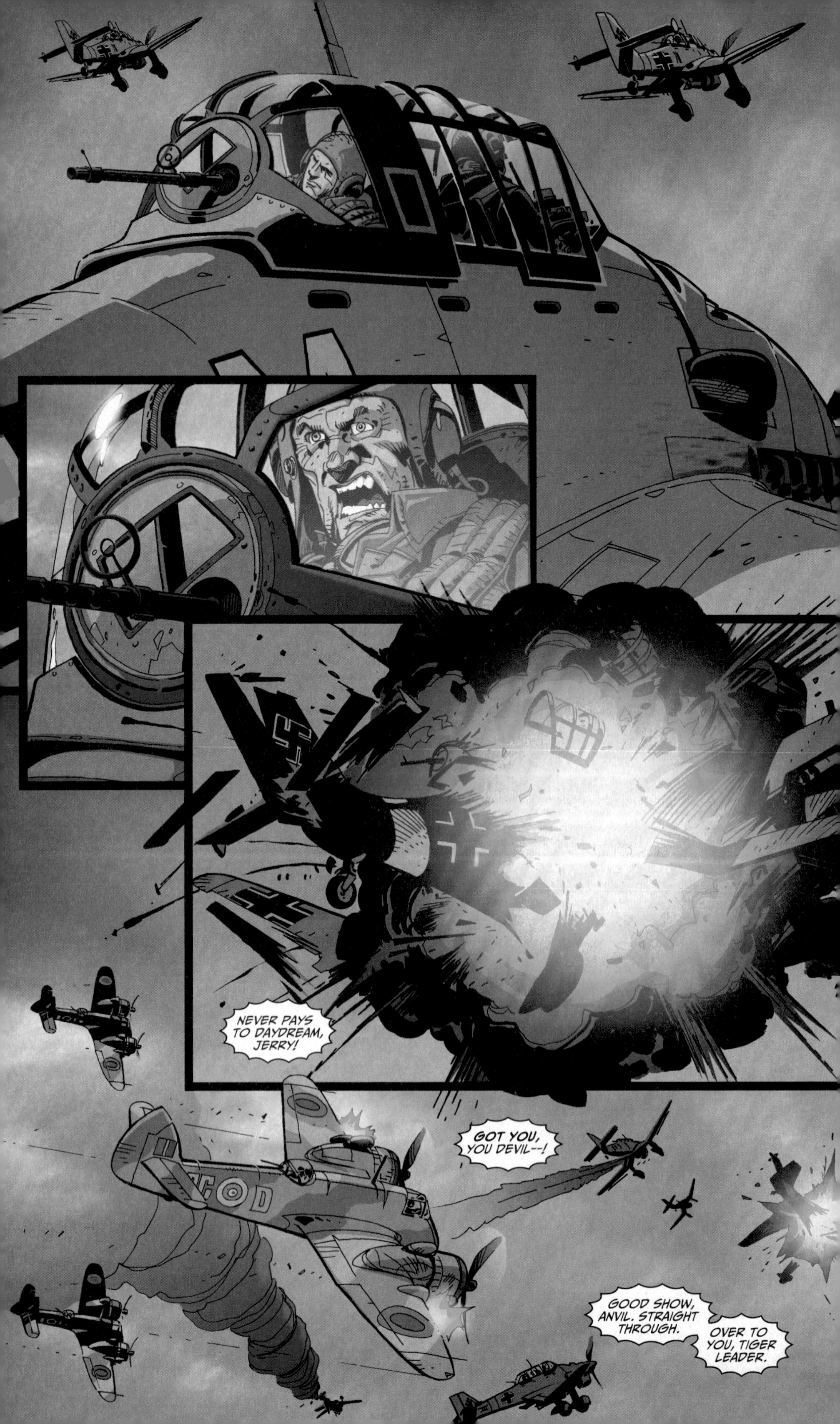
NEVER PAYS TO DAYDREAM, JERRY!
GOT YOU, YOU DEVIL--!
GOOD SHOW, ANVIL. STRAIGHT THROUGH.
OVER TO YOU, TIGER LEADER.

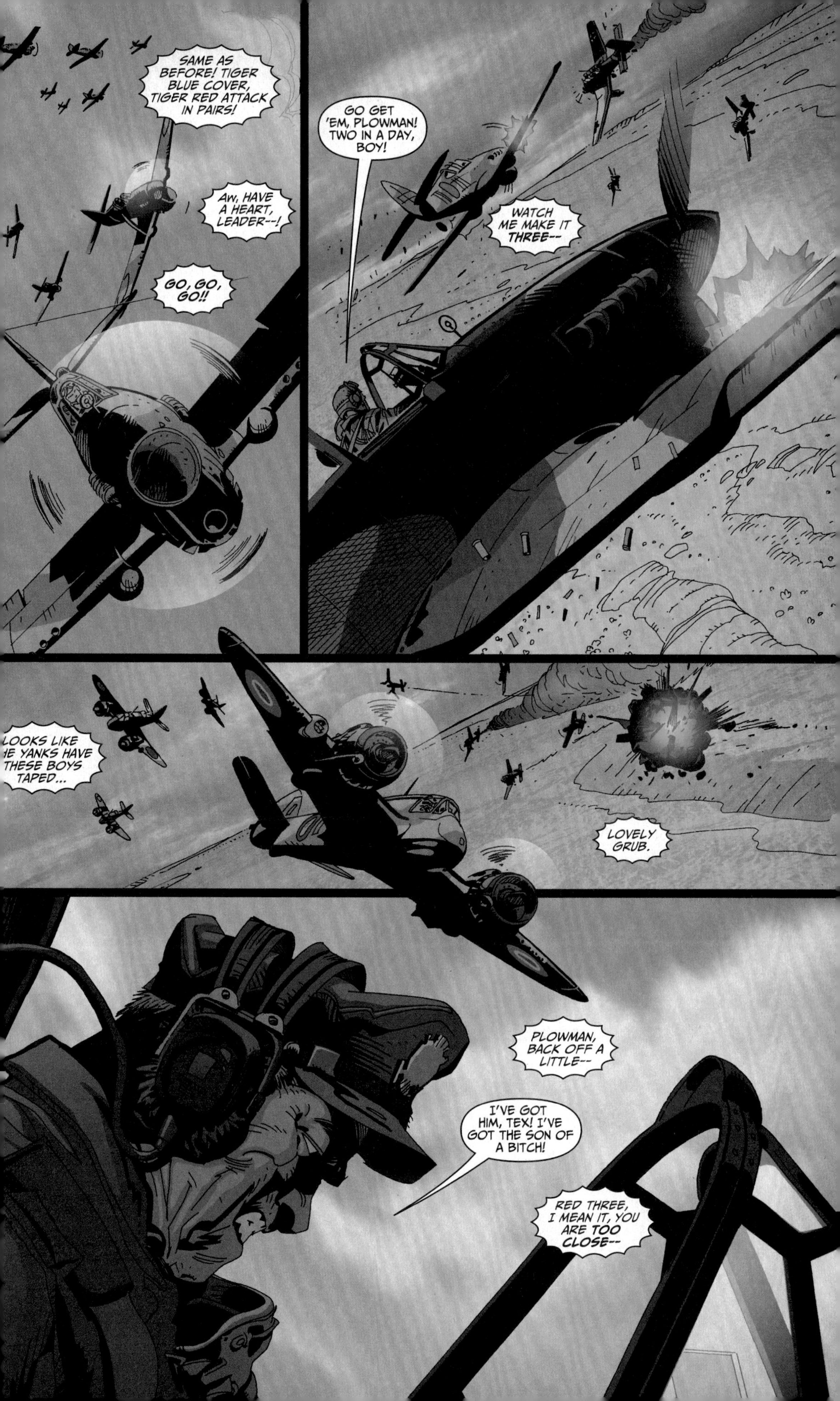
SAME AS BEFORE! TIGER BLUE COVER, TIGER RED ATTACK IN PAIRS!
AW, HAVE A HEART, LEADER--!
GO, GO, GO!!
GO GET 'EM, PLOWMAN! TWO IN A DAY, BOY!
WATCH ME MAKE IT THREE--
LOOKS LIKE HE YANKS HAVE THESE BOYS TAPED...
LOVELY GRUB.
PLOWMAN, BACK OFF A LITTLE--
I'VE GOT HIM, TEX! I'VE GOT THE SON OF A BITCH!
RED THREE, I MEAN IT, YOU ARE TOO CLOSE--

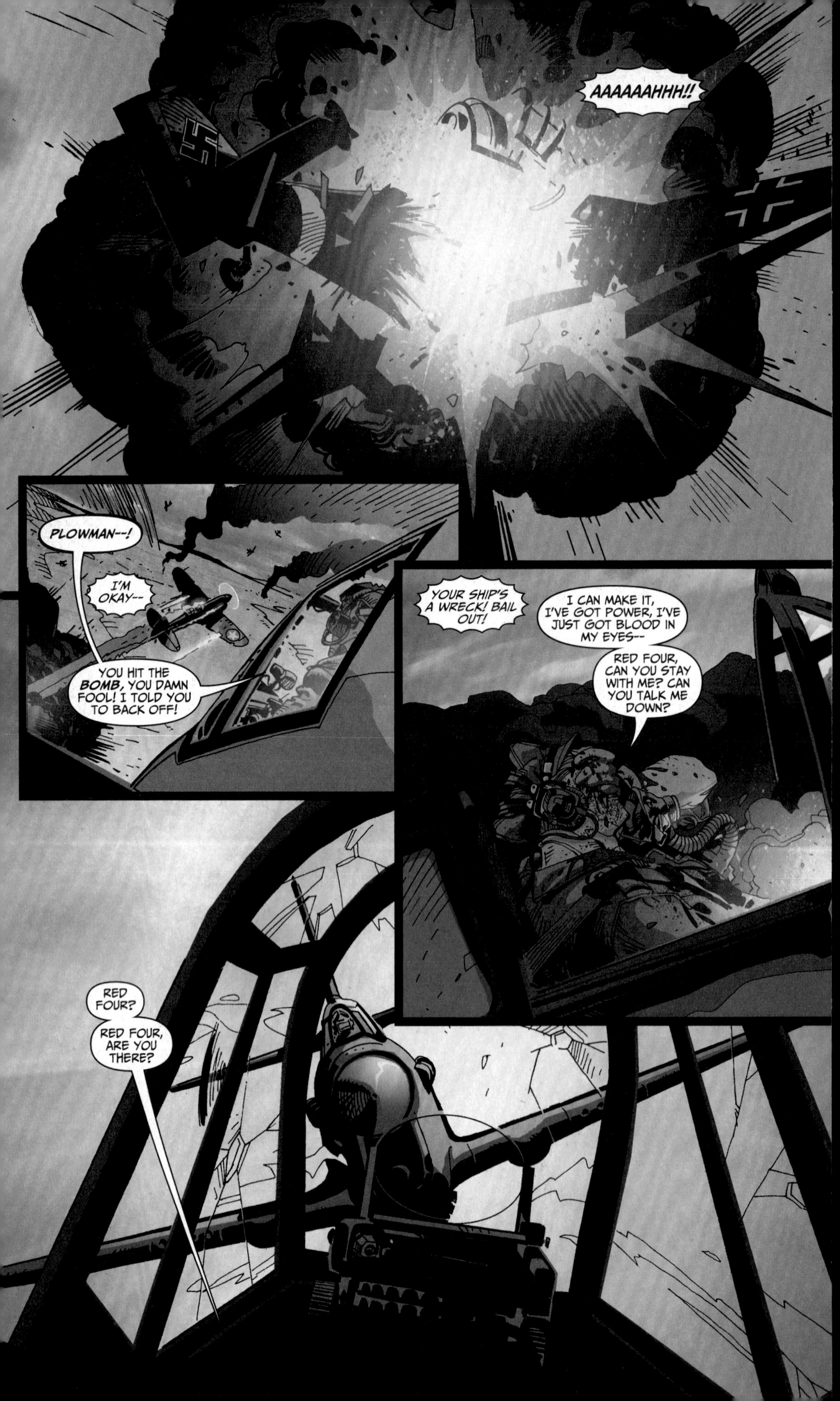
AAAAAAHHH!!
PLOWMAN--!
I'M OKAY--
YOU HIT THE BOMB, YOU DAMN FOOL! I TOLD YOU TO BACK OFF!
YOUR SHIP'S A WRECK! BAIL OUT!
I CAN MAKE IT, I'VE GOT POWER, I'VE JUST GOT BLOOD IN MY EYES--
RED FOUR, CAN YOU STAY WITH ME? CAN YOU TALK ME DOWN?
RED FOUR?
RED FOUR, ARE YOU THERE?

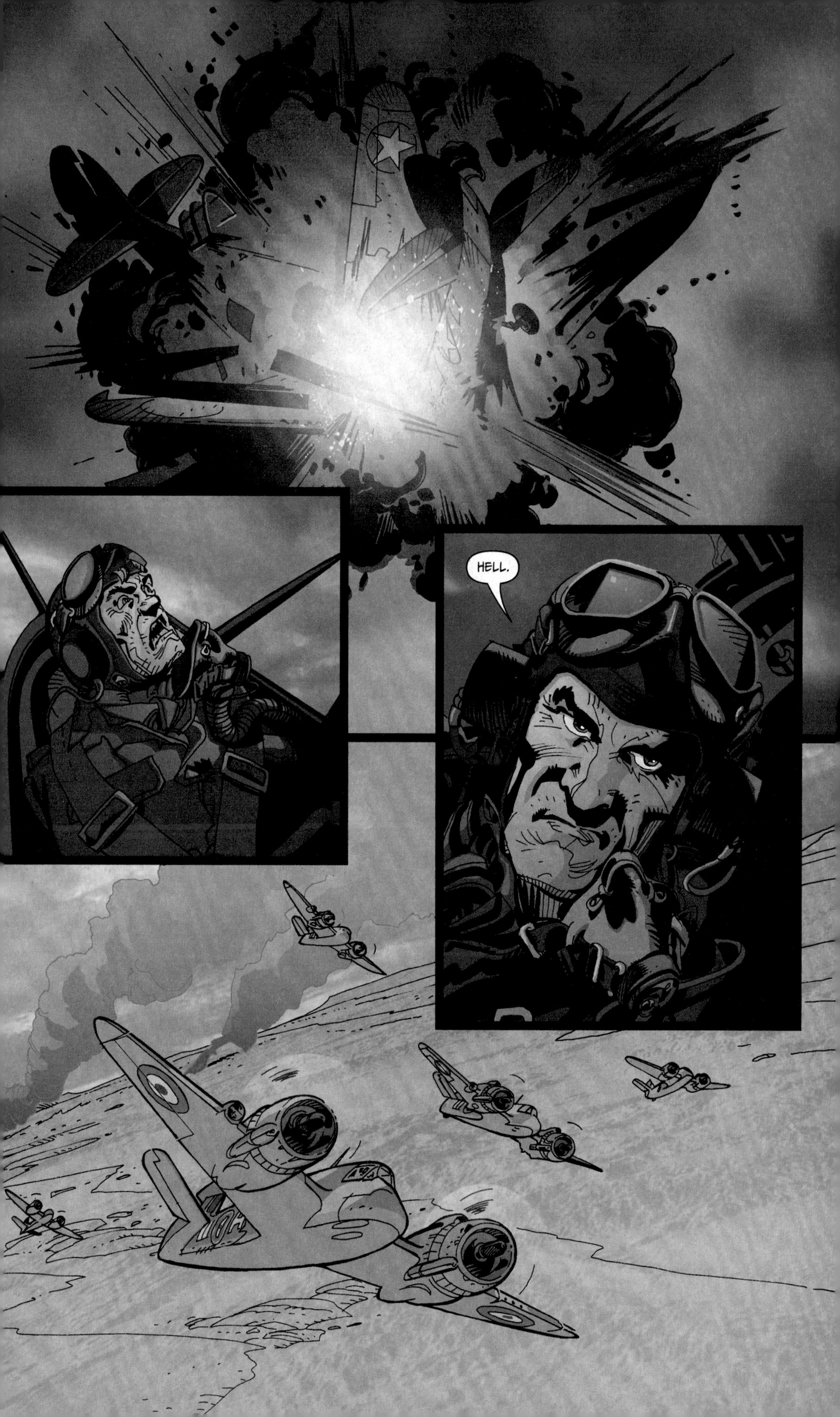
HELL.

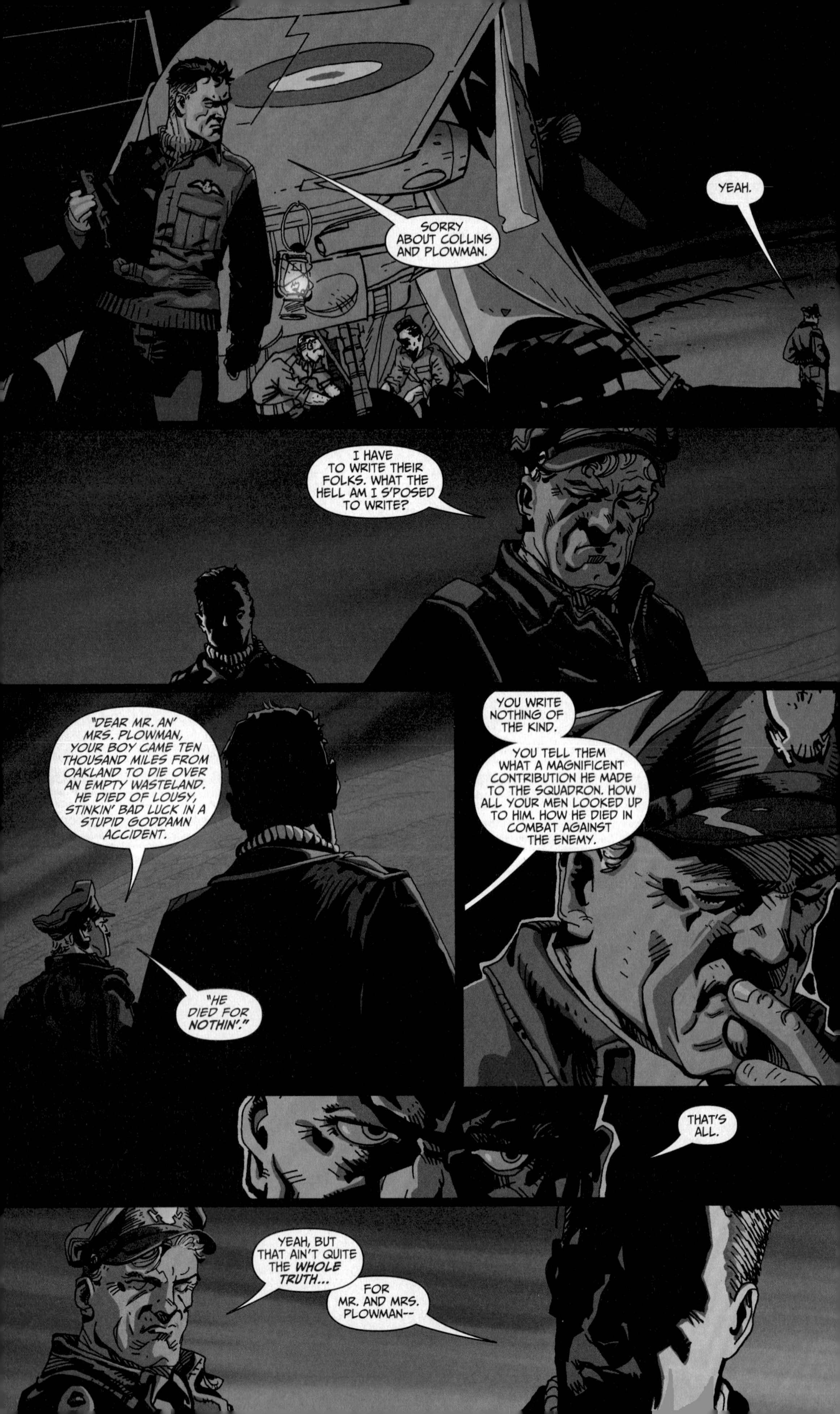
SORRY ABOUT COLLINS AND PLOWMAN.
YEAH.
I HAVE TO WRITE THEIR FOLKS. WHAT THE HELL AM I S'POSED TO WRITE?
"DEAR MR. AN' MRS. PLOWMAN, YOUR BOY CAME TEN THOUSAND MILES FROM OAKLAND TO DIE OVER AN EMPTY WASTELAND. HE DIED OF LOUSY, STINKIN' BAD LUCK IN A STUPID GODDAMN ACCIDENT.
"HE DIED FOR NOTHIN'."
YOU WRITE NOTHING OF THE KIND.
YOU TELL THEM WHAT A MAGNIFICENT CONTRIBUTION HE MADE TO THE SQUADRON. HOW ALL YOUR MEN LOOKED UP TO HIM. HOW HE DIED IN COMBAT AGAINST THE ENEMY.
THAT'S ALL.
YEAH, BUT THAT AIN'T QUITE THE WHOLE TRUTH...
FOR MR. AND MRS. PLOWMAN--

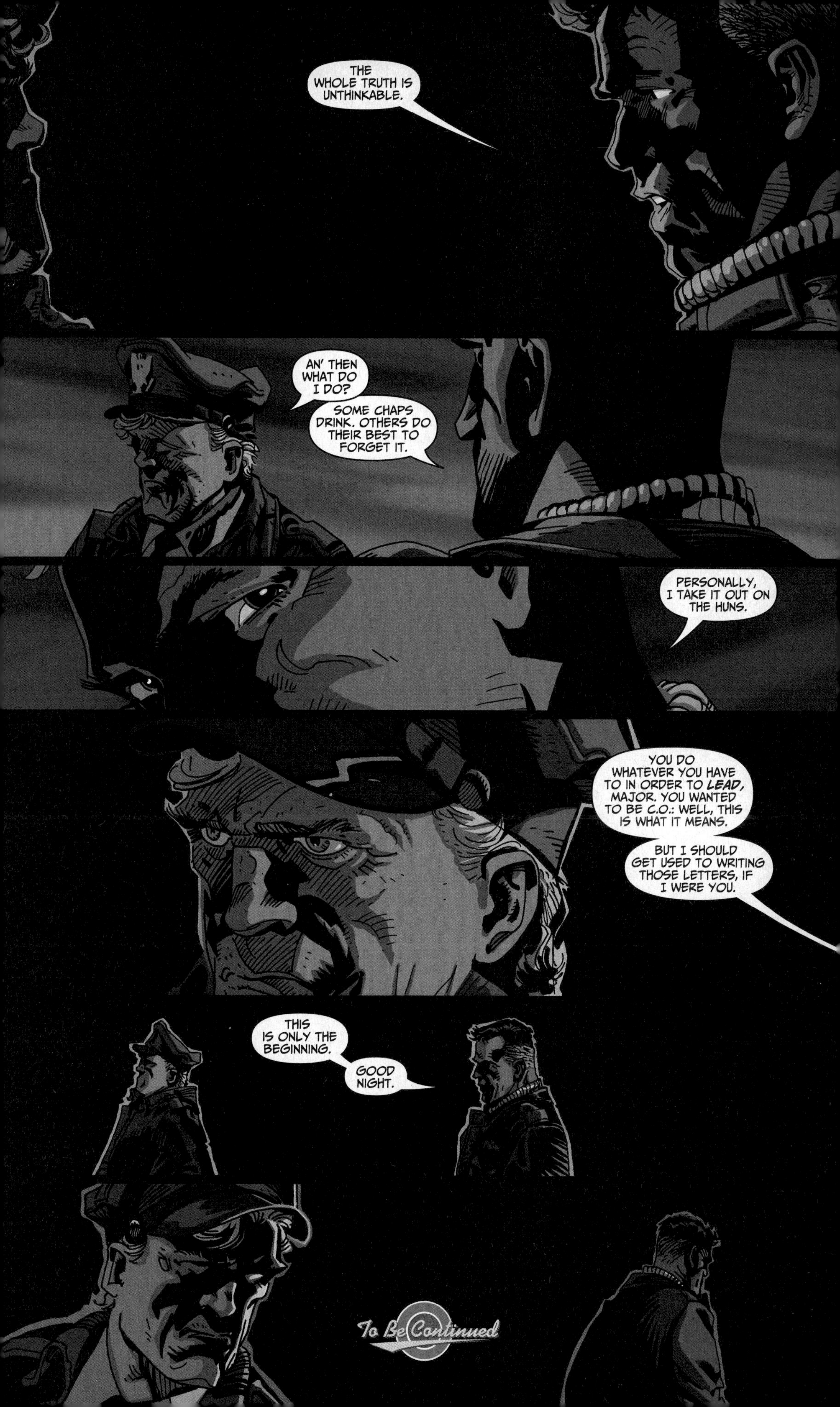
THE WHOLE TRUTH IS UNTHINKABLE.
AN' THEN WHAT DO I DO?
SOME CHAPS DRINK. OTHERS DO THEIR BEST TO FORGET IT.
PERSONALLY, I TAKE IT OUT ON THE HUNS.
YOU DO WHATEVER YOU HAVE TO IN ORDER TO *LEAD,* MAJOR. YOU WANTED TO BE C.O.: WELL, THIS IS WHAT IT MEANS.
BUT I SHOULD GET USED TO WRITING THOSE LETTERS, IF I WERE YOU.
THIS IS ONLY THE BEGINNING.
GOOD NIGHT.
To Be Continued

CHAPTER 3

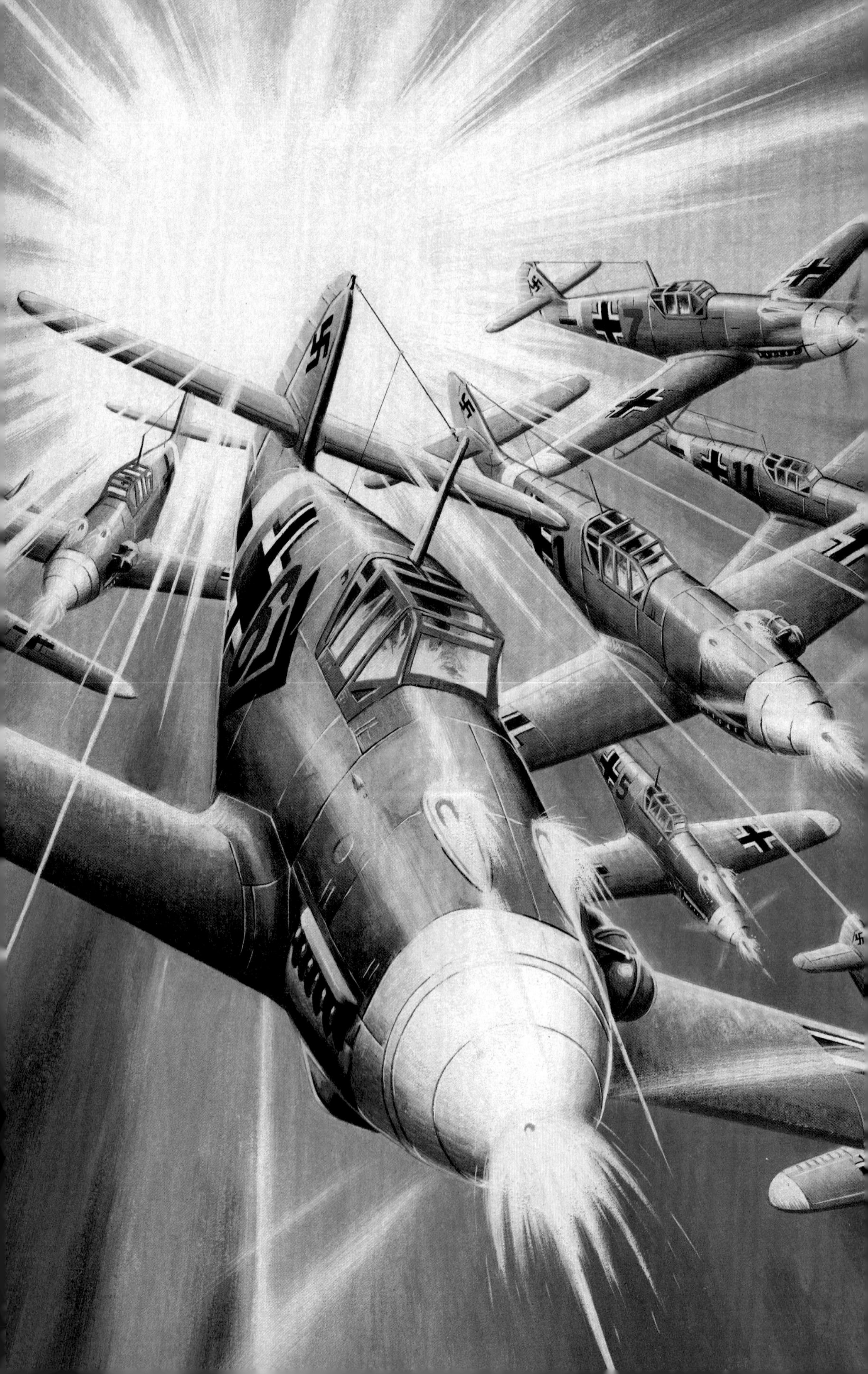

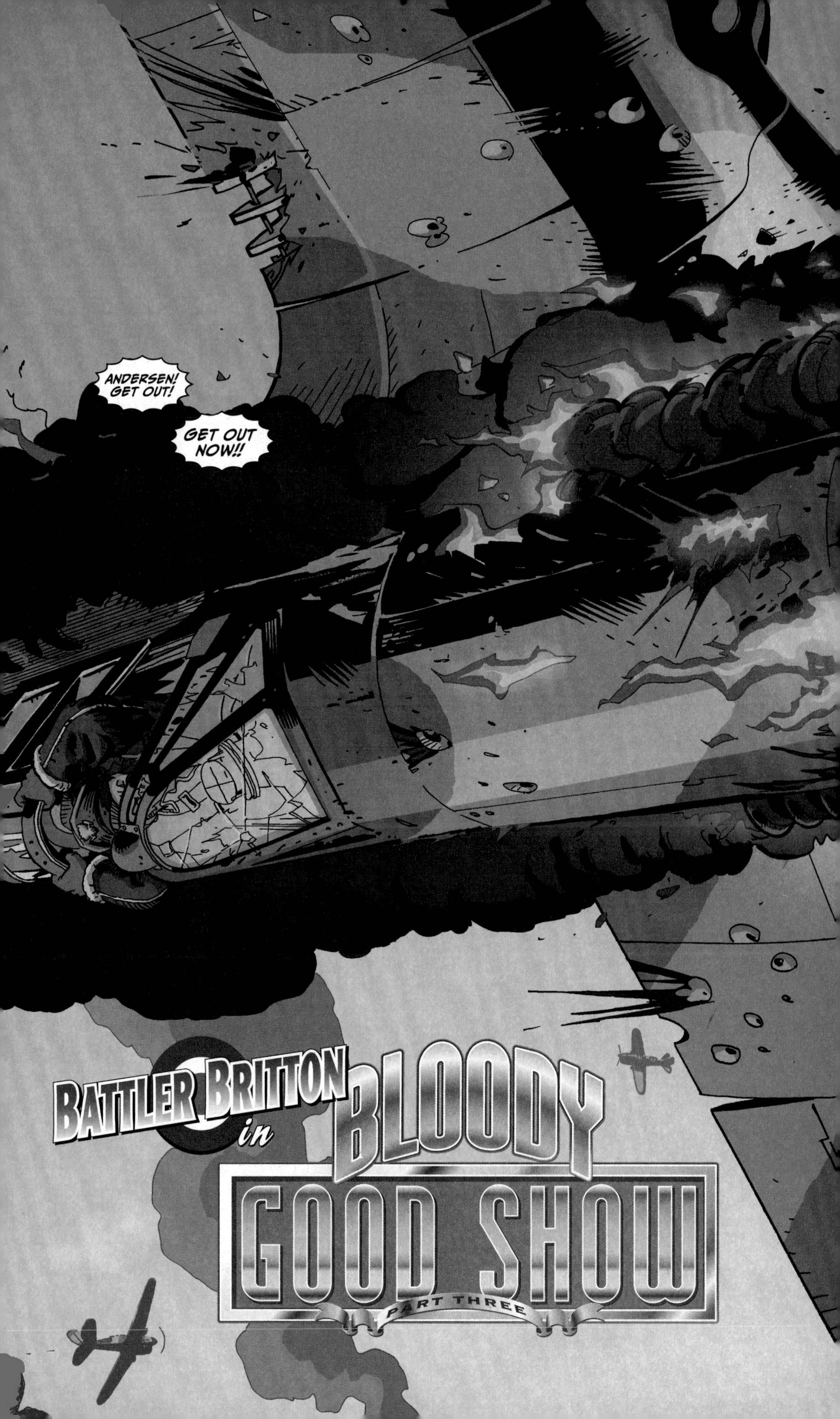
ANDERSEN! GET OUT!
GET OUT NOW!!
BATTLER BRITTON in
BLOODY
GOOD SHOW
PART THREE

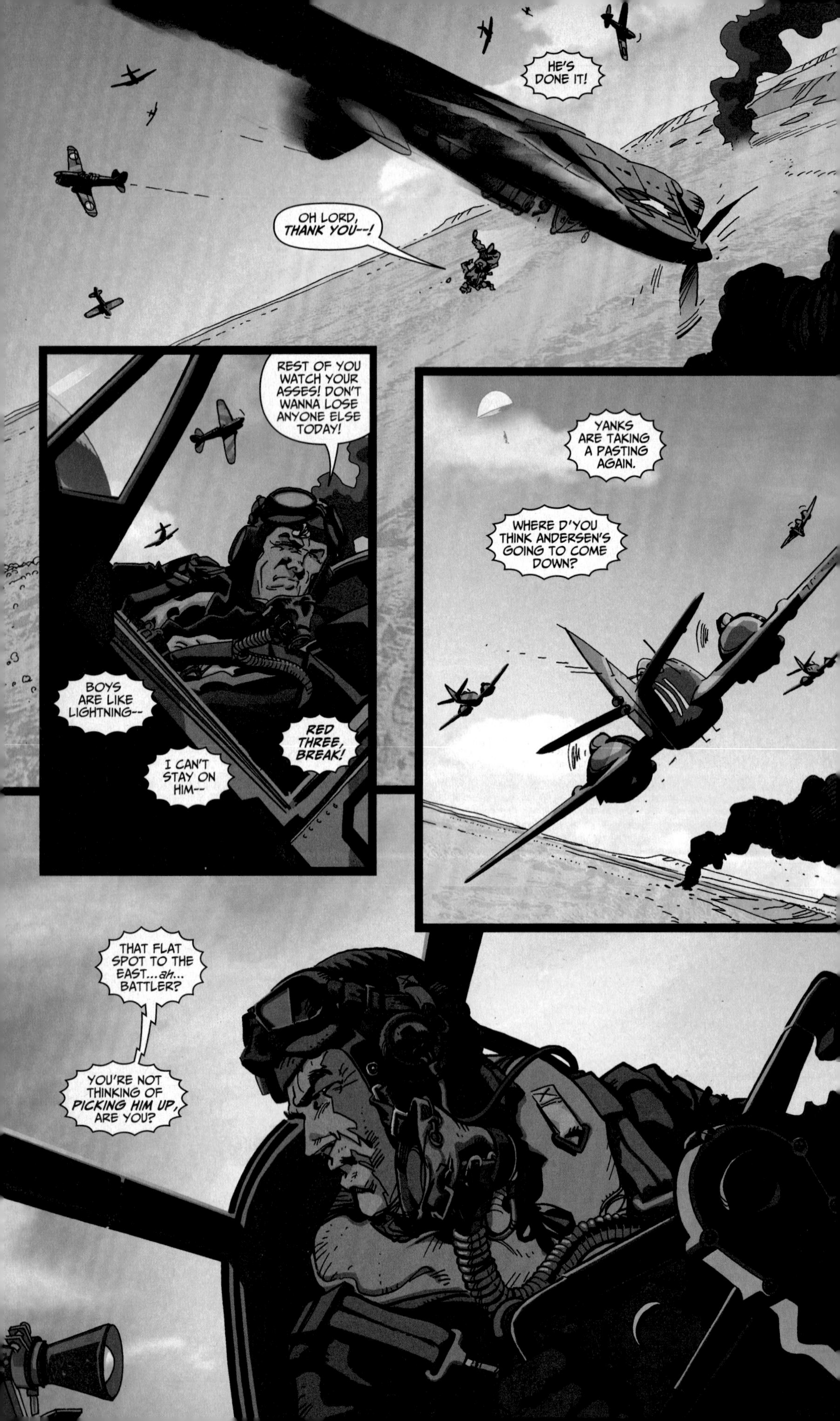
HE'S DONE IT!
OH LORD, *THANK YOU*--!
REST OF YOU WATCH YOUR ASSES! DON'T WANNA LOSE ANYONE ELSE TODAY!
BOYS ARE LIKE LIGHTNING--
RED THREE, BREAK!
I CAN'T STAY ON HIM--
YANKS ARE TAKING A PASTING AGAIN.
WHERE D'YOU THINK ANDERSEN'S GOING TO COME DOWN?
THAT FLAT SPOT TO THE EAST...*ah*... BATTLER?
YOU'RE NOT THINKING OF *PICKING HIM UP*, ARE YOU?

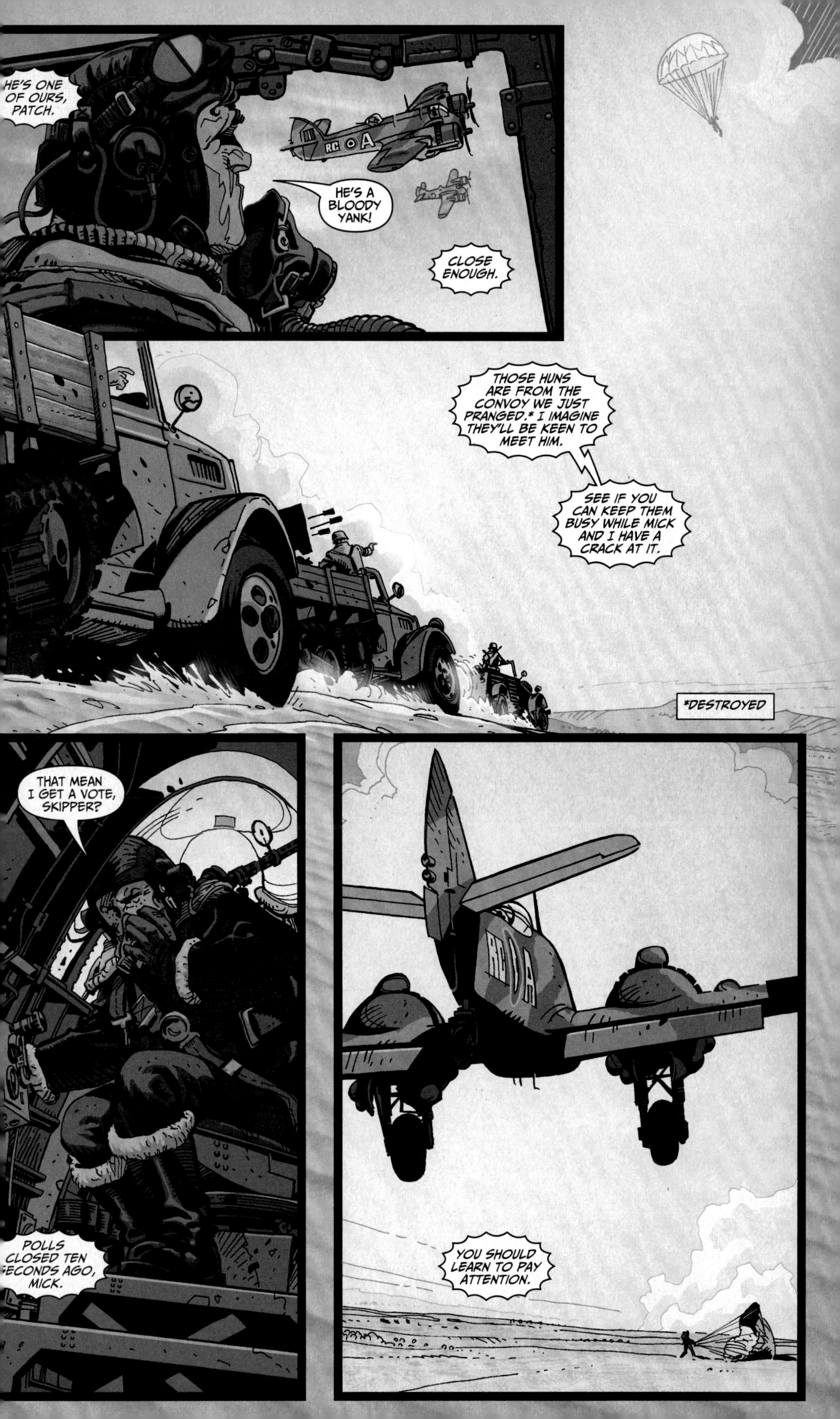
HE'S ONE OF OURS, PATCH.
HE'S A BLOODY YANK!
CLOSE ENOUGH.
THOSE HUNS ARE FROM THE CONVOY WE JUST PRANGED.* I IMAGINE THEY'LL BE KEEN TO MEET HIM.
SEE IF YOU CAN KEEP THEM BUSY WHILE MICK AND I HAVE A CRACK AT IT.
*DESTROYED
THAT MEAN I GET A VOTE, SKIPPER?
POLLS CLOSED TEN SECONDS AGO, MICK.
YOU SHOULD LEARN TO PAY ATTENTION.

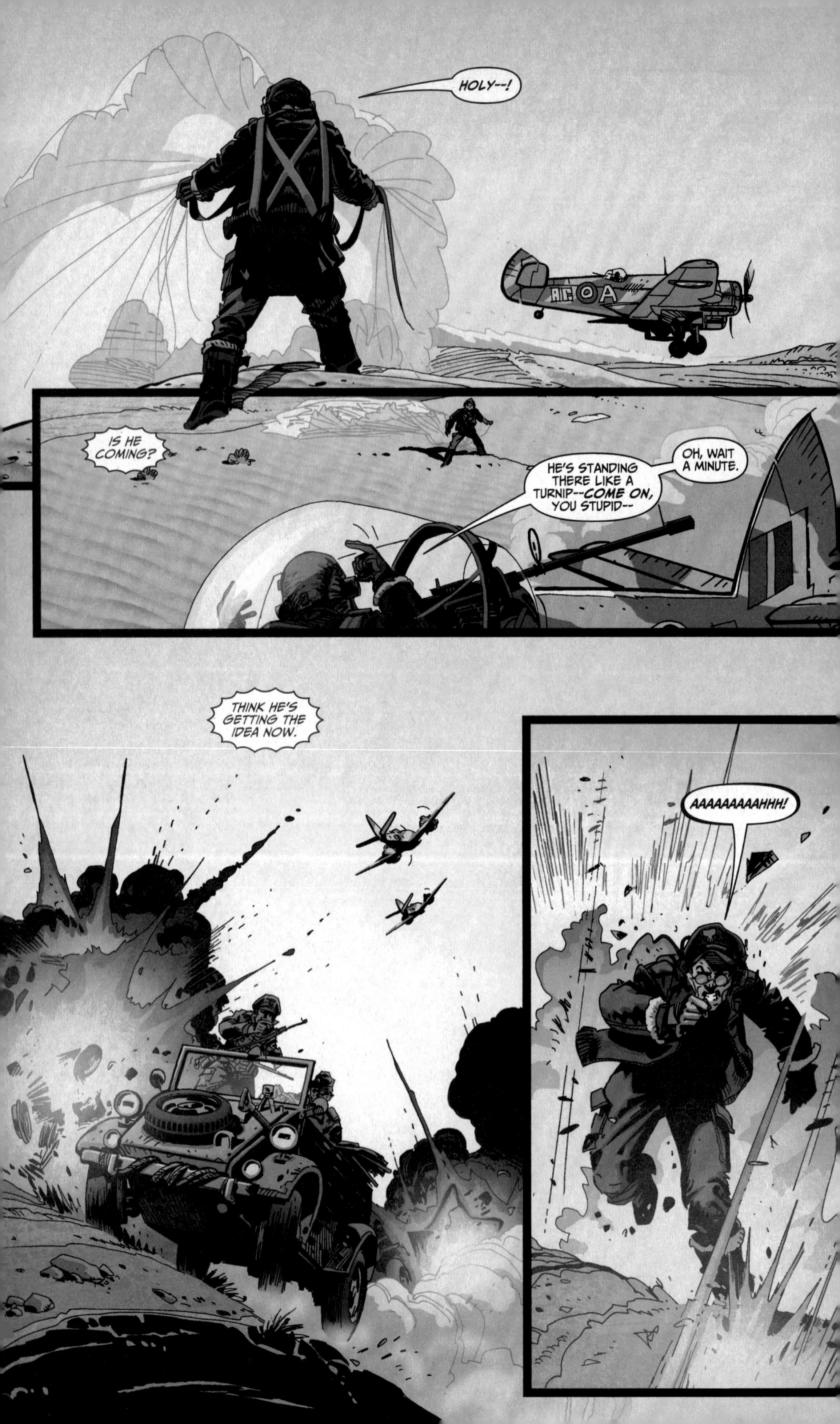
HOLY--!
IS HE COMING?
HE'S STANDING THERE LIKE A TURNIP--**COME ON,** YOU STUPID--
OH, WAIT A MINUTE.
THINK HE'S GETTING THE IDEA NOW.
AAAAAAAAAHHH!

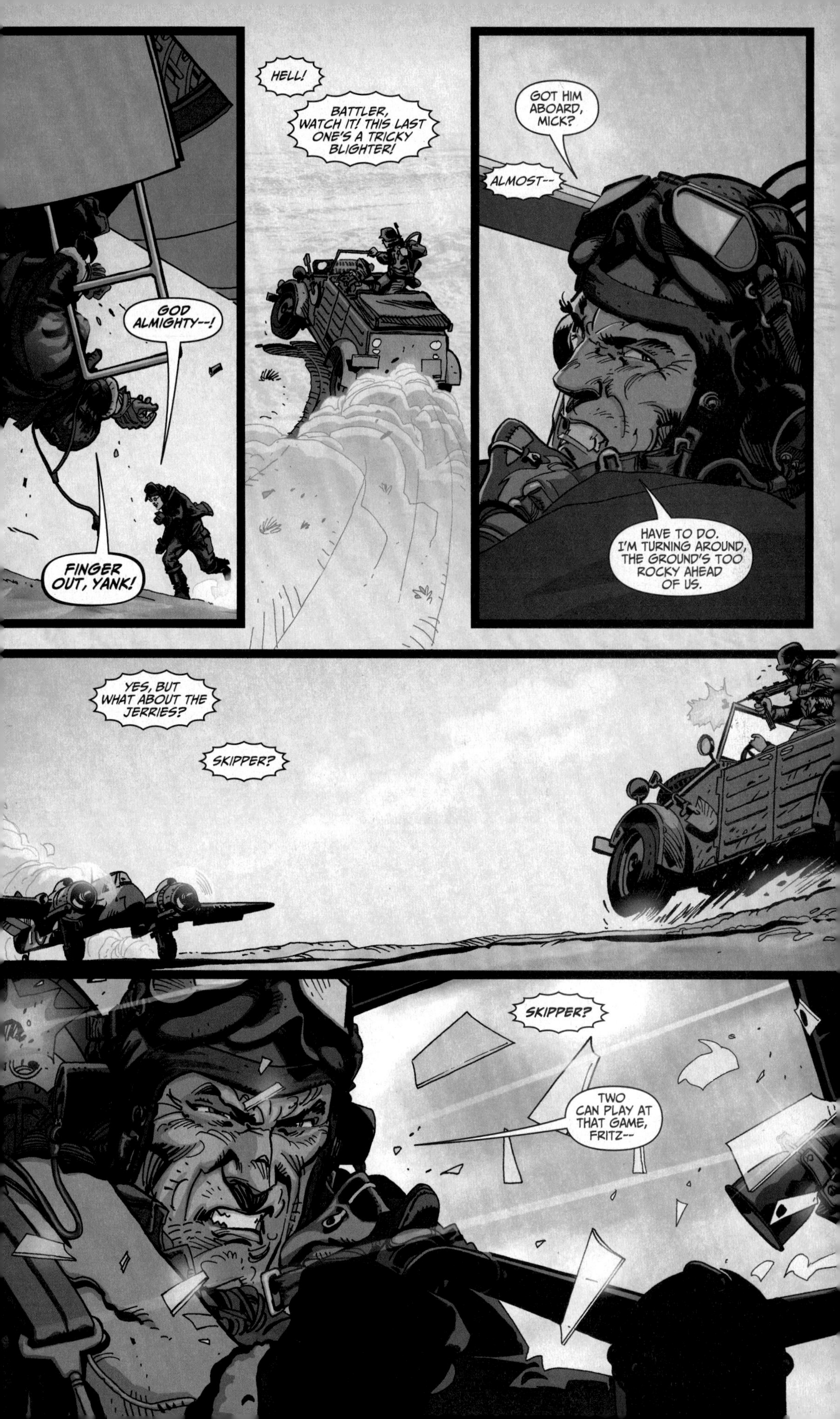
HELL!
BATTLER, WATCH IT! THIS LAST ONE'S A TRICKY BLIGHTER!
GOD ALMIGHTY--!
FINGER OUT, YANK!
GOT HIM ABOARD, MICK?
ALMOST--
HAVE TO DO. I'M TURNING AROUND, THE GROUND'S TOO ROCKY AHEAD OF US.
YES, BUT WHAT ABOUT THE JERRIES?
SKIPPER?
SKIPPER?
TWO CAN PLAY AT THAT GAME, FRITZ--

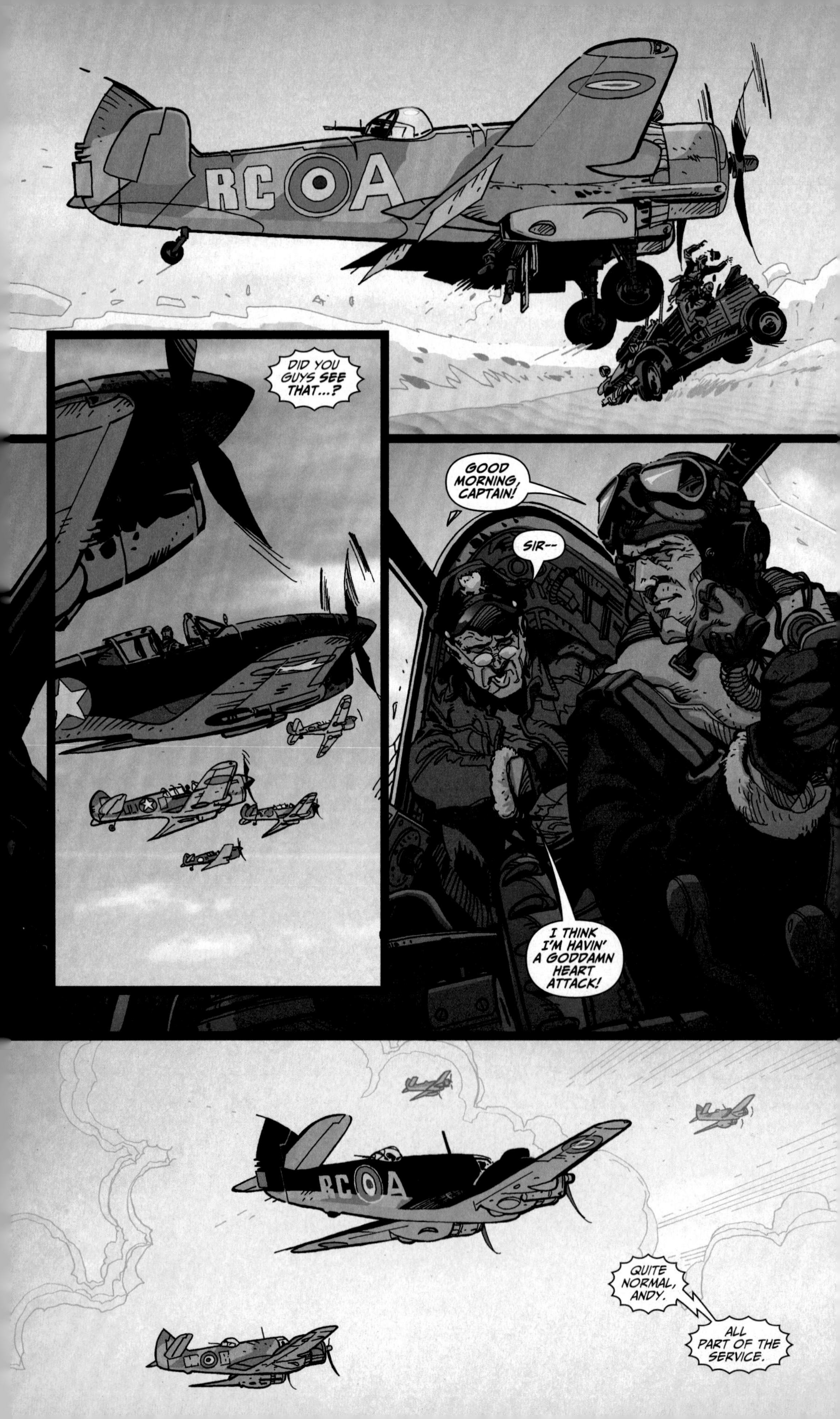
RC A
DID YOU GUYS SEE THAT...?
GOOD MORNING CAPTAIN!
SIR--
I THINK I'M HAVIN' A GODDAMN HEART ATTACK!
RC A
QUITE NORMAL, ANDY.
ALL PART OF THE SERVICE.

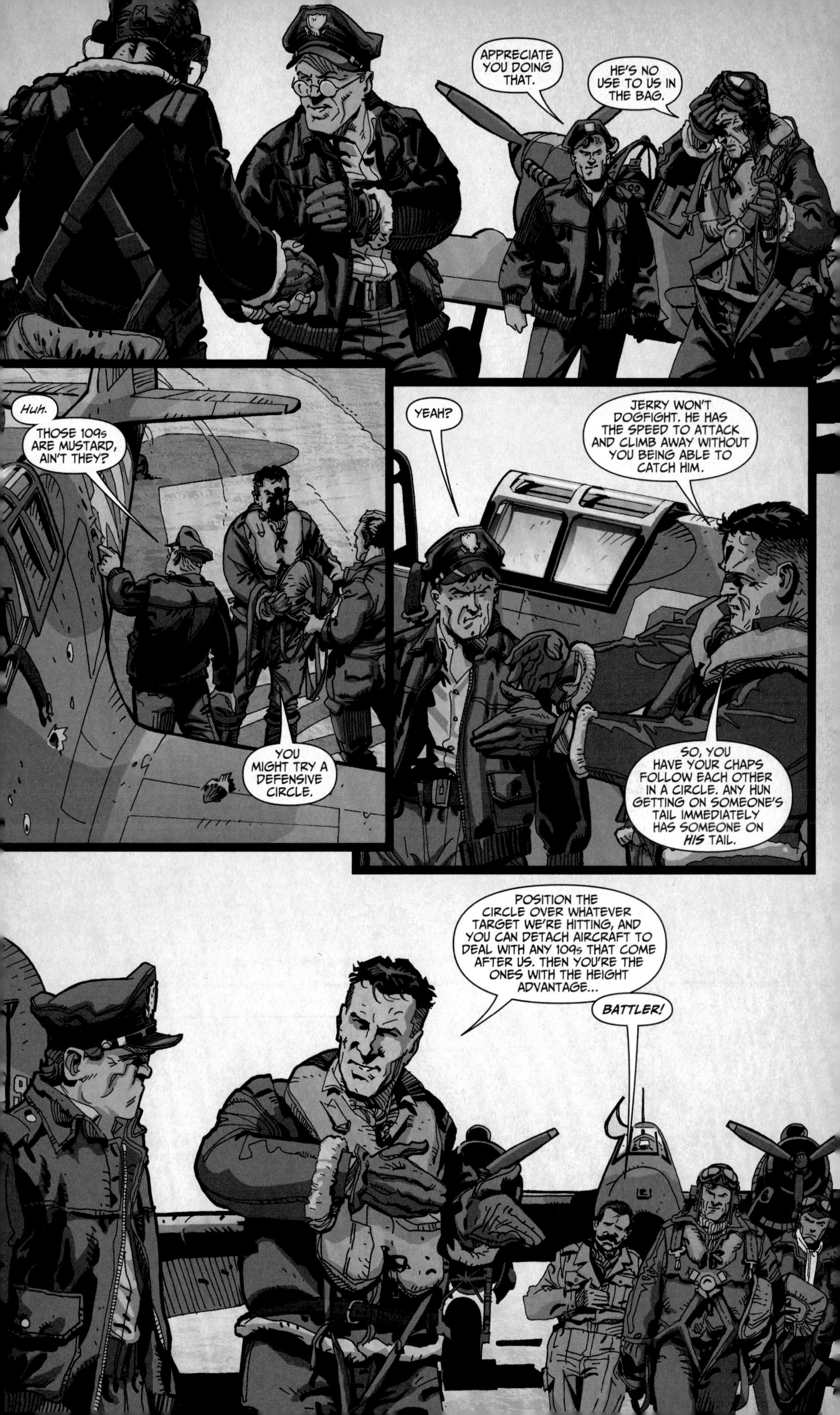
APPRECIATE YOU DOING THAT.
HE'S NO USE TO US IN THE BAG.
Huh.
THOSE 109s ARE MUSTARD, AIN'T THEY?
YOU MIGHT TRY A DEFENSIVE CIRCLE.
YEAH?
JERRY WON'T DOGFIGHT. HE HAS THE SPEED TO ATTACK AND CLIMB AWAY WITHOUT YOU BEING ABLE TO CATCH HIM.
SO, YOU HAVE YOUR CHAPS FOLLOW EACH OTHER IN A CIRCLE. ANY HUN GETTING ON SOMEONE'S TAIL IMMEDIATELY HAS SOMEONE ON *HIS* TAIL.
POSITION THE CIRCLE OVER WHATEVER TARGET WE'RE HITTING, AND YOU CAN DETACH AIRCRAFT TO DEAL WITH ANY 109s THAT COME AFTER US. THEN YOU'RE THE ONES WITH THE HEIGHT ADVANTAGE...
BATTLER!

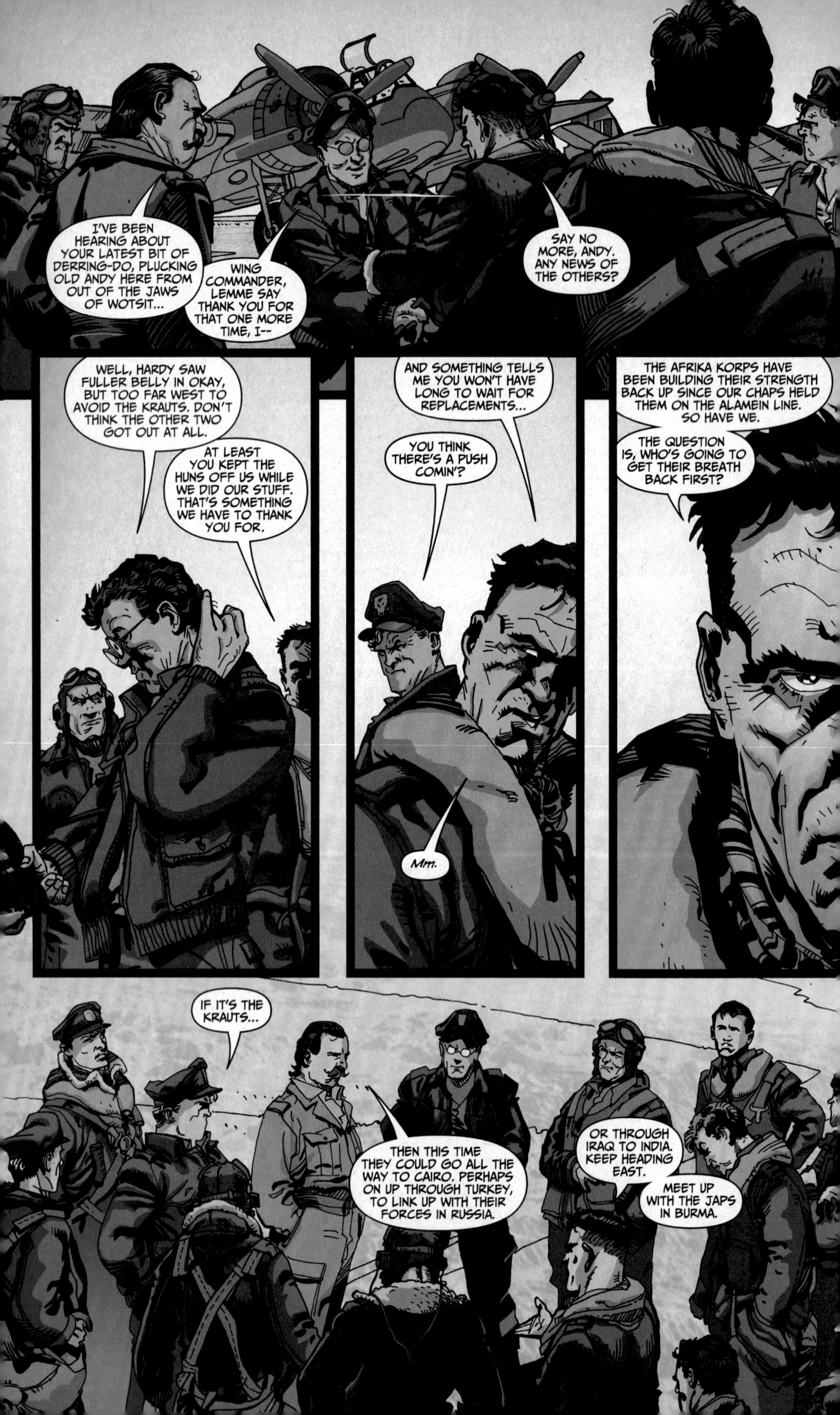
I'VE BEEN HEARING ABOUT YOUR LATEST BIT OF DERRING-DO, PLUCKING OLD ANDY HERE FROM OUT OF THE JAWS OF WOTSIT...
WING COMMANDER, LEMME SAY THANK YOU FOR THAT ONE MORE TIME, I--
SAY NO MORE, ANDY. ANY NEWS OF THE OTHERS?
WELL, HARDY SAW FULLER BELLY IN OKAY, BUT TOO FAR WEST TO AVOID THE KRAUTS. DON'T THINK THE OTHER TWO GOT OUT AT ALL.
AT LEAST YOU KEPT THE HUNS OFF US WHILE WE DID OUR STUFF. THAT'S SOMETHING WE HAVE TO THANK YOU FOR.
AND SOMETHING TELLS ME YOU WON'T HAVE LONG TO WAIT FOR REPLACEMENTS...
YOU THINK THERE'S A PUSH COMIN'?
Mm.
THE AFRIKA KORPS HAVE BEEN BUILDING THEIR STRENGTH BACK UP SINCE OUR CHAPS HELD THEM ON THE ALAMEIN LINE. SO HAVE WE.
THE QUESTION IS, WHO'S GOING TO GET THEIR BREATH BACK FIRST?
IF IT'S THE KRAUTS...
THEN THIS TIME THEY COULD GO ALL THE WAY TO CAIRO. PERHAPS ON UP THROUGH TURKEY, TO LINK UP WITH THEIR FORCES IN RUSSIA.
OR THROUGH IRAQ TO INDIA. KEEP HEADING EAST.
MEET UP WITH THE JAPS IN BURMA.

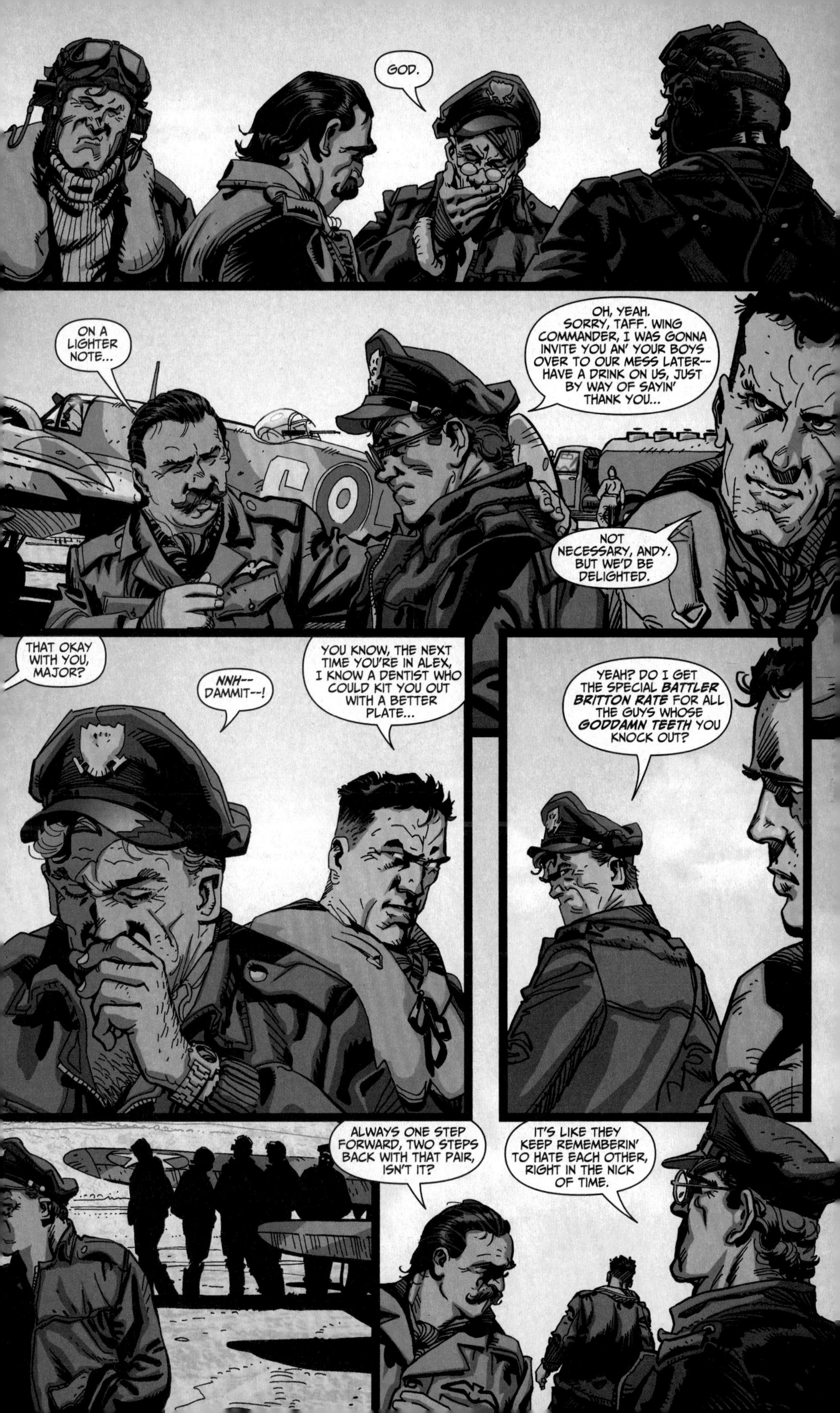
GOD.
ON A LIGHTER NOTE...
OH, YEAH. SORRY, TAFF. WING COMMANDER, I WAS GONNA INVITE YOU AN' YOUR BOYS OVER TO OUR MESS LATER-- HAVE A DRINK ON US, JUST BY WAY OF SAYIN' THANK YOU...
NOT NECESSARY, ANDY. BUT WE'D BE DELIGHTED.
THAT OKAY WITH YOU, MAJOR?
NNH-- DAMMIT--!
YOU KNOW, THE NEXT TIME YOU'RE IN ALEX, I KNOW A DENTIST WHO COULD KIT YOU OUT WITH A BETTER PLATE...
YEAH? DO I GET THE SPECIAL BATTLER BRITTON RATE FOR ALL THE GUYS WHOSE GODDAMN TEETH YOU KNOCK OUT?
ALWAYS ONE STEP FORWARD, TWO STEPS BACK WITH THAT PAIR, ISN'T IT?
IT'S LIKE THEY KEEP REMEMBERIN' TO HATE EACH OTHER, RIGHT IN THE NICK OF TIME.

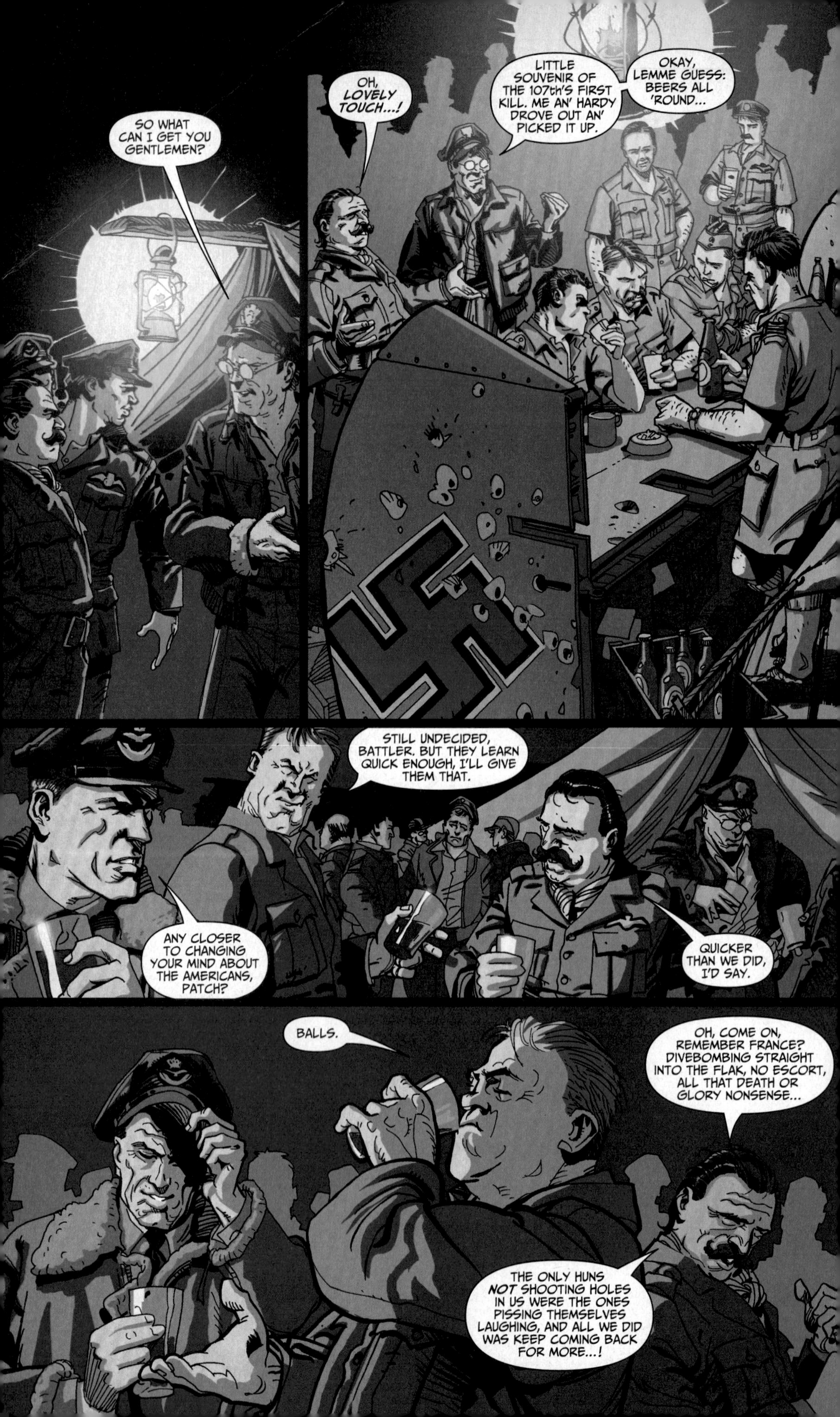
SO WHAT CAN I GET YOU GENTLEMEN?
OH, LOVELY TOUCH...!
LITTLE SOUVENIR OF THE 107th'S FIRST KILL. ME AN' HARDY DROVE OUT AN' PICKED IT UP.
OKAY, LEMME GUESS: BEERS ALL 'ROUND...
ANY CLOSER TO CHANGING YOUR MIND ABOUT THE AMERICANS, PATCH?
STILL UNDECIDED, BATTLER. BUT THEY LEARN QUICK ENOUGH, I'LL GIVE THEM THAT.
QUICKER THAN WE DID, I'D SAY.
BALLS.
OH, COME ON, REMEMBER FRANCE? DIVEBOMBING STRAIGHT INTO THE FLAK, NO ESCORT, ALL THAT DEATH OR GLORY NONSENSE...
THE ONLY HUNS NOT SHOOTING HOLES IN US WERE THE ONES PISSING THEMSELVES LAUGHING, AND ALL WE DID WAS KEEP COMING BACK FOR MORE...!

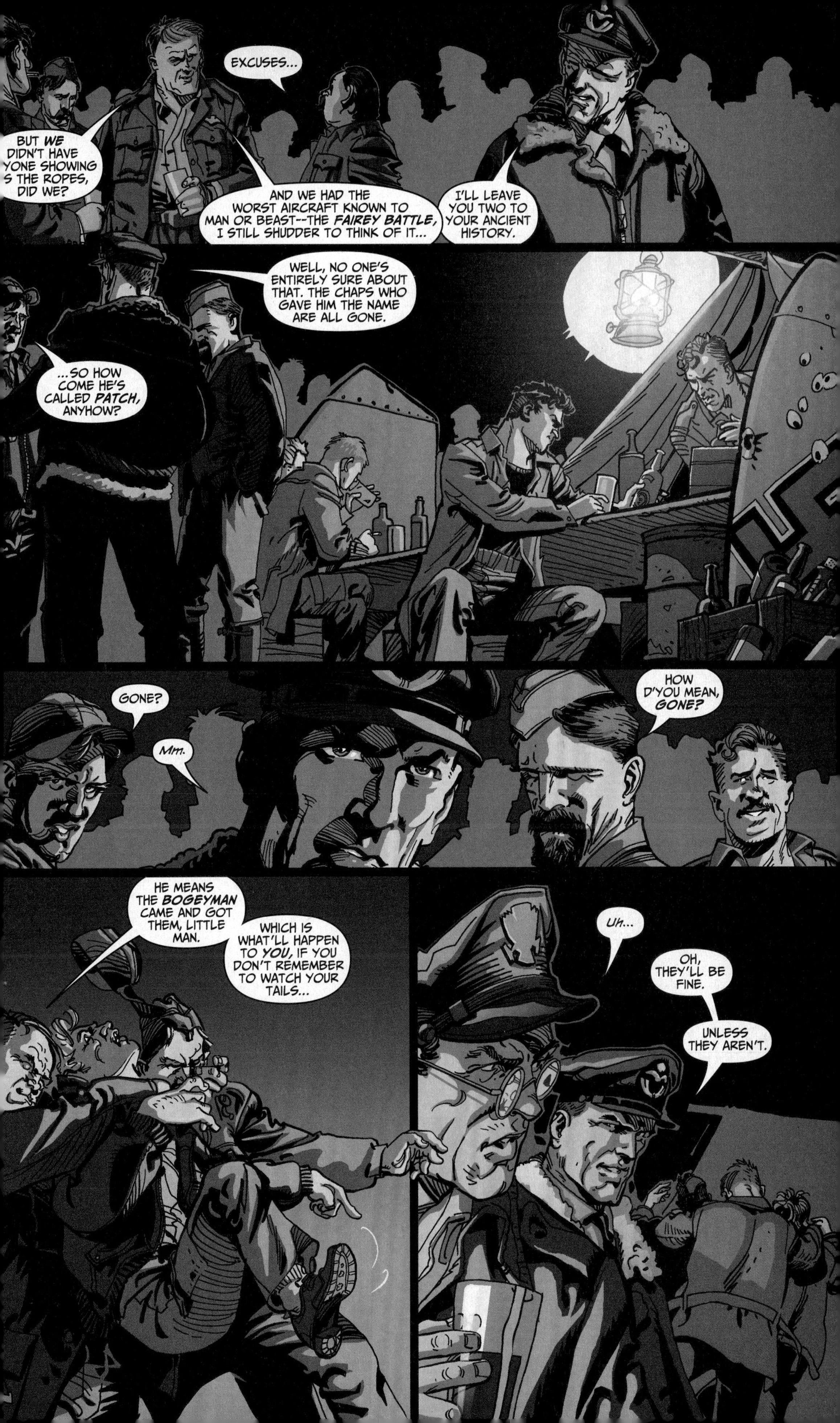
EXCUSES...
BUT WE DIDN'T HAVE YONE SHOWING S THE ROPES, DID WE?
AND WE HAD THE WORST AIRCRAFT KNOWN TO MAN OR BEAST--THE FAIREY BATTLE, I STILL SHUDDER TO THINK OF IT...
I'LL LEAVE YOU TWO TO YOUR ANCIENT HISTORY.
...SO HOW COME HE'S CALLED PATCH, ANYHOW?
WELL, NO ONE'S ENTIRELY SURE ABOUT THAT. THE CHAPS WHO GAVE HIM THE NAME ARE ALL GONE.
GONE?
Mm.
HOW D'YOU MEAN, GONE?
HE MEANS THE BOGEYMAN CAME AND GOT THEM, LITTLE MAN.
WHICH IS WHAT'LL HAPPEN TO YOU, IF YOU DON'T REMEMBER TO WATCH YOUR TAILS...
Uh...
OH, THEY'LL BE FINE.
UNLESS THEY AREN'T.

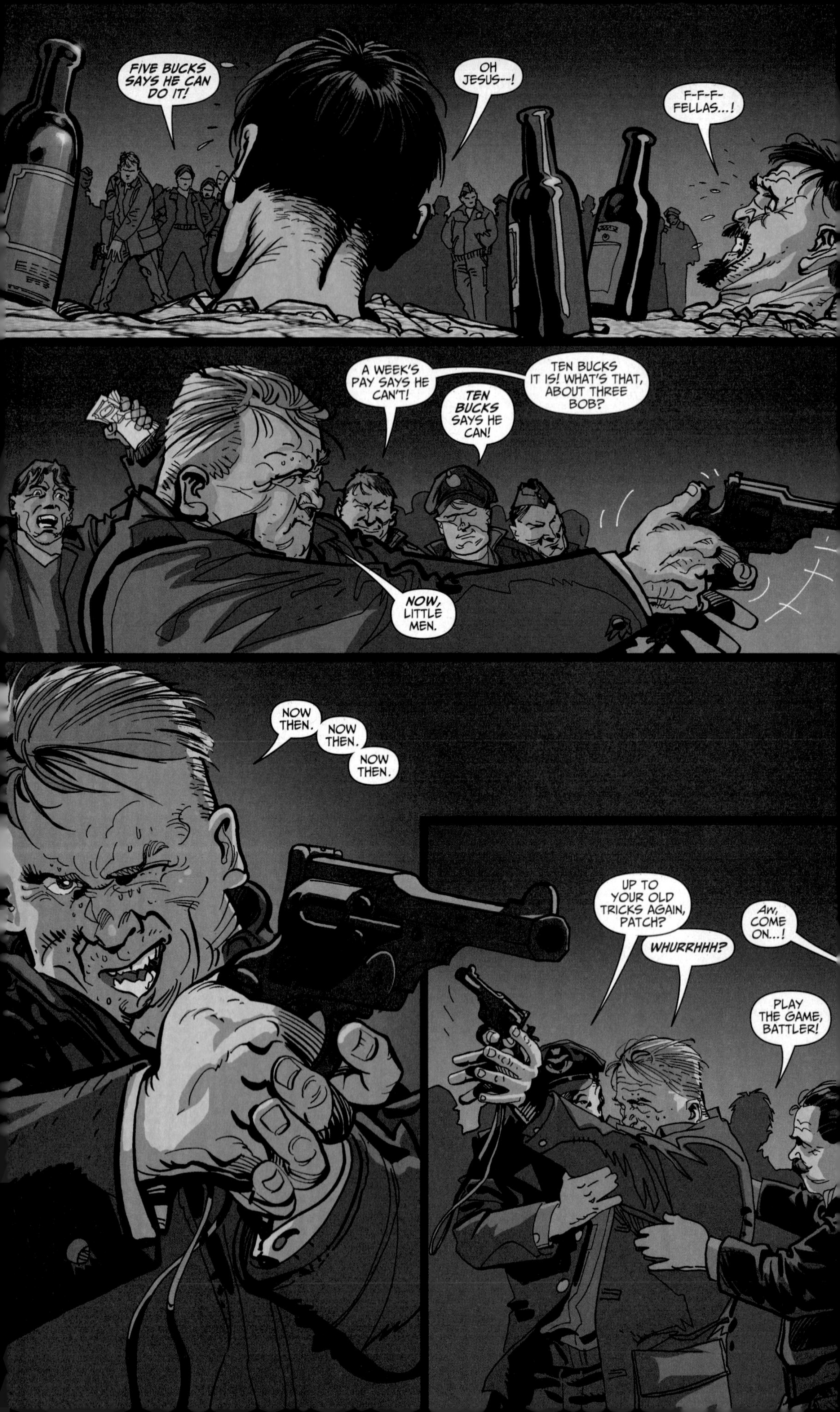
FIVE BUCKS SAYS HE CAN DO IT!
OH JESUS--!
F-F-F-FELLAS...!
A WEEK'S PAY SAYS HE CAN'T!
TEN BUCKS SAYS HE CAN!
TEN BUCKS IT IS! WHAT'S THAT, ABOUT THREE BOB?
NOW, LITTLE MEN.
NOW THEN.
NOW THEN.
NOW THEN.
UP TO YOUR OLD TRICKS AGAIN, PATCH?
WHURRHHH?
AW, COME ON...!
PLAY THE GAME, BATTLER!

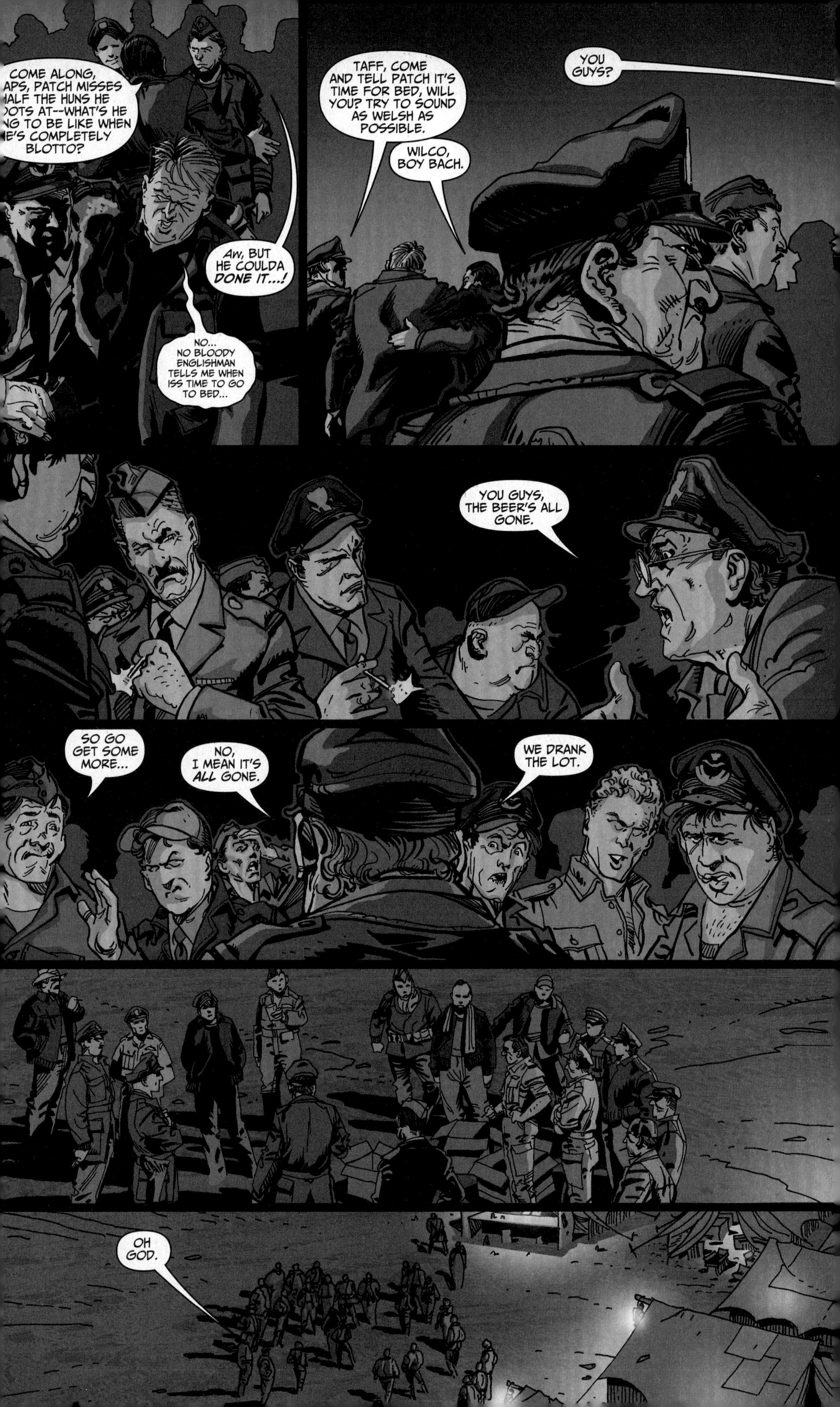
COME ALONG, CHAPS, PATCH MISSES HALF THE HUNS HE SHOOTS AT--WHAT'S HE GOING TO BE LIKE WHEN HE'S COMPLETELY BLOTTO?
AW, BUT HE COULDA DONE IT...!
NO... NO BLOODY ENGLISHMAN TELLS ME WHEN ISS TIME TO GO TO BED...
TAFF, COME AND TELL PATCH IT'S TIME FOR BED, WILL YOU? TRY TO SOUND AS WELSH AS POSSIBLE.
WILCO, BOY BACH.
YOU GUYS?
YOU GUYS, THE BEER'S ALL GONE.
SO GO GET SOME MORE...
NO, I MEAN IT'S ALL GONE.
WE DRANK THE LOT.
OH GOD.

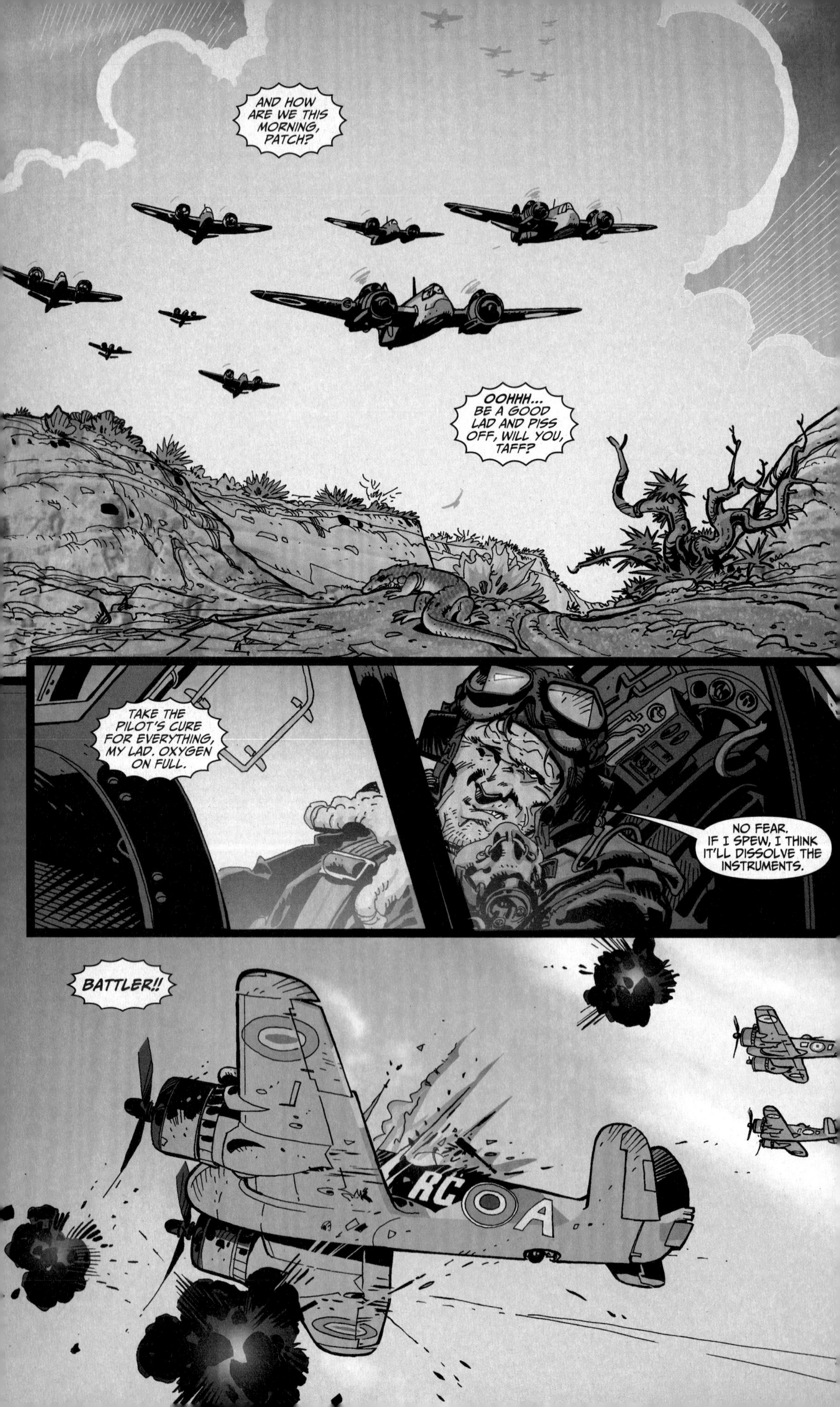
AND HOW ARE WE THIS MORNING, PATCH?
OOHHH... BE A GOOD LAD AND PISS OFF, WILL YOU, TAFF?
TAKE THE PILOT'S CURE FOR EVERYTHING, MY LAD. OXYGEN ON FULL.
NO FEAR. IF I SPEW, I THINK IT'LL DISSOLVE THE INSTRUMENTS.
BATTLER!!
RC
A

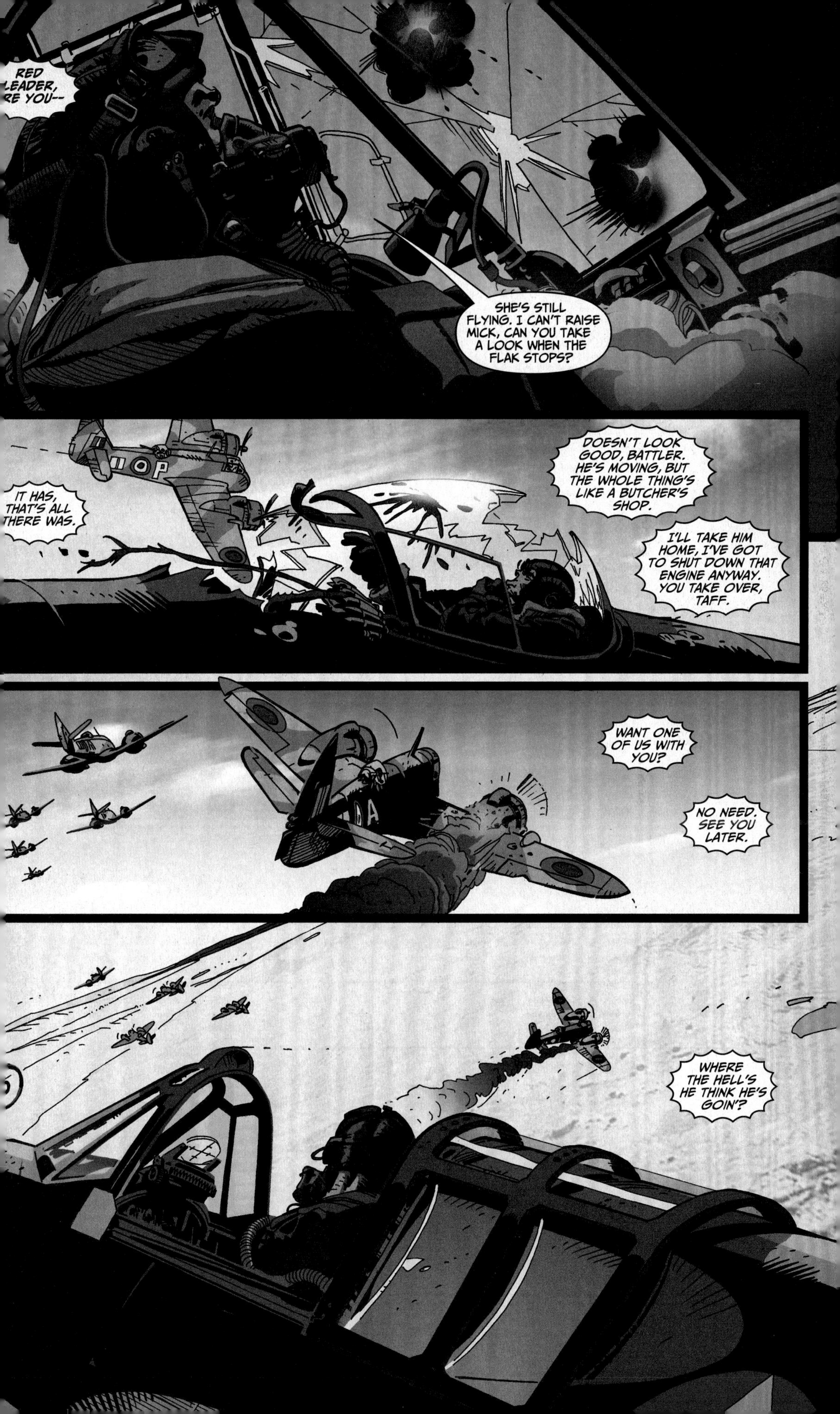

RED LEADER, ARE YOU--
SHE'S STILL FLYING. I CAN'T RAISE MICK, CAN YOU TAKE A LOOK WHEN THE FLAK STOPS?
IT HAS, THAT'S ALL THERE WAS.
DOESN'T LOOK GOOD, BATTLER. HE'S MOVING, BUT THE WHOLE THING'S LIKE A BUTCHER'S SHOP.
I'LL TAKE HIM HOME, I'VE GOT TO SHUT DOWN THAT ENGINE ANYWAY. YOU TAKE OVER, TAFF.
WANT ONE OF US WITH YOU?
NO NEED. SEE YOU LATER.
WHERE THE HELL'S HE THINK HE'S GOIN'?

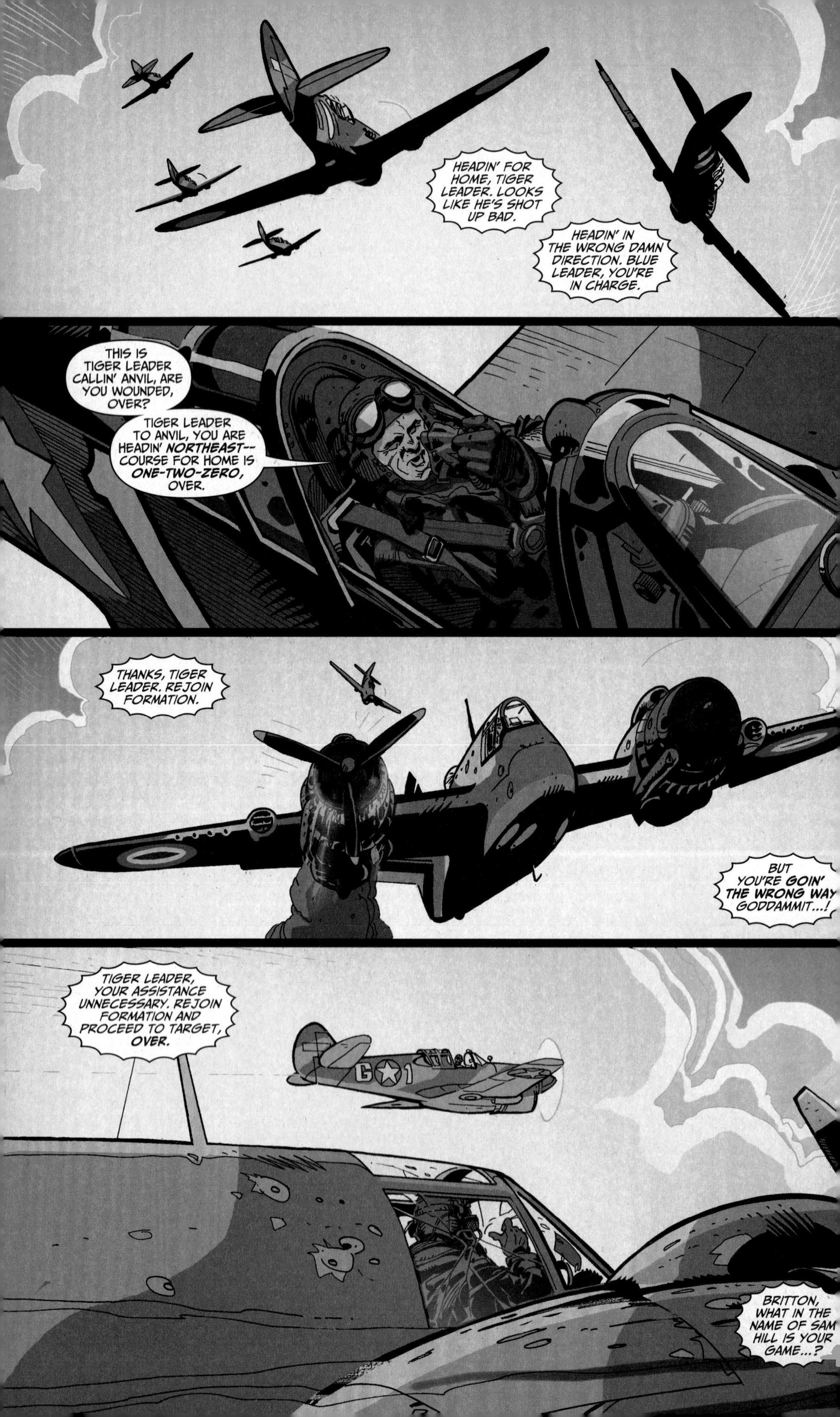
HEADIN' FOR HOME, TIGER LEADER. LOOKS LIKE HE'S SHOT UP BAD.
HEADIN' IN THE WRONG DAMN DIRECTION. BLUE LEADER, YOU'RE IN CHARGE.
THIS IS TIGER LEADER CALLIN' ANVIL, ARE YOU WOUNDED, OVER?
TIGER LEADER TO ANVIL, YOU ARE HEADIN' NORTHEAST-- COURSE FOR HOME IS ONE-TWO-ZERO, OVER.
THANKS, TIGER LEADER. REJOIN FORMATION.
BUT YOU'RE GOIN' THE WRONG WAY GODDAMMIT...!
TIGER LEADER, YOUR ASSISTANCE UNNECESSARY. REJOIN FORMATION AND PROCEED TO TARGET, OVER.
BRITTON, WHAT IN THE NAME OF SAM HILL IS YOUR GAME...?

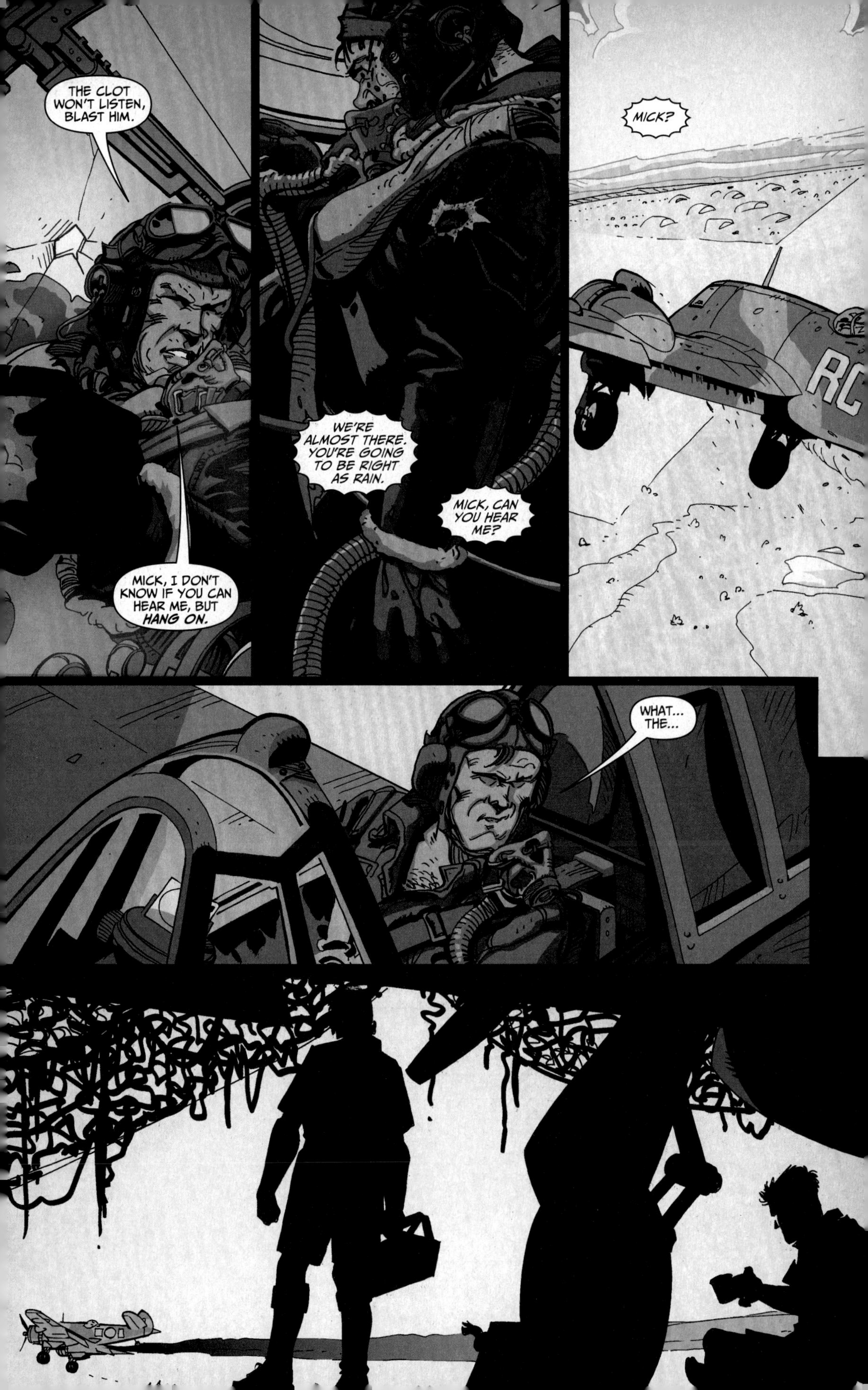
THE CLOT WON'T LISTEN, BLAST HIM.
MICK, I DON'T KNOW IF YOU CAN HEAR ME, BUT HANG ON.
WE'RE ALMOST THERE. YOU'RE GOING TO BE RIGHT AS RAIN.
MICK, CAN YOU HEAR ME?
MICK?
RC
WHAT... THE...

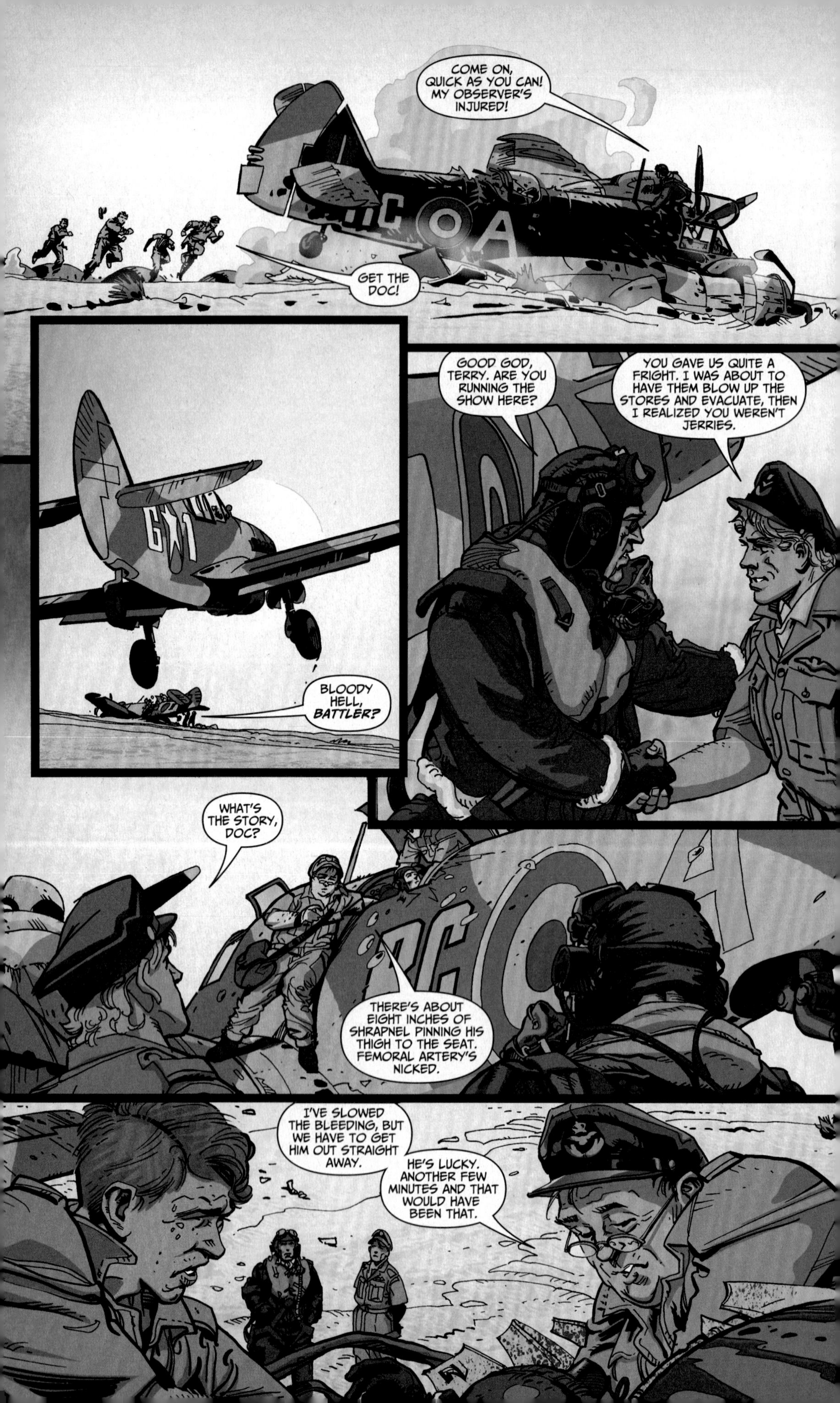
COME ON, QUICK AS YOU CAN! MY OBSERVER'S INJURED!
GET THE DOC!
BLOODY HELL, *BATTLER?*
GOOD GOD, TERRY. ARE YOU RUNNING THE SHOW HERE?
YOU GAVE US QUITE A FRIGHT. I WAS ABOUT TO HAVE THEM BLOW UP THE STORES AND EVACUATE, THEN I REALIZED YOU WEREN'T JERRIES.
WHAT'S THE STORY, DOC?
THERE'S ABOUT EIGHT INCHES OF SHRAPNEL PINNING HIS THIGH TO THE SEAT. FEMORAL ARTERY'S NICKED.
I'VE SLOWED THE BLEEDING, BUT WE HAVE TO GET HIM OUT STRAIGHT AWAY.
HE'S LUCKY. ANOTHER FEW MINUTES AND THAT WOULD HAVE BEEN THAT.

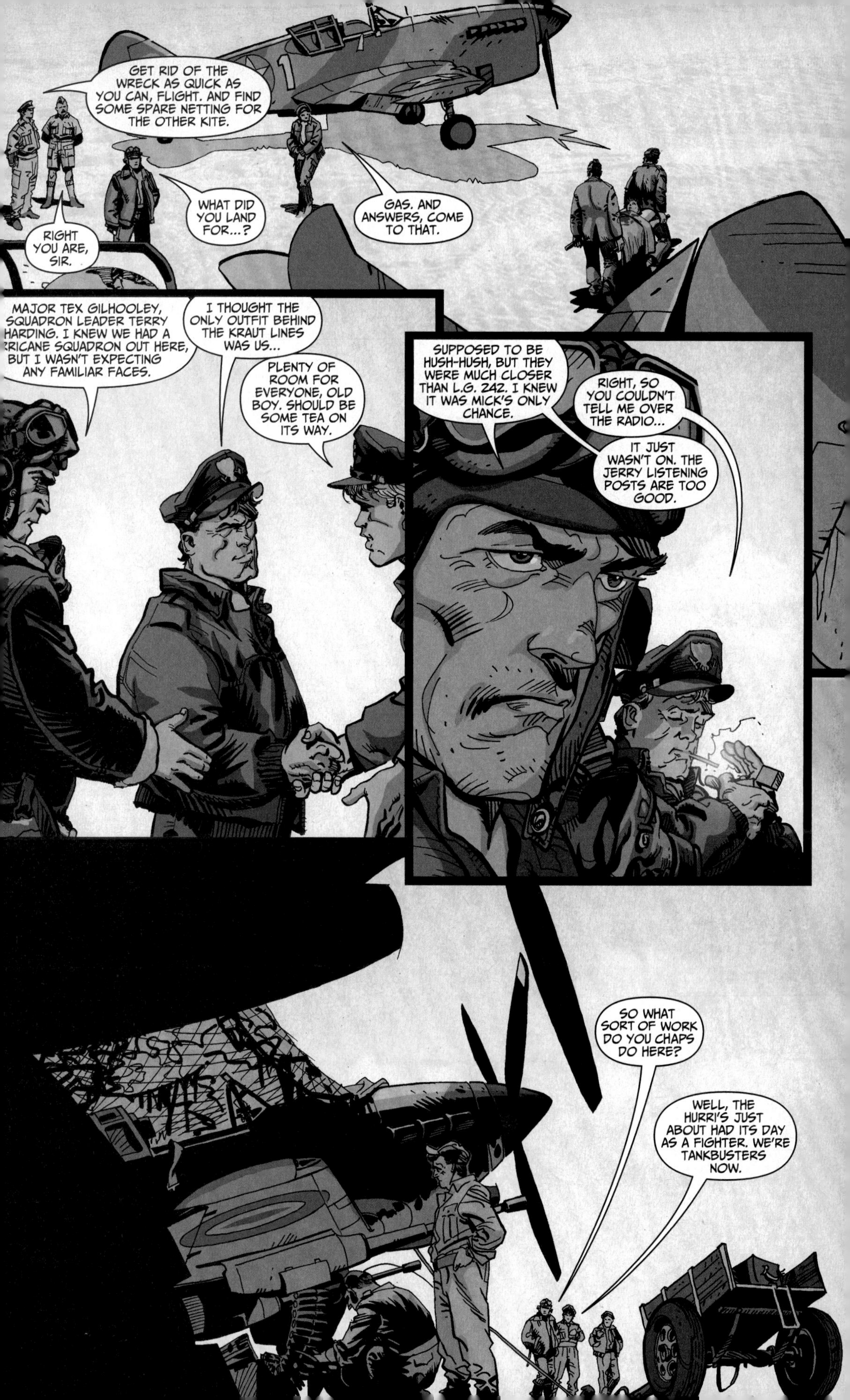
GET RID OF THE WRECK AS QUICK AS YOU CAN, FLIGHT. AND FIND SOME SPARE NETTING FOR THE OTHER KITE.
RIGHT YOU ARE, SIR.
WHAT DID YOU LAND FOR...?
GAS. AND ANSWERS, COME TO THAT.
MAJOR TEX GILHOOLEY, SQUADRON LEADER TERRY HARDING. I KNEW WE HAD A RICANE SQUADRON OUT HERE, BUT I WASN'T EXPECTING ANY FAMILIAR FACES.
I THOUGHT THE ONLY OUTFIT BEHIND THE KRAUT LINES WAS US...
PLENTY OF ROOM FOR EVERYONE, OLD BOY. SHOULD BE SOME TEA ON ITS WAY.
SUPPOSED TO BE HUSH-HUSH, BUT THEY WERE MUCH CLOSER THAN L.G. 242. I KNEW IT WAS MICK'S ONLY CHANCE.
RIGHT, SO YOU COULDN'T TELL ME OVER THE RADIO...
IT JUST WASN'T ON. THE JERRY LISTENING POSTS ARE TOO GOOD.
SO WHAT SORT OF WORK DO YOU CHAPS DO HERE?
WELL, THE HURRI'S JUST ABOUT HAD ITS DAY AS A FIGHTER. WE'RE TANKBUSTERS NOW.

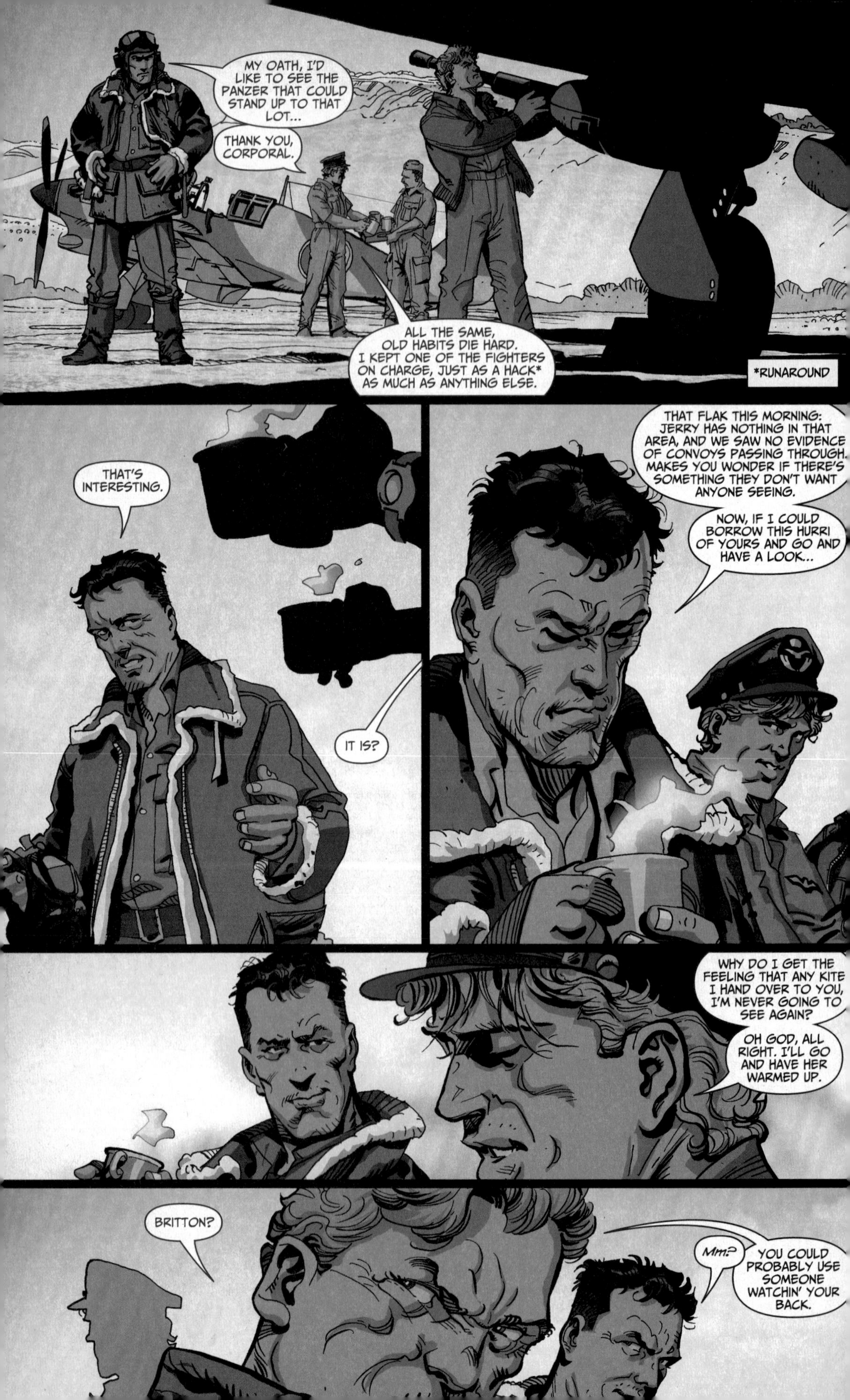
MY OATH, I'D LIKE TO SEE THE PANZER THAT COULD STAND UP TO THAT LOT...
THANK YOU, CORPORAL.
ALL THE SAME, OLD HABITS DIE HARD. I KEPT ONE OF THE FIGHTERS ON CHARGE, JUST AS A HACK* AS MUCH AS ANYTHING ELSE.
*RUNAROUND
THAT'S INTERESTING.
IT IS?
THAT FLAK THIS MORNING: JERRY HAS NOTHING IN THAT AREA, AND WE SAW NO EVIDENCE OF CONVOYS PASSING THROUGH. MAKES YOU WONDER IF THERE'S SOMETHING THEY DON'T WANT ANYONE SEEING.
NOW, IF I COULD BORROW THIS HURRI OF YOURS AND GO AND HAVE A LOOK...
WHY DO I GET THE FEELING THAT ANY KITE I HAND OVER TO YOU, I'M NEVER GOING TO SEE AGAIN?
OH GOD, ALL RIGHT. I'LL GO AND HAVE HER WARMED UP.
BRITTON?
Mm?
YOU COULD PROBABLY USE SOMEONE WATCHIN' YOUR BACK.

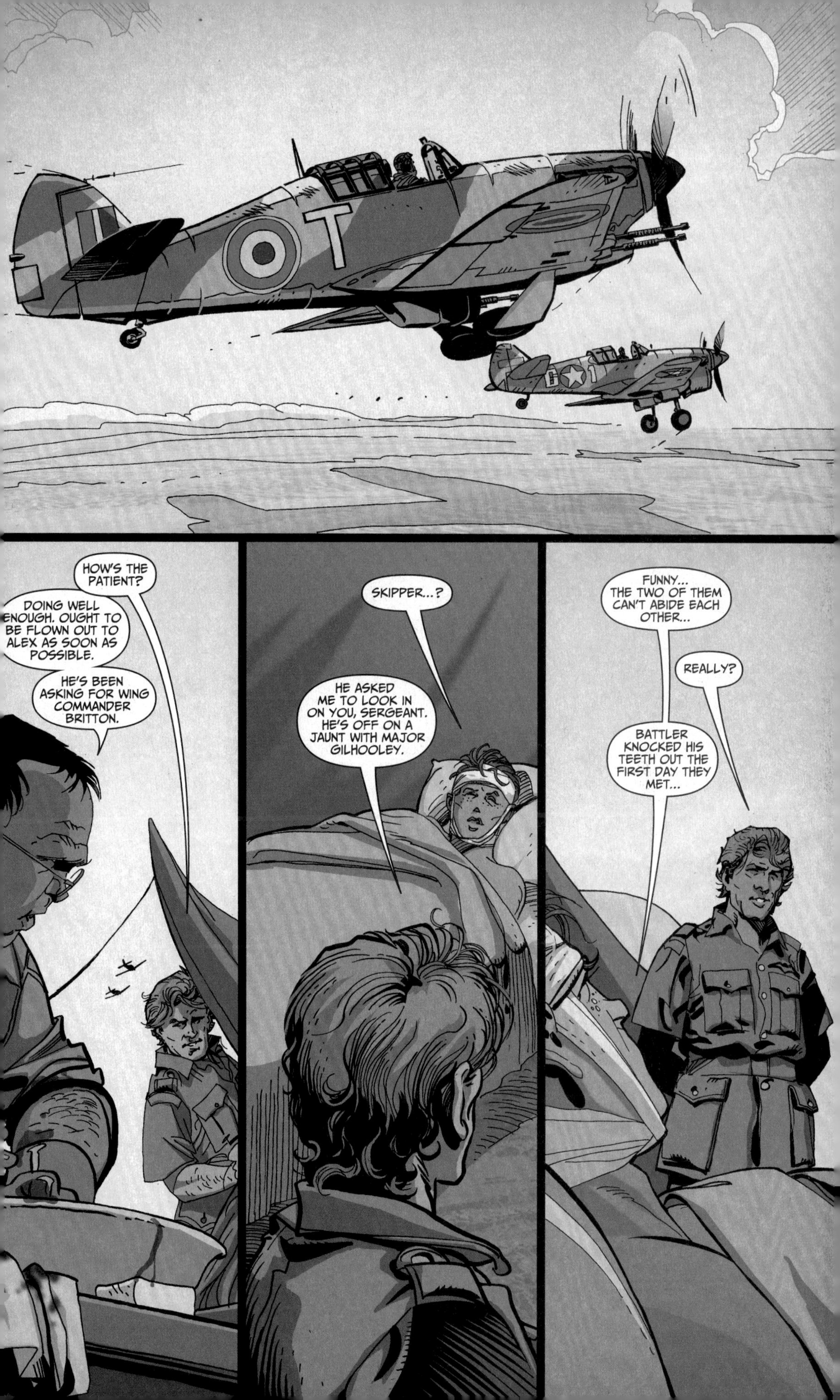
HOW'S THE PATIENT?
DOING WELL ENOUGH. OUGHT TO BE FLOWN OUT TO ALEX AS SOON AS POSSIBLE.
HE'S BEEN ASKING FOR WING COMMANDER BRITTON.
SKIPPER...?
HE ASKED ME TO LOOK IN ON YOU, SERGEANT. HE'S OFF ON A JAUNT WITH MAJOR GILHOOLEY.
FUNNY... THE TWO OF THEM CAN'T ABIDE EACH OTHER...
REALLY?
BATTLER KNOCKED HIS TEETH OUT THE FIRST DAY THEY MET...

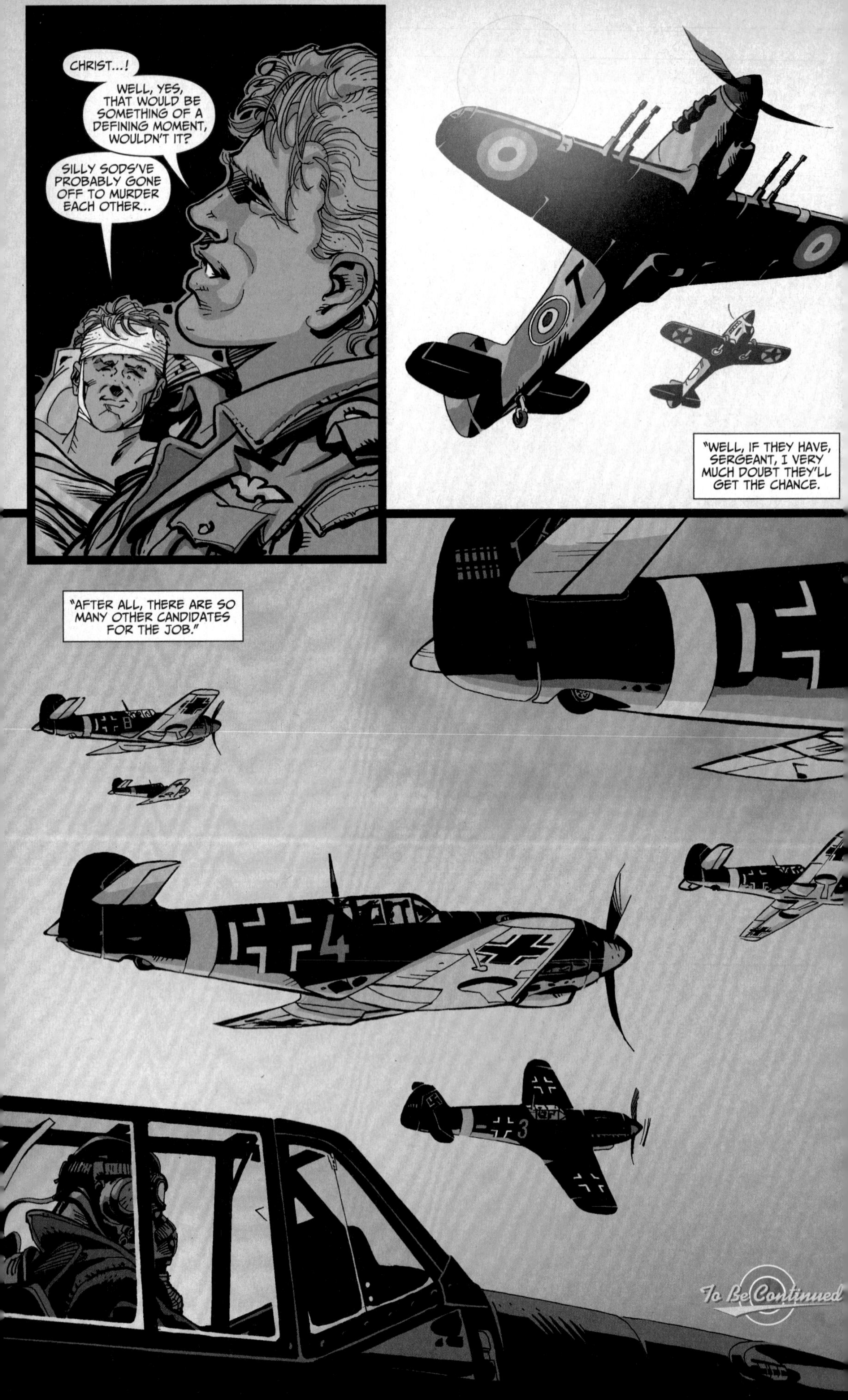
CHRIST...!
WELL, YES, THAT WOULD BE SOMETHING OF A DEFINING MOMENT, WOULDN'T IT?
SILLY SODS'VE PROBABLY GONE OFF TO MURDER EACH OTHER...
"WELL, IF THEY HAVE, SERGEANT, I VERY MUCH DOUBT THEY'LL GET THE CHANCE.
"AFTER ALL, THERE ARE SO MANY OTHER CANDIDATES FOR THE JOB."
To Be Continued

CHAPTER 4

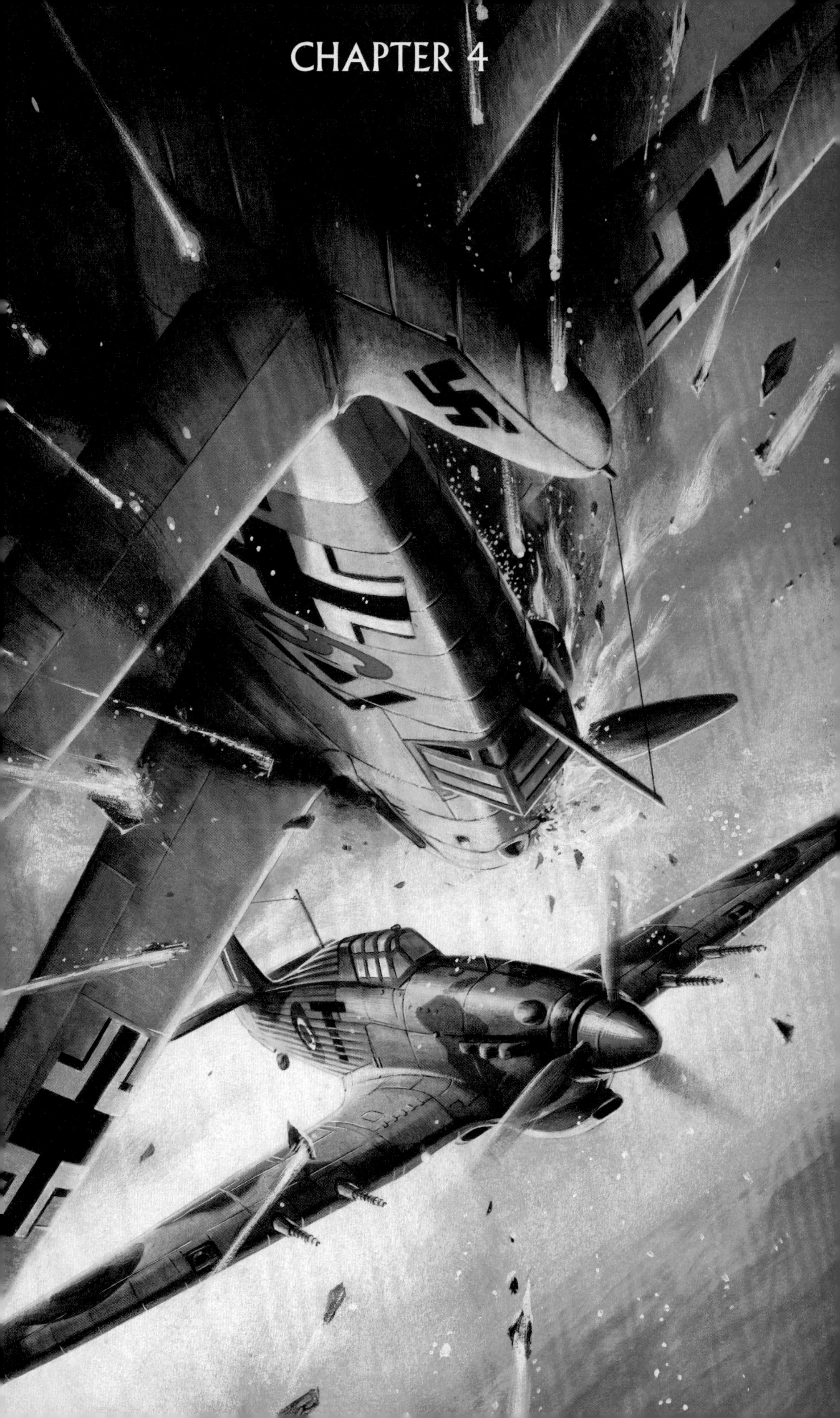

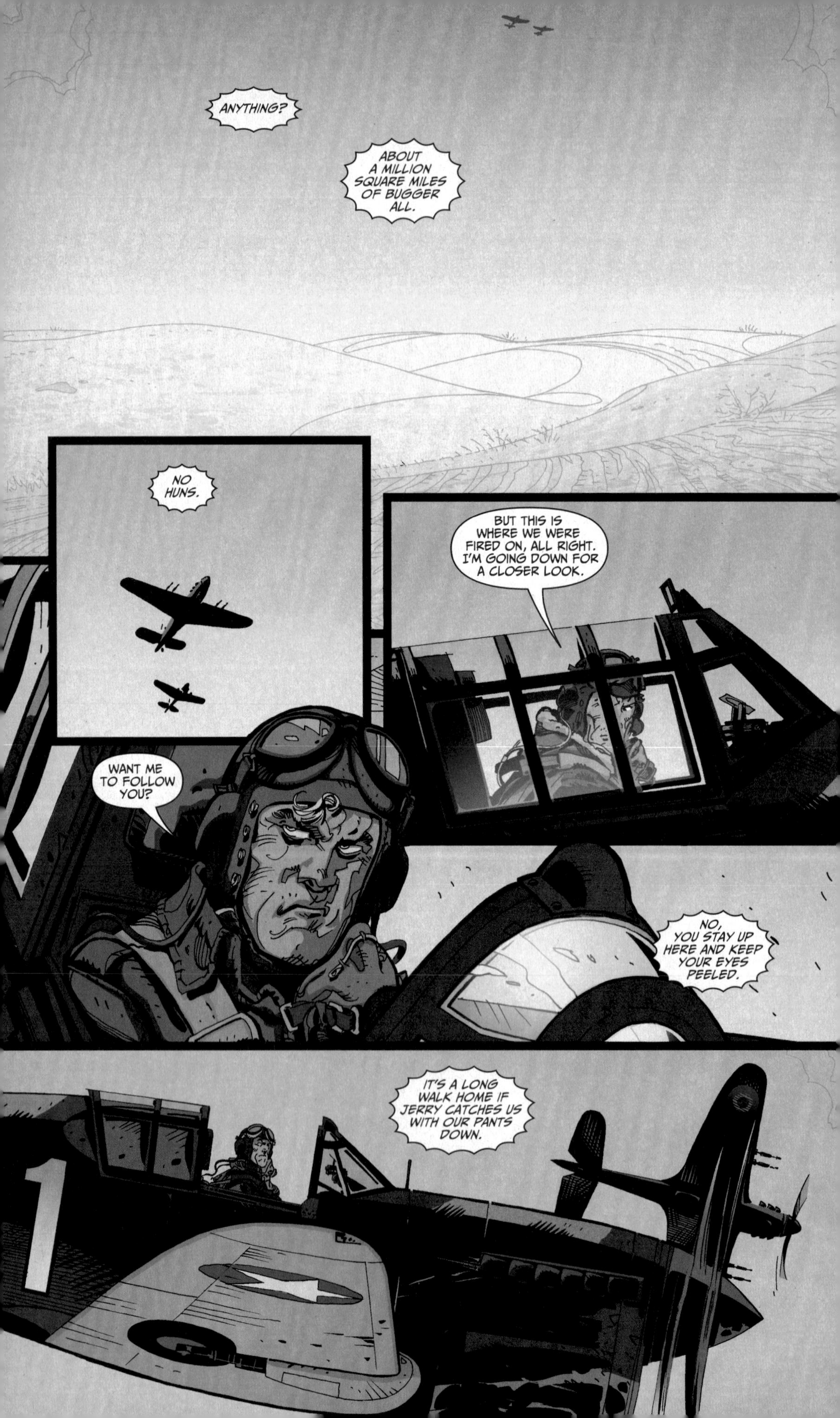
ANYTHING?
ABOUT A MILLION SQUARE MILES OF BUGGER ALL.
NO HUNS.
BUT THIS IS WHERE WE WERE FIRED ON, ALL RIGHT. I'M GOING DOWN FOR A CLOSER LOOK.
WANT ME TO FOLLOW YOU?
NO, YOU STAY UP HERE AND KEEP YOUR EYES PEELED.
IT'S A LONG WALK HOME IF JERRY CATCHES US WITH OUR PANTS DOWN.

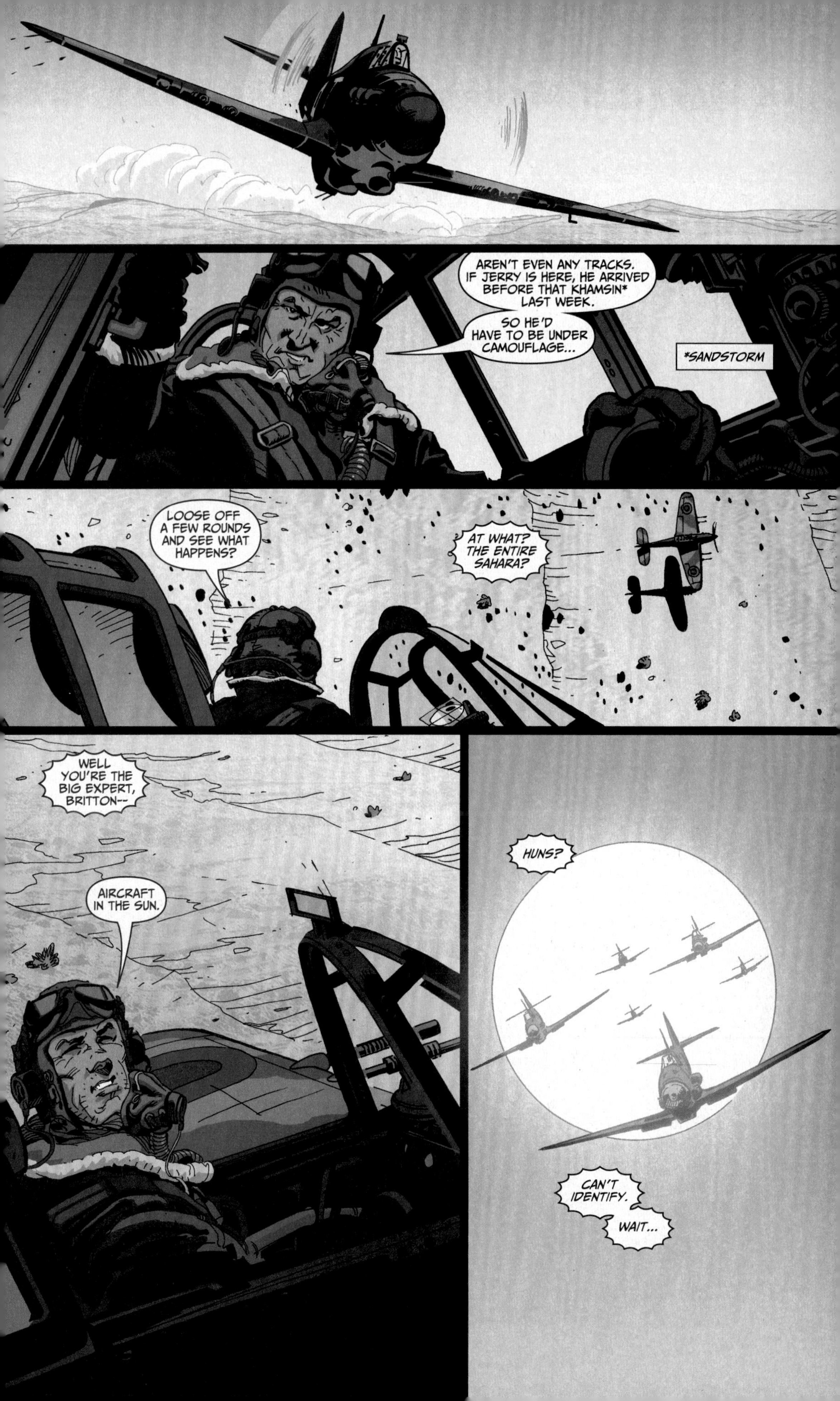

AREN'T EVEN ANY TRACKS. IF JERRY IS HERE, HE ARRIVED BEFORE THAT KHAMSIN* LAST WEEK.
SO HE'D HAVE TO BE UNDER CAMOUFLAGE...
*SANDSTORM
LOOSE OFF A FEW ROUNDS AND SEE WHAT HAPPENS?
AT WHAT? THE ENTIRE SAHARA?
WELL YOU'RE THE BIG EXPERT, BRITTON--
AIRCRAFT IN THE SUN.
HUNS?
CAN'T IDENTIFY.
WAIT...

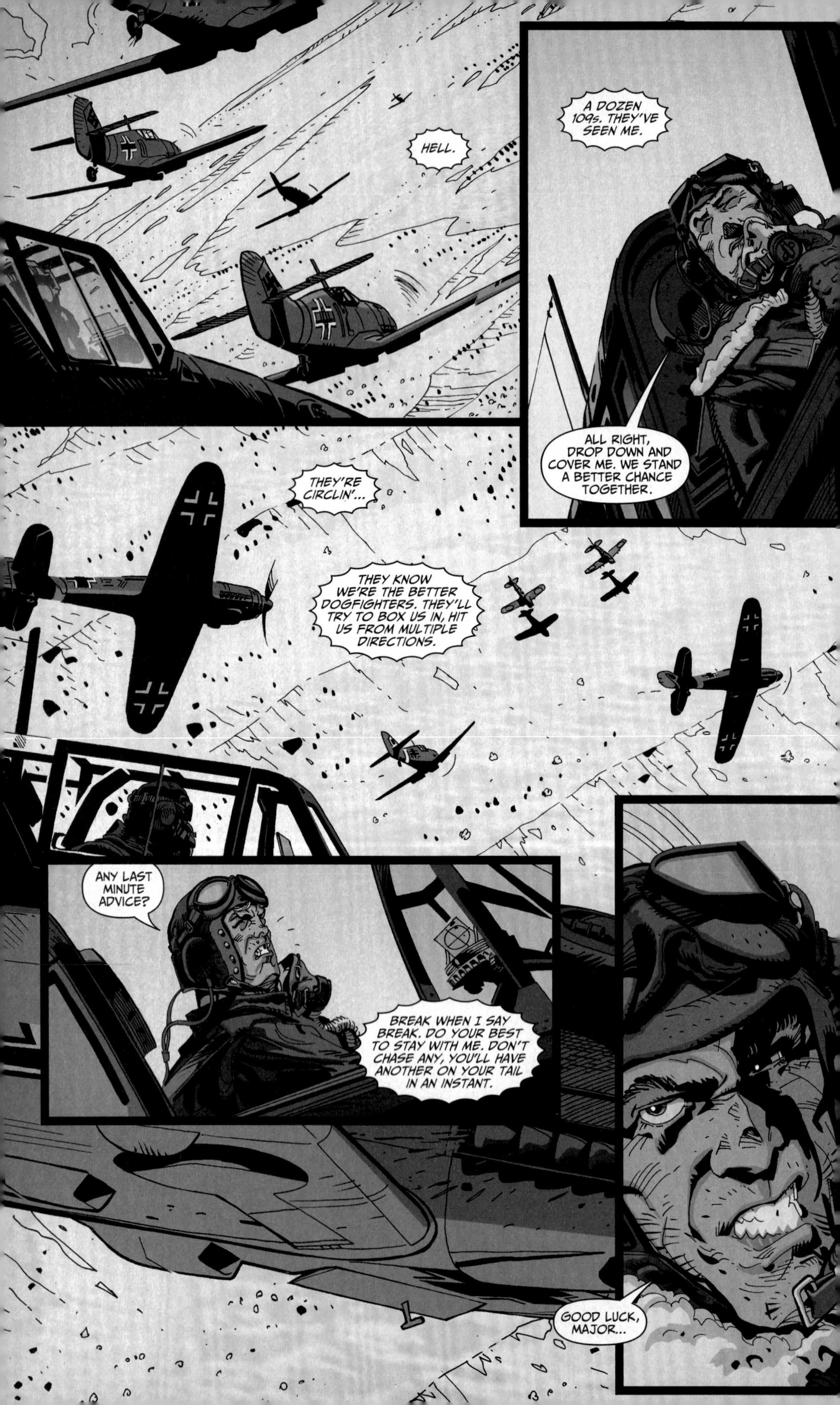
HELL.
A DOZEN 109s. THEY'VE SEEN ME.
ALL RIGHT, DROP DOWN AND COVER ME. WE STAND A BETTER CHANCE TOGETHER.
THEY'RE CIRCLIN'...
THEY KNOW WE'RE THE BETTER DOGFIGHTERS. THEY'LL TRY TO BOX US IN, HIT US FROM MULTIPLE DIRECTIONS.
ANY LAST MINUTE ADVICE?
BREAK WHEN I SAY BREAK. DO YOUR BEST TO STAY WITH ME. DON'T CHASE ANY, YOU'LL HAVE ANOTHER ON YOUR TAIL IN AN INSTANT.
GOOD LUCK, MAJOR...

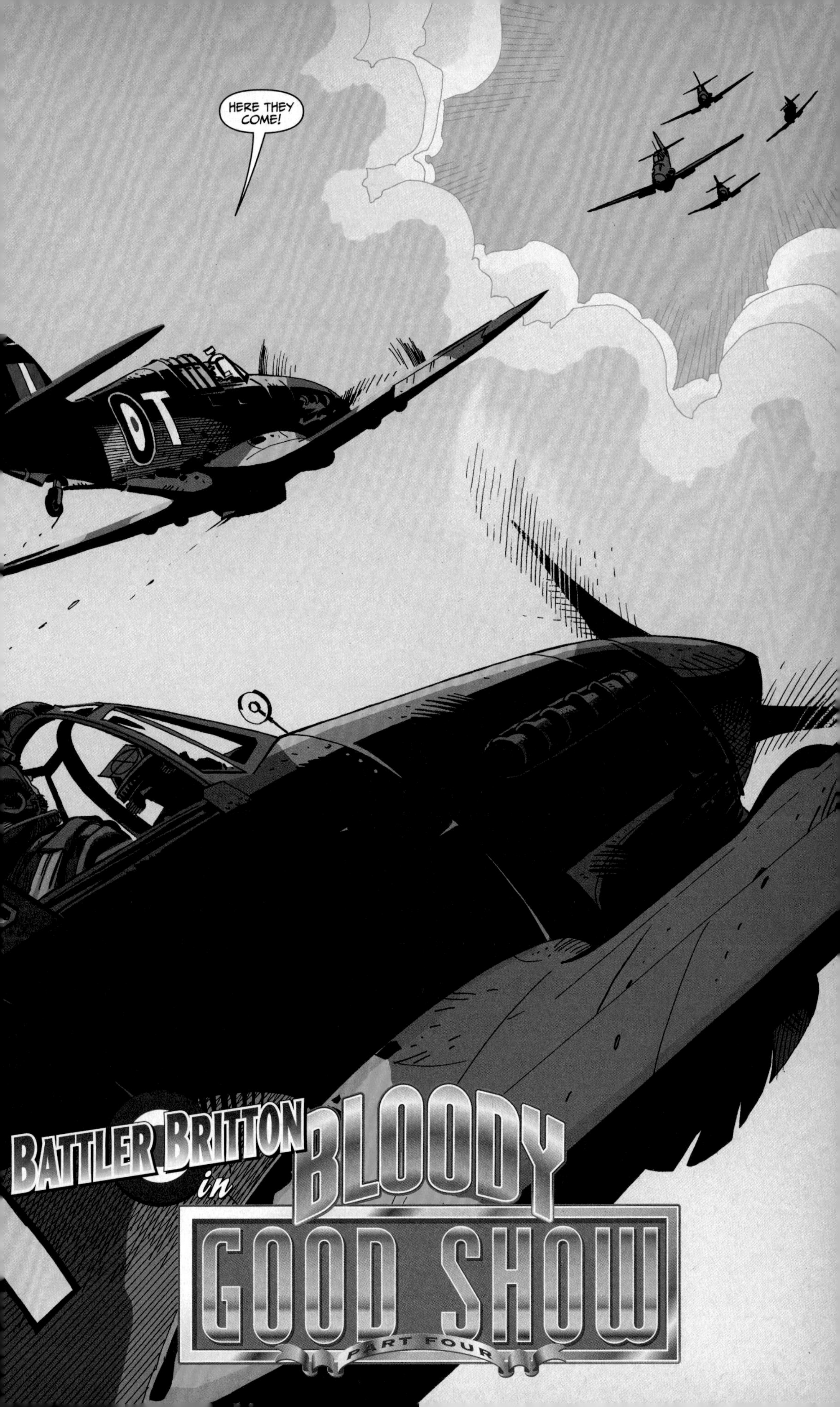
HERE THEY COME!
BATTLER BRITTON in
BLOODY GOOD SHOW
PART FOUR

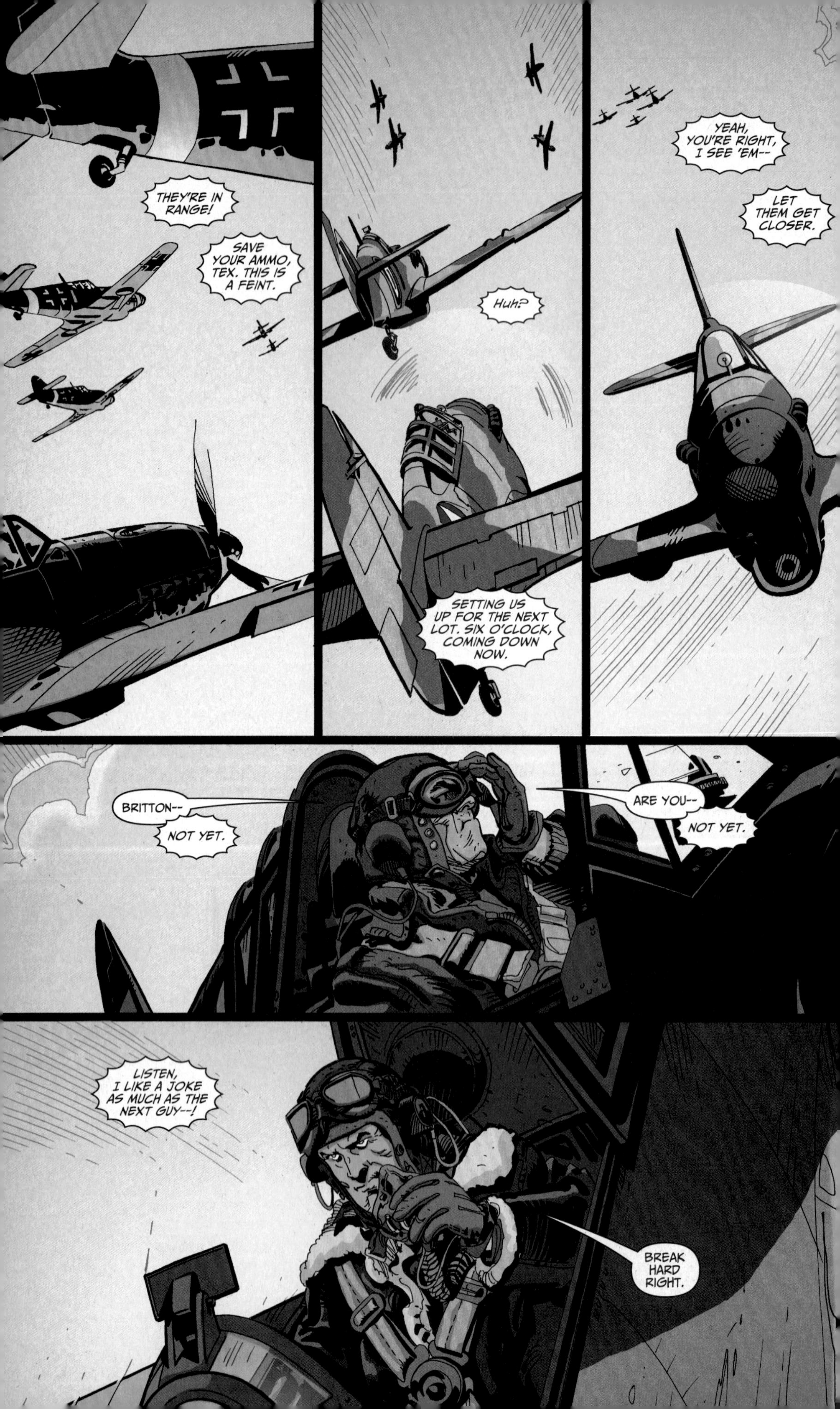
THEY'RE IN RANGE!
SAVE YOUR AMMO, TEX. THIS IS A FEINT.
Huh?
SETTING US UP FOR THE NEXT LOT. SIX O'CLOCK, COMING DOWN NOW.
YEAH, YOU'RE RIGHT, I SEE 'EM--
LET THEM GET CLOSER.
BRITTON--
NOT YET.
ARE YOU--
NOT YET.
LISTEN, I LIKE A JOKE AS MUCH AS THE NEXT GUY--!
BREAK HARD RIGHT.

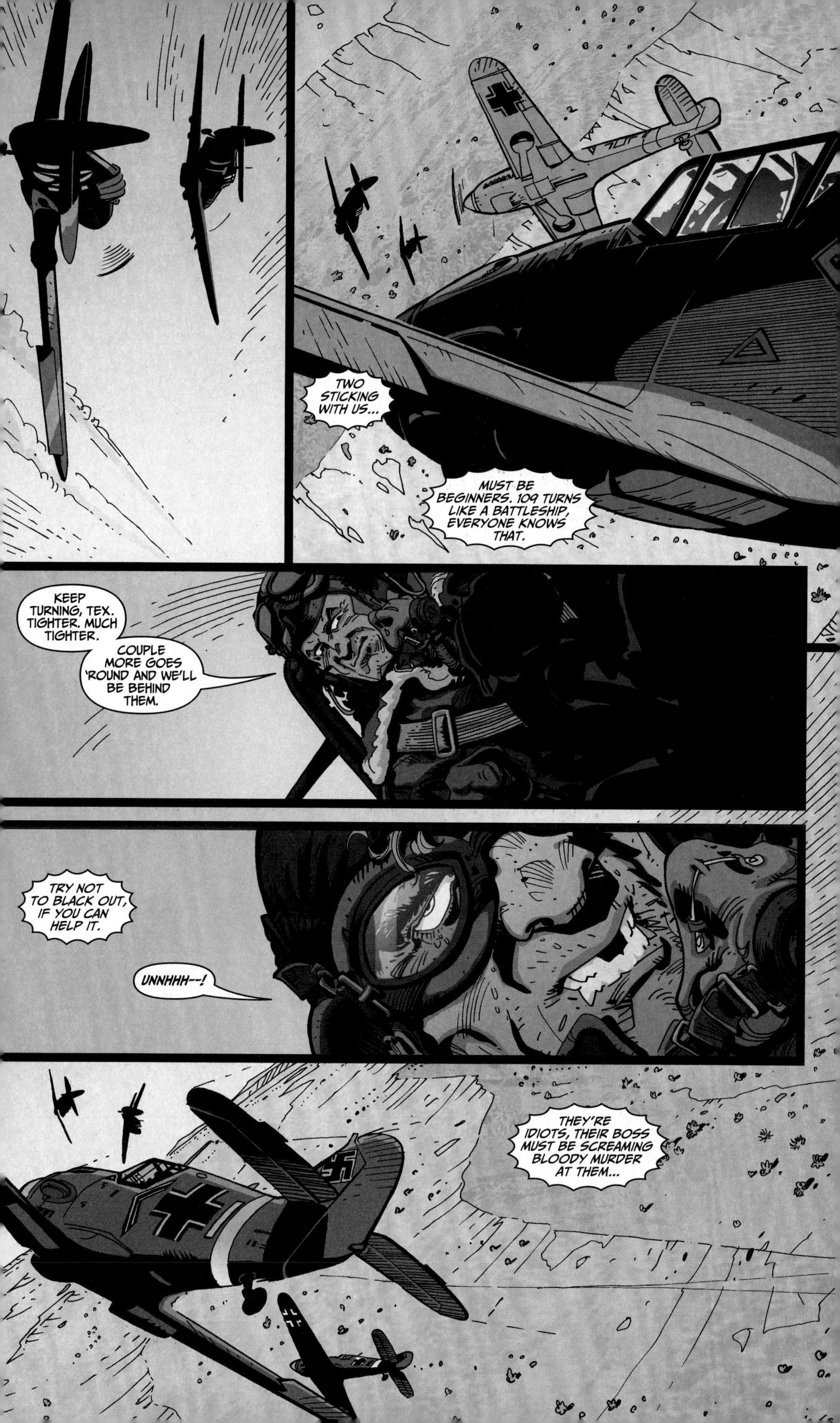
TWO STICKING WITH US...
MUST BE BEGINNERS. 109 TURNS LIKE A BATTLESHIP, EVERYONE KNOWS THAT.
KEEP TURNING, TEX. TIGHTER. MUCH TIGHTER.
COUPLE MORE GOES 'ROUND AND WE'LL BE BEHIND THEM.
TRY NOT TO BLACK OUT, IF YOU CAN HELP IT.
UNNHHH--!
THEY'RE IDIOTS, THEIR BOSS MUST BE SCREAMING BLOODY MURDER AT THEM...

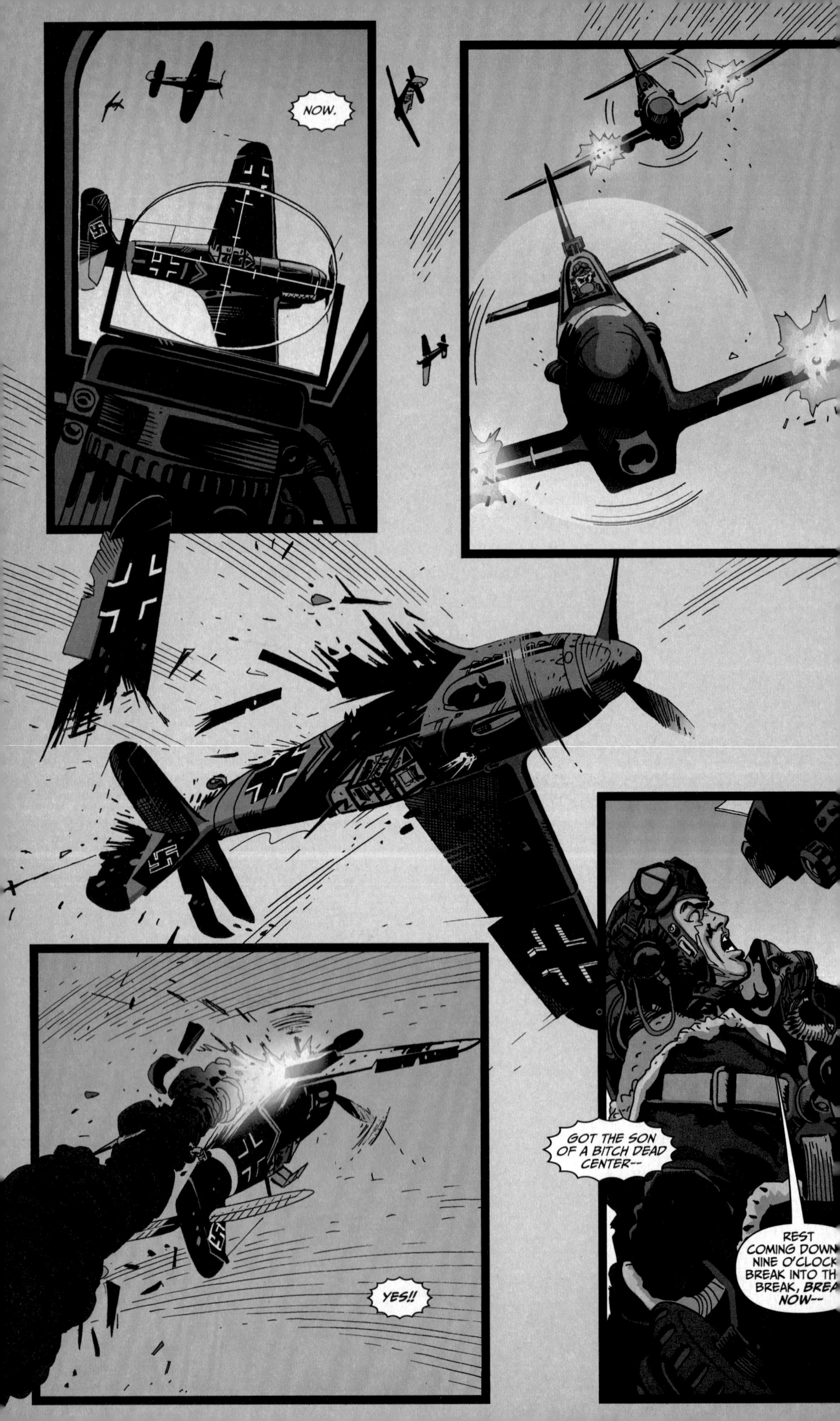
NOW.
YES!!
GOT THE SON OF A BITCH DEAD CENTER--
REST COMING DOWN NINE O'CLOCK BREAK INTO TH BREAK, BREA NOW--

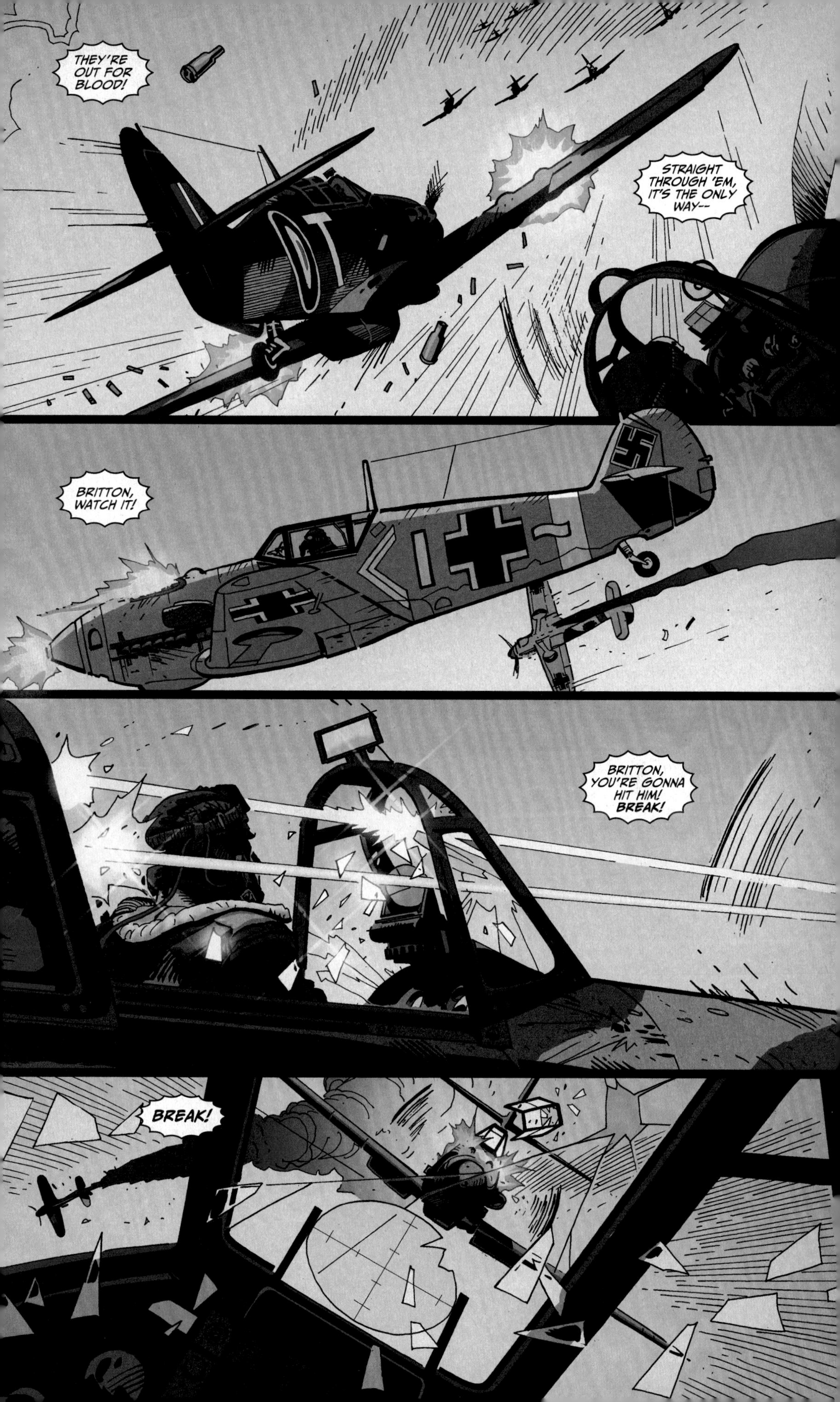
THEY'RE OUT FOR BLOOD!
STRAIGHT THROUGH 'EM, IT'S THE ONLY WAY--
BRITTON, WATCH IT!
BRITTON, YOU'RE GONNA HIT HIM! BREAK!
BREAK!

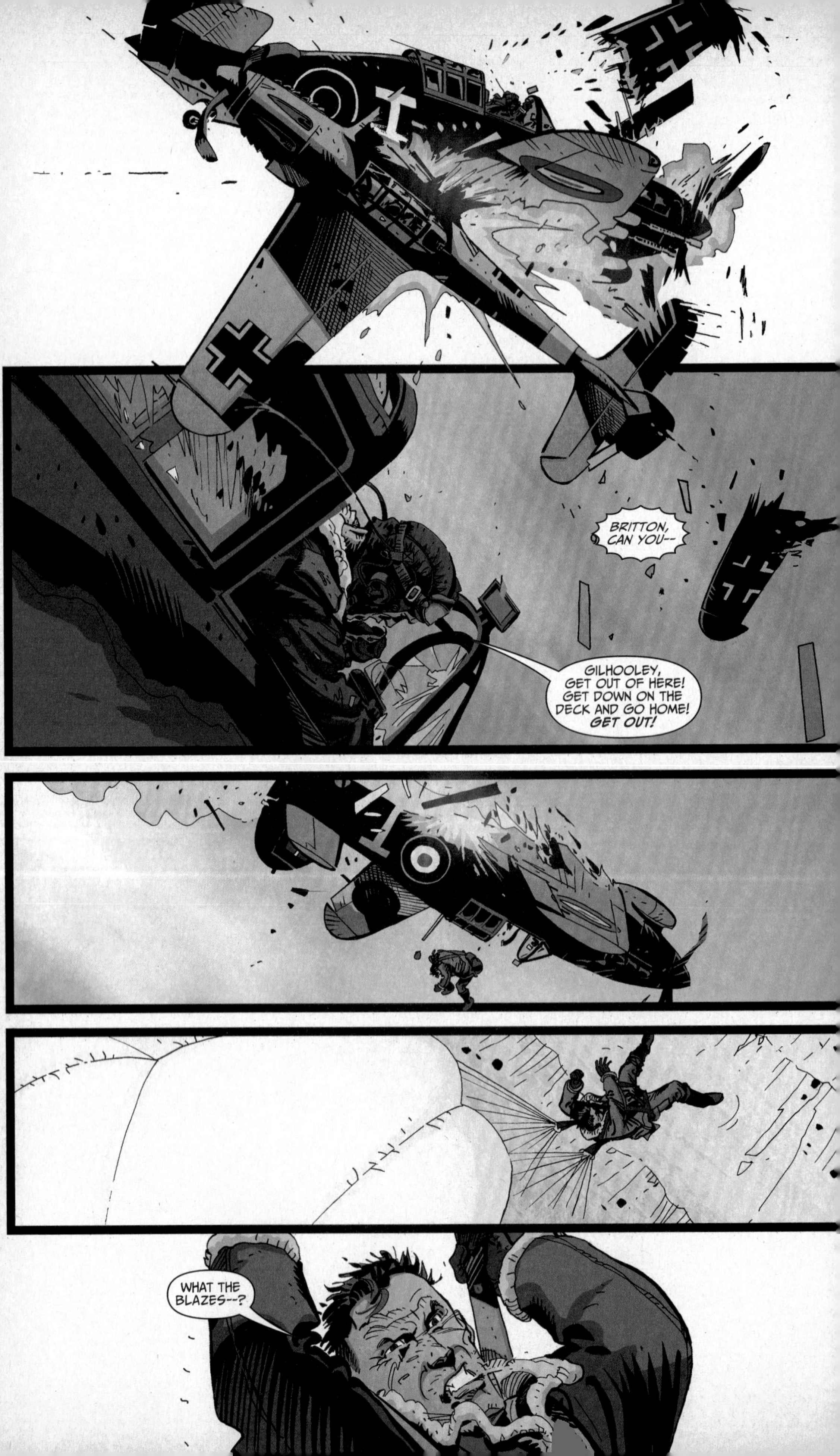
BRITTON, CAN YOU--
GILHOOLEY, GET OUT OF HERE! GET DOWN ON THE DECK AND GO HOME! GET OUT!
WHAT THE BLAZES--?

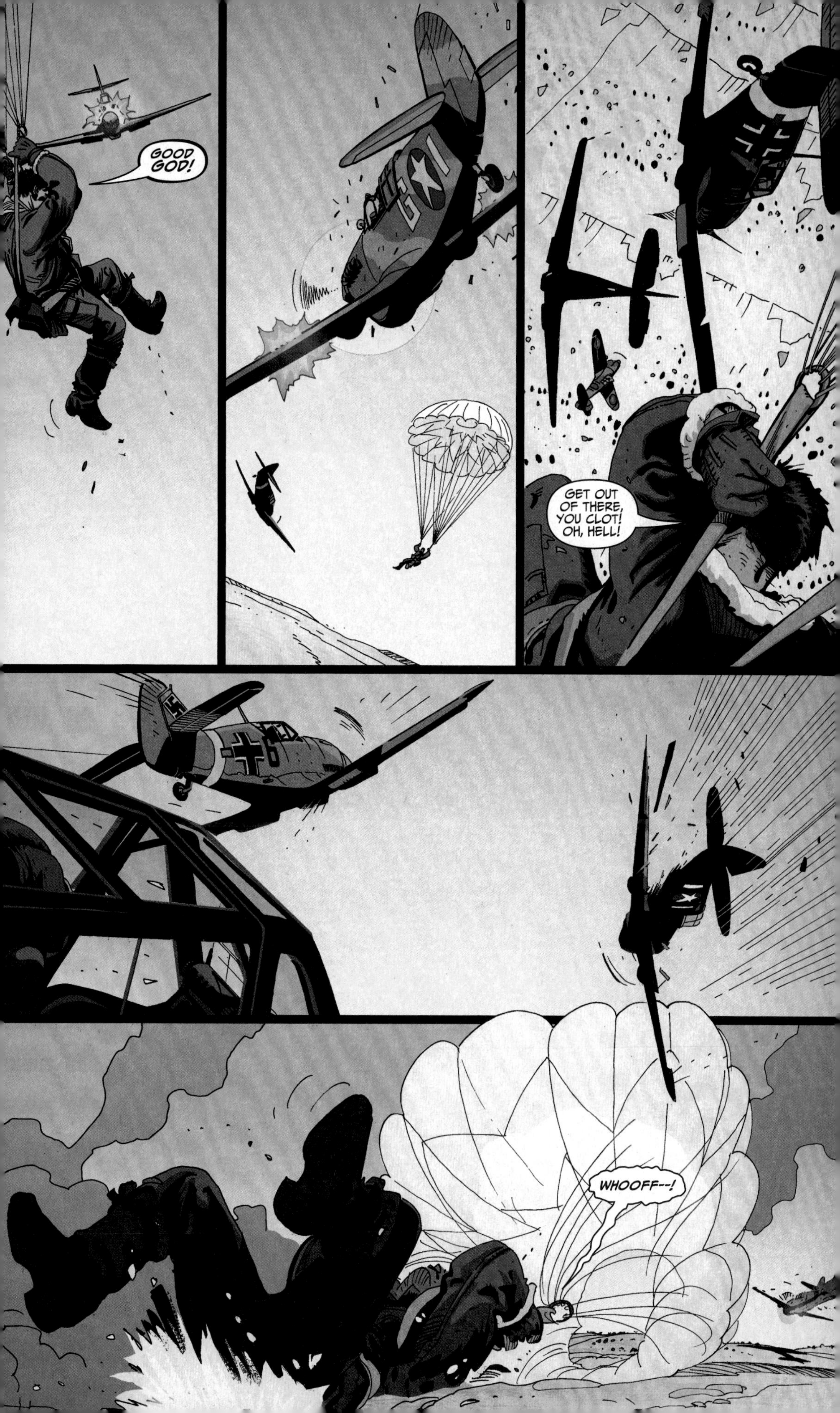
GOOD GOD!
GET OUT OF THERE, YOU CLOT! OH, HELL!
WHOOFF--!

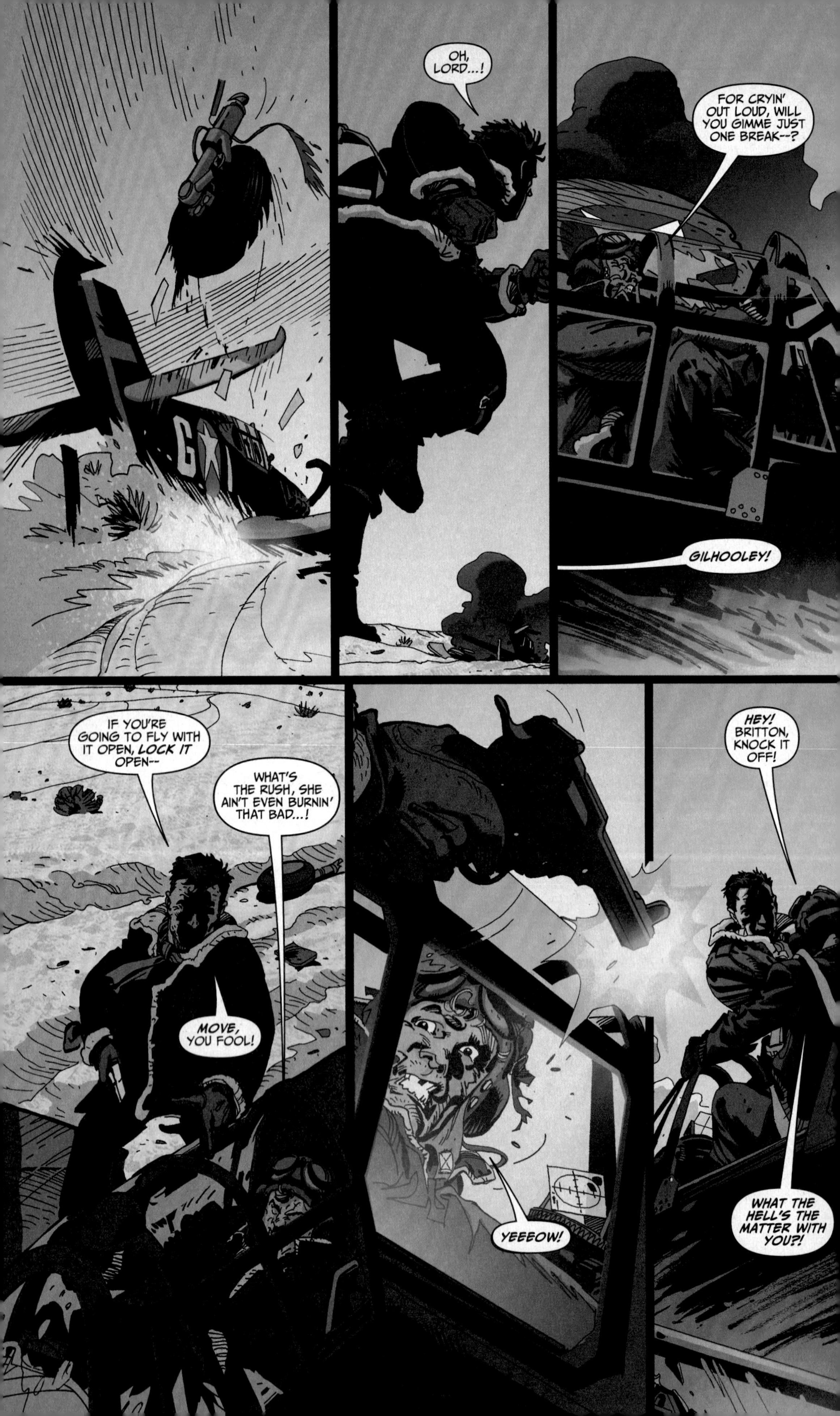
OH, LORD...!
FOR CRYIN' OUT LOUD, WILL YOU GIMME JUST ONE BREAK--?
GILHOOLEY!
IF YOU'RE GOING TO FLY WITH IT OPEN, *LOCK IT* OPEN--
WHAT'S THE RUSH, SHE AIN'T EVEN BURNIN' THAT BAD...!
MOVE, YOU FOOL!
YEEEOW!
HEY! BRITTON, KNOCK IT OFF!
WHAT THE HELL'S THE MATTER WITH YOU?!

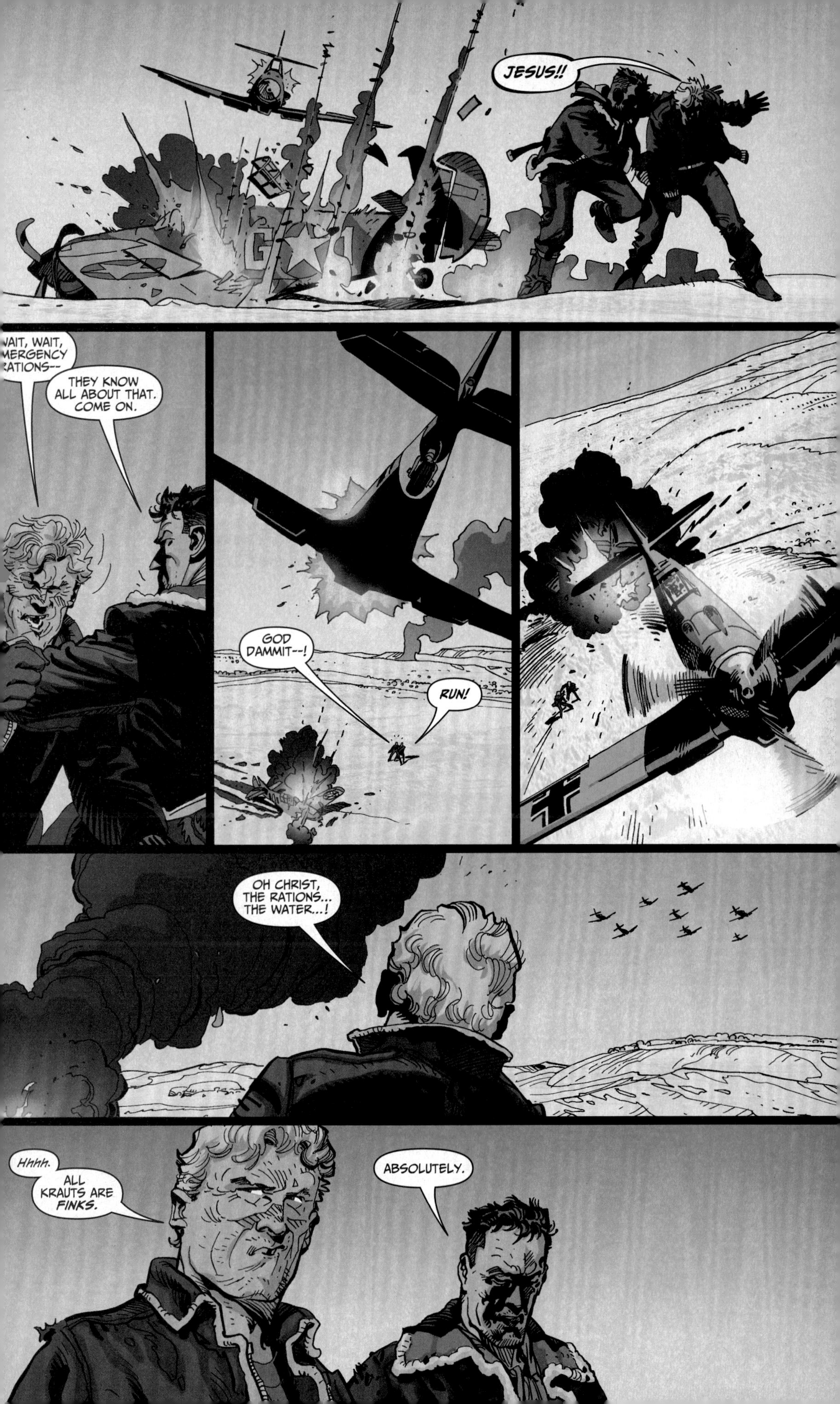
JESUS!!
AIT, WAIT, MERGENCY ATIONS--
THEY KNOW ALL ABOUT THAT. COME ON.
GOD DAMMIT--!
RUN!
OH CHRIST, THE RATIONS... THE WATER...!
Hhhh. ALL KRAUTS ARE FINKS.
ABSOLUTELY.

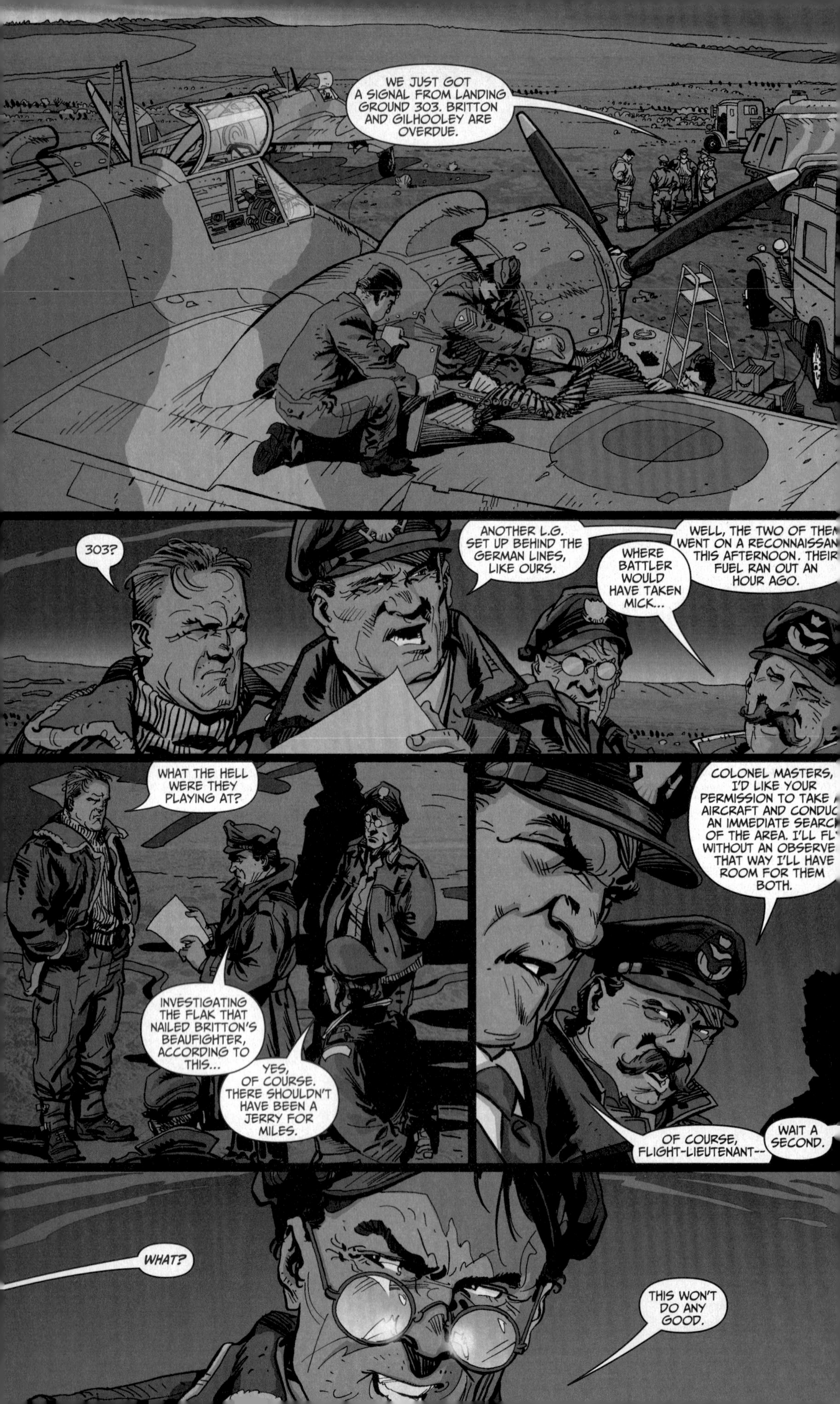
WE JUST GOT A SIGNAL FROM LANDING GROUND 303. BRITTON AND GILHOOLEY ARE OVERDUE.
303?
ANOTHER L.G. SET UP BEHIND THE GERMAN LINES, LIKE OURS.
WHERE BATTLER WOULD HAVE TAKEN MICK...
WELL, THE TWO OF THEM WENT ON A RECONNAISSAN THIS AFTERNOON. THEIR FUEL RAN OUT AN HOUR AGO.
WHAT THE HELL WERE THEY PLAYING AT?
INVESTIGATING THE FLAK THAT NAILED BRITTON'S BEAUFIGHTER, ACCORDING TO THIS...
YES, OF COURSE. THERE SHOULDN'T HAVE BEEN A JERRY FOR MILES.
COLONEL MASTERS, I'D LIKE YOUR PERMISSION TO TAKE AIRCRAFT AND CONDUC AN IMMEDIATE SEARC OF THE AREA. I'LL FL WITHOUT AN OBSERVE THAT WAY I'LL HAVE ROOM FOR THEM BOTH.
OF COURSE, FLIGHT-LIEUTENANT--
WAIT A SECOND.
WHAT?
THIS WON'T DO ANY GOOD.

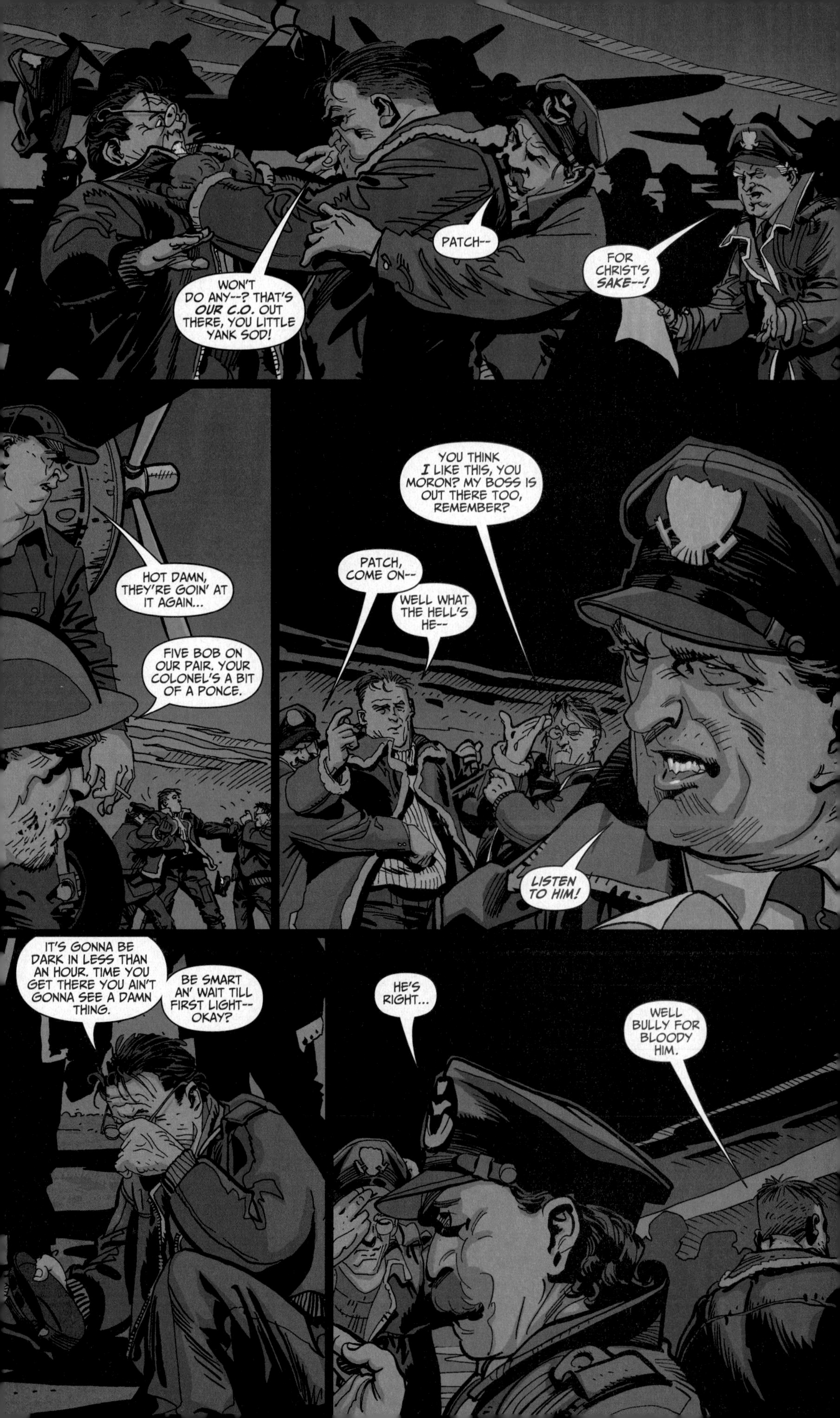
WON'T DO ANY--? THAT'S OUR C.O. OUT THERE, YOU LITTLE YANK SOD!
PATCH--
FOR CHRIST'S SAKE--!
HOT DAMN, THEY'RE GOIN' AT IT AGAIN...
FIVE BOB ON OUR PAIR. YOUR COLONEL'S A BIT OF A PONCE.
YOU THINK I LIKE THIS, YOU MORON? MY BOSS IS OUT THERE TOO, REMEMBER?
PATCH, COME ON--
WELL WHAT THE HELL'S HE--
LISTEN TO HIM!
IT'S GONNA BE DARK IN LESS THAN AN HOUR. TIME YOU GET THERE YOU AIN'T GONNA SEE A DAMN THING.
BE SMART AN' WAIT TILL FIRST LIGHT-- OKAY?
HE'S RIGHT...
WELL BULLY FOR BLOODY HIM.

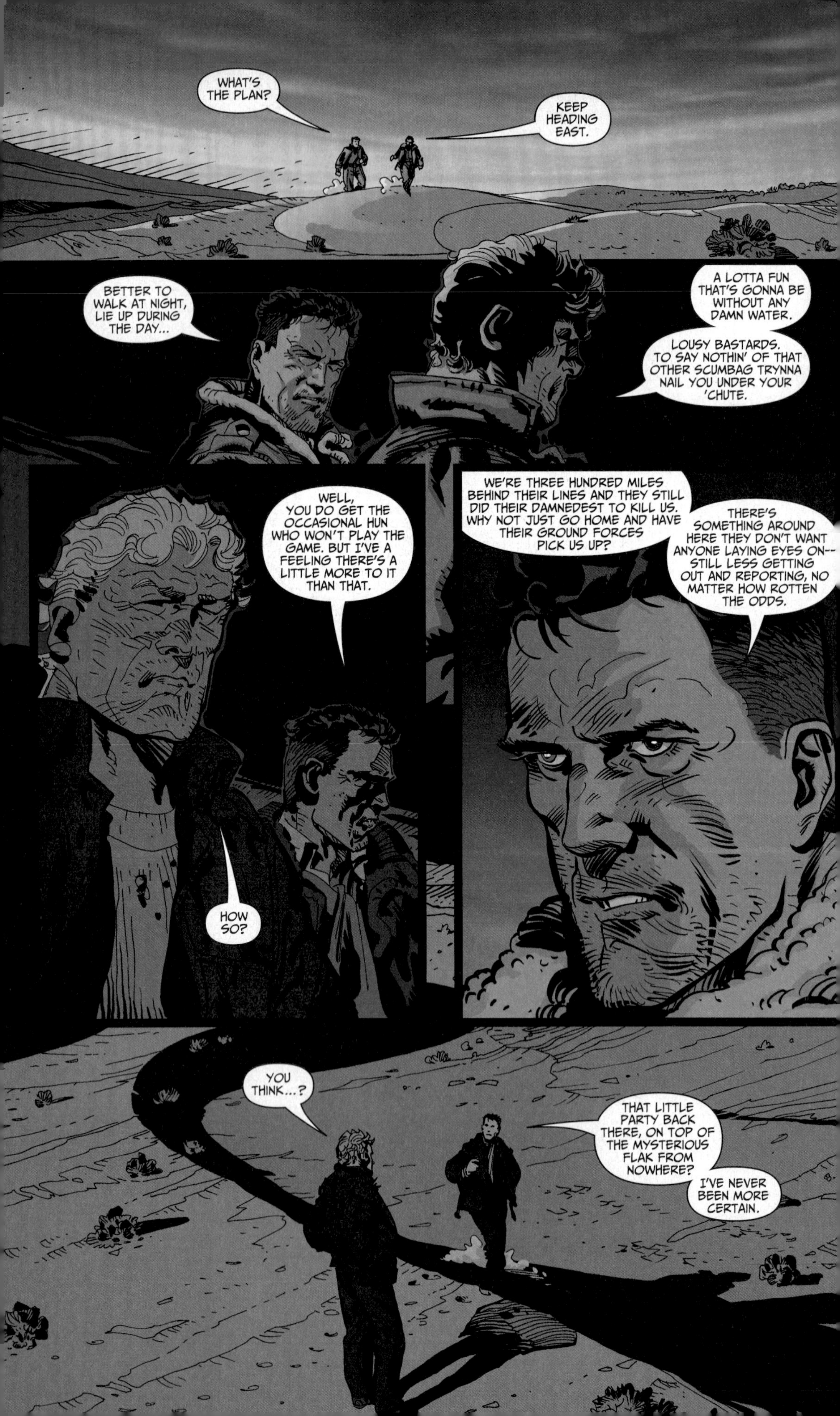
WHAT'S THE PLAN?
KEEP HEADING EAST.
BETTER TO WALK AT NIGHT, LIE UP DURING THE DAY...
A LOTTA FUN THAT'S GONNA BE WITHOUT ANY DAMN WATER.
LOUSY BASTARDS. TO SAY NOTHIN' OF THAT OTHER SCUMBAG TRYNNA NAIL YOU UNDER YOUR 'CHUTE.
WELL, YOU DO GET THE OCCASIONAL HUN WHO WON'T PLAY THE GAME. BUT I'VE A FEELING THERE'S A LITTLE MORE TO IT THAN THAT.
HOW SO?
WE'RE THREE HUNDRED MILES BEHIND THEIR LINES AND THEY STILL DID THEIR DAMNEDEST TO KILL US. WHY NOT JUST GO HOME AND HAVE THEIR GROUND FORCES PICK US UP?
THERE'S SOMETHING AROUND HERE THEY DON'T WANT ANYONE LAYING EYES ON-- STILL LESS GETTING OUT AND REPORTING, NO MATTER HOW ROTTEN THE ODDS.
YOU THINK...?
THAT LITTLE PARTY BACK THERE, ON TOP OF THE MYSTERIOUS FLAK FROM NOWHERE?
I'VE NEVER BEEN MORE CERTAIN.

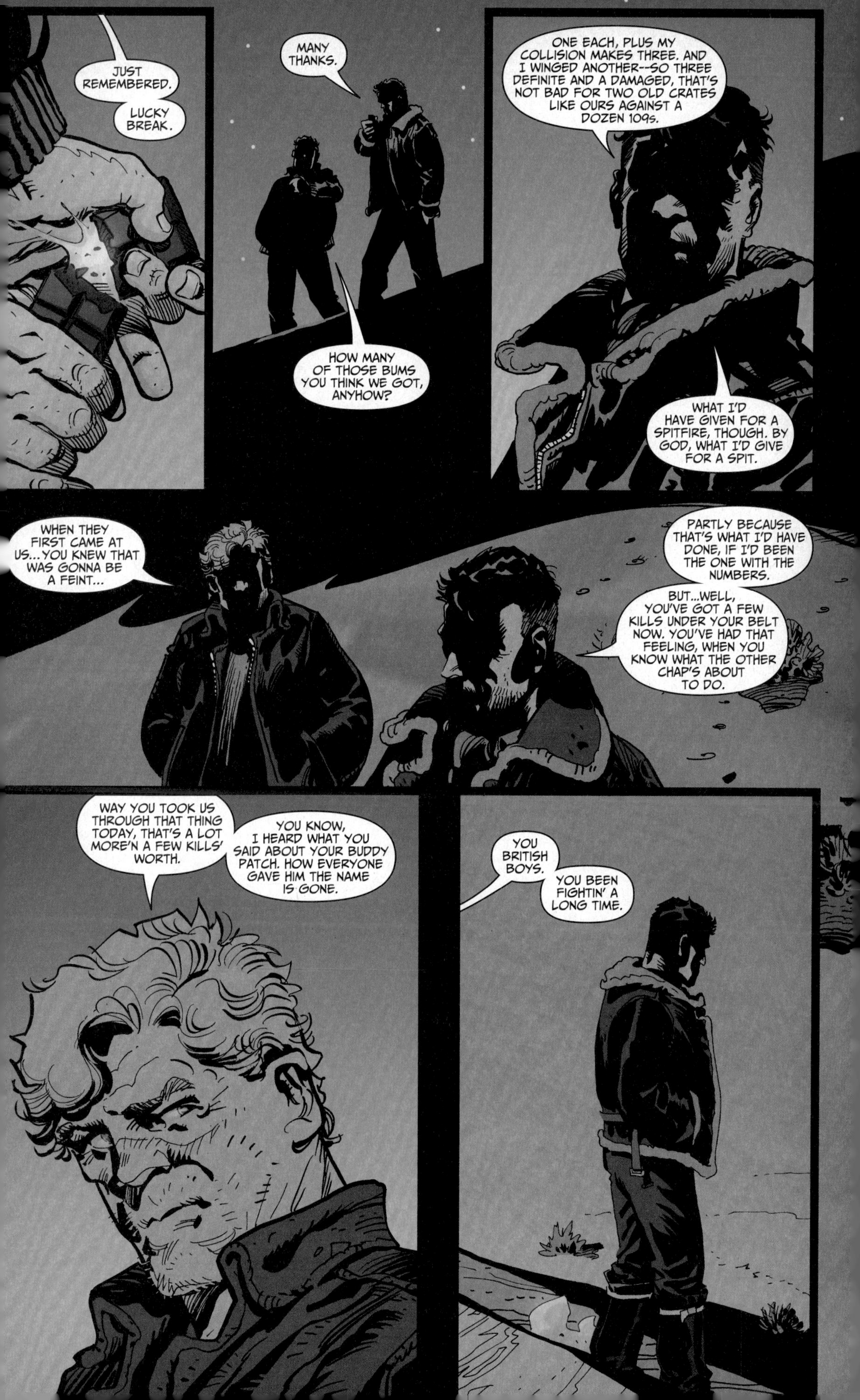
JUST REMEMBERED.
LUCKY BREAK.
MANY THANKS.
HOW MANY OF THOSE BUMS YOU THINK WE GOT, ANYHOW?
ONE EACH, PLUS MY COLLISION MAKES THREE. AND I WINGED ANOTHER--SO THREE DEFINITE AND A DAMAGED, THAT'S NOT BAD FOR TWO OLD CRATES LIKE OURS AGAINST A DOZEN 109s.
WHAT I'D HAVE GIVEN FOR A SPITFIRE, THOUGH. BY GOD, WHAT I'D GIVE FOR A SPIT.
WHEN THEY FIRST CAME AT US...YOU KNEW THAT WAS GONNA BE A FEINT...
PARTLY BECAUSE THAT'S WHAT I'D HAVE DONE, IF I'D BEEN THE ONE WITH THE NUMBERS.
BUT...WELL, YOU'VE GOT A FEW KILLS UNDER YOUR BELT NOW. YOU'VE HAD THAT FEELING, WHEN YOU KNOW WHAT THE OTHER CHAP'S ABOUT TO DO.
WAY YOU TOOK US THROUGH TODAY THAT THING TODAY, THAT'S A LOT MORE'N A FEW KILLS' WORTH.
YOU KNOW, I HEARD WHAT YOU SAID ABOUT YOUR BUDDY PATCH. HOW EVERYONE GAVE HIM THE NAME IS GONE.
YOU BRITISH BOYS.
YOU BEEN FIGHTIN' A LONG TIME.

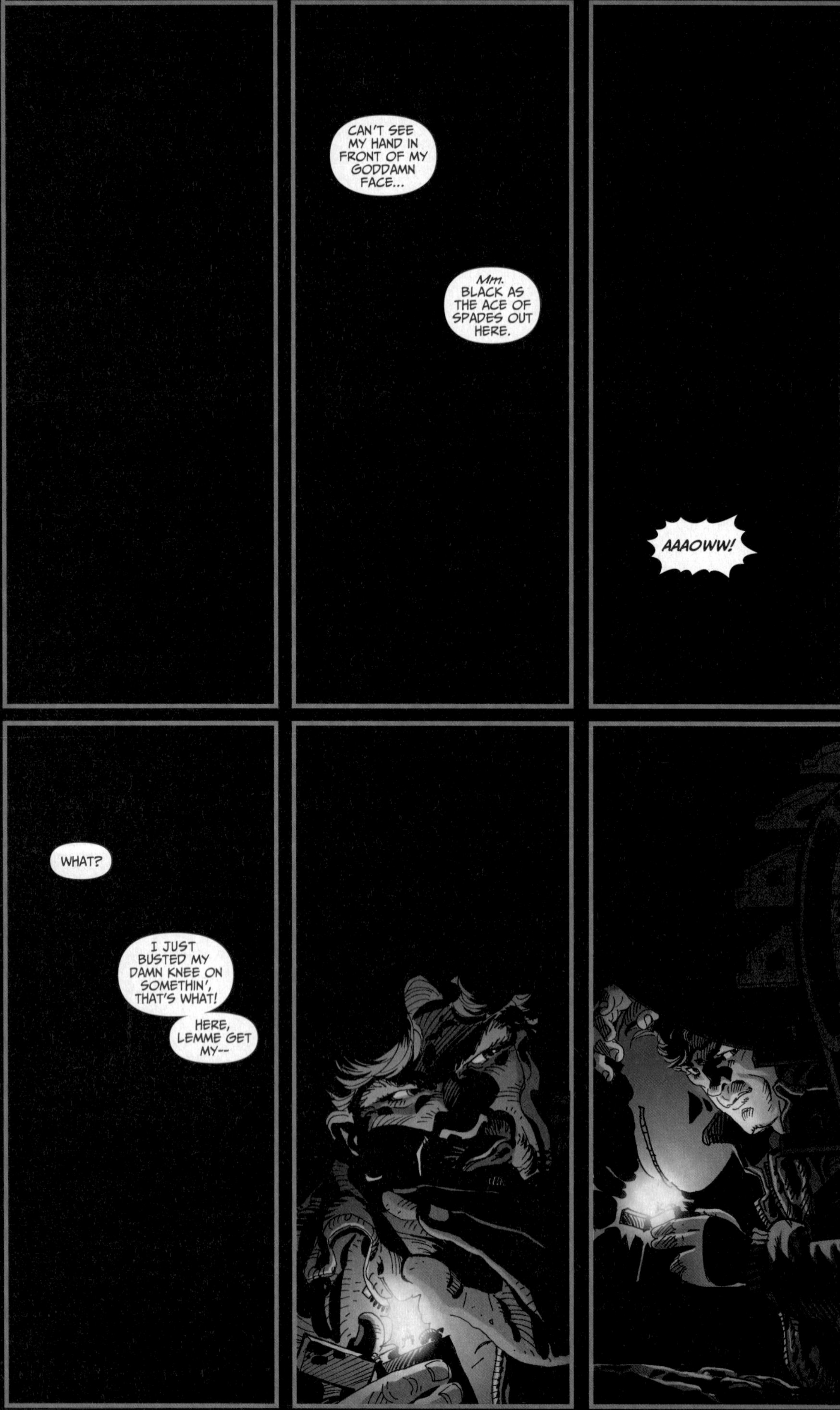
CAN'T SEE MY HAND IN FRONT OF MY GODDAMN FACE...
Mm. BLACK AS THE ACE OF SPADES OUT HERE.
AAAOWW!
WHAT?
I JUST BUSTED MY DAMN KNEE ON SOMETHIN', THAT'S WHAT!
HERE, LEMME GET MY--

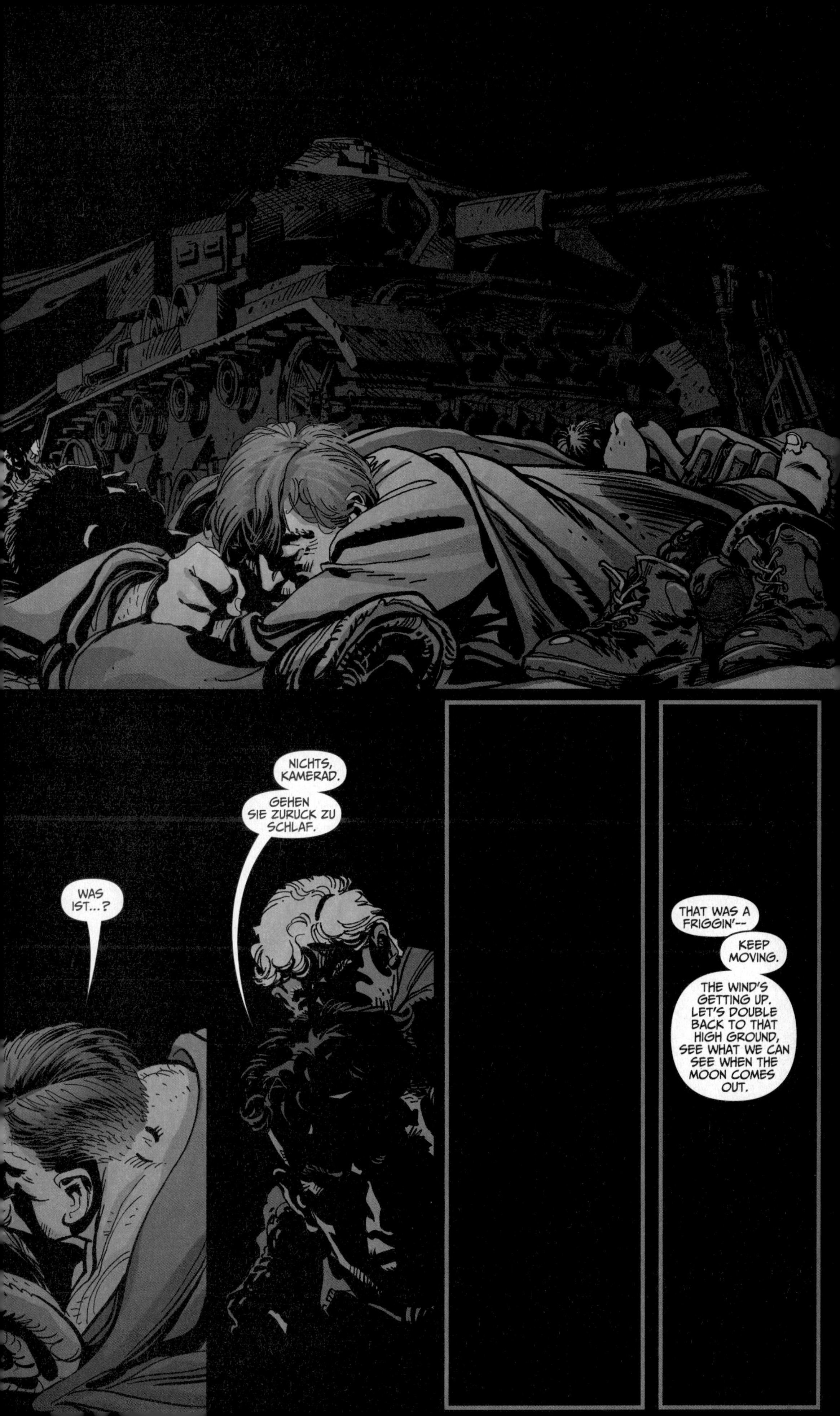
WAS IST...?
NICHTS, KAMERAD.
GEHEN SIE ZURUCK ZU SCHLAF.
THAT WAS A FRIGGIN'--
KEEP MOVING.
THE WIND'S GETTING UP. LET'S DOUBLE BACK TO THAT HIGH GROUND, SEE WHAT WE CAN SEE WHEN THE MOON COMES OUT.

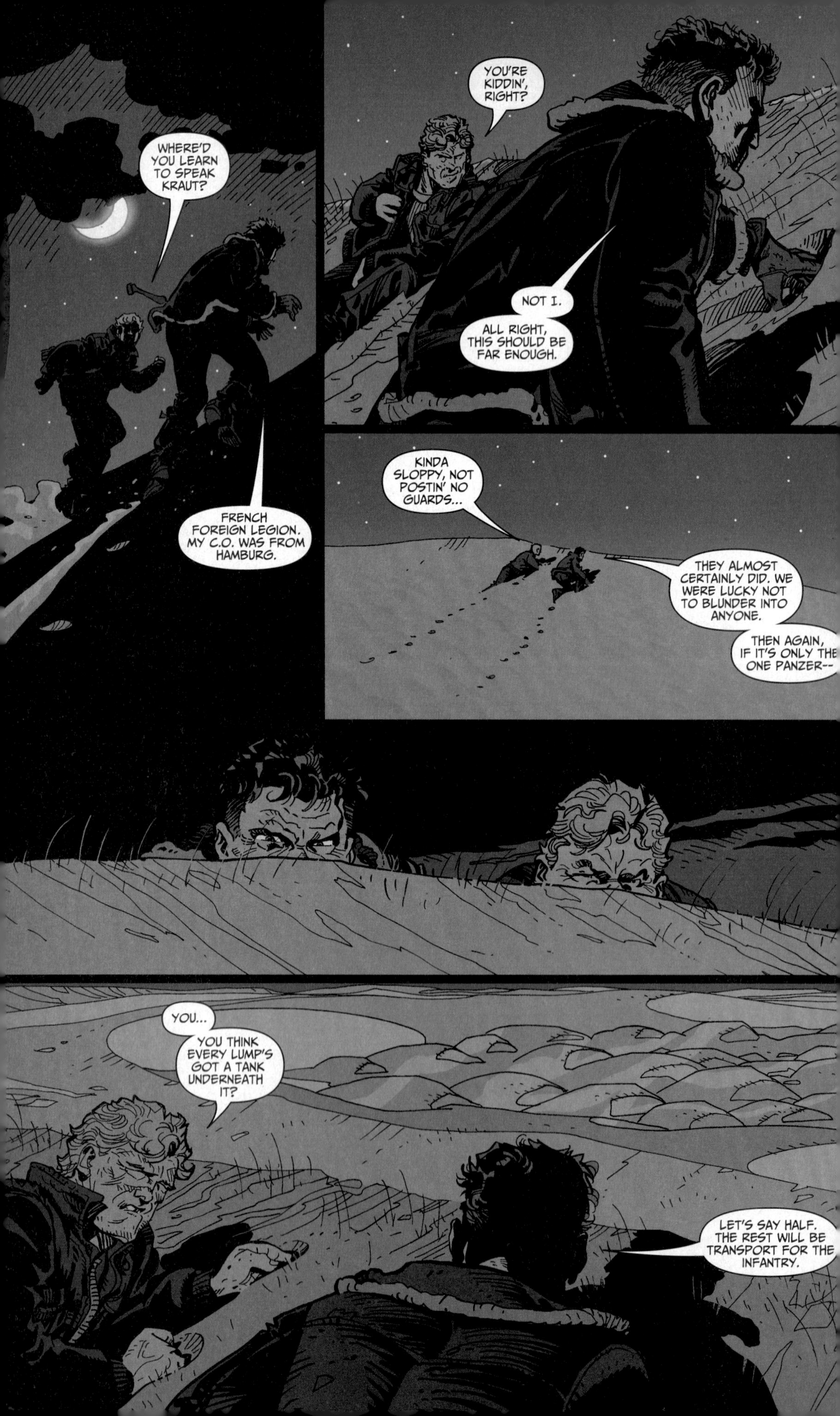
WHERE'D YOU LEARN TO SPEAK KRAUT?
FRENCH FOREIGN LEGION. MY C.O. WAS FROM HAMBURG.
YOU'RE KIDDIN', RIGHT?
NOT I.
ALL RIGHT, THIS SHOULD BE FAR ENOUGH.
KINDA SLOPPY, NOT POSTIN' NO GUARDS...
THEY ALMOST CERTAINLY DID. WE WERE LUCKY NOT TO BLUNDER INTO ANYONE.
THEN AGAIN, IF IT'S ONLY THE ONE PANZER--
YOU...
YOU THINK EVERY LUMP'S GOT A TANK UNDERNEATH IT?
LET'S SAY HALF. THE REST WILL BE TRANSPORT FOR THE INFANTRY.

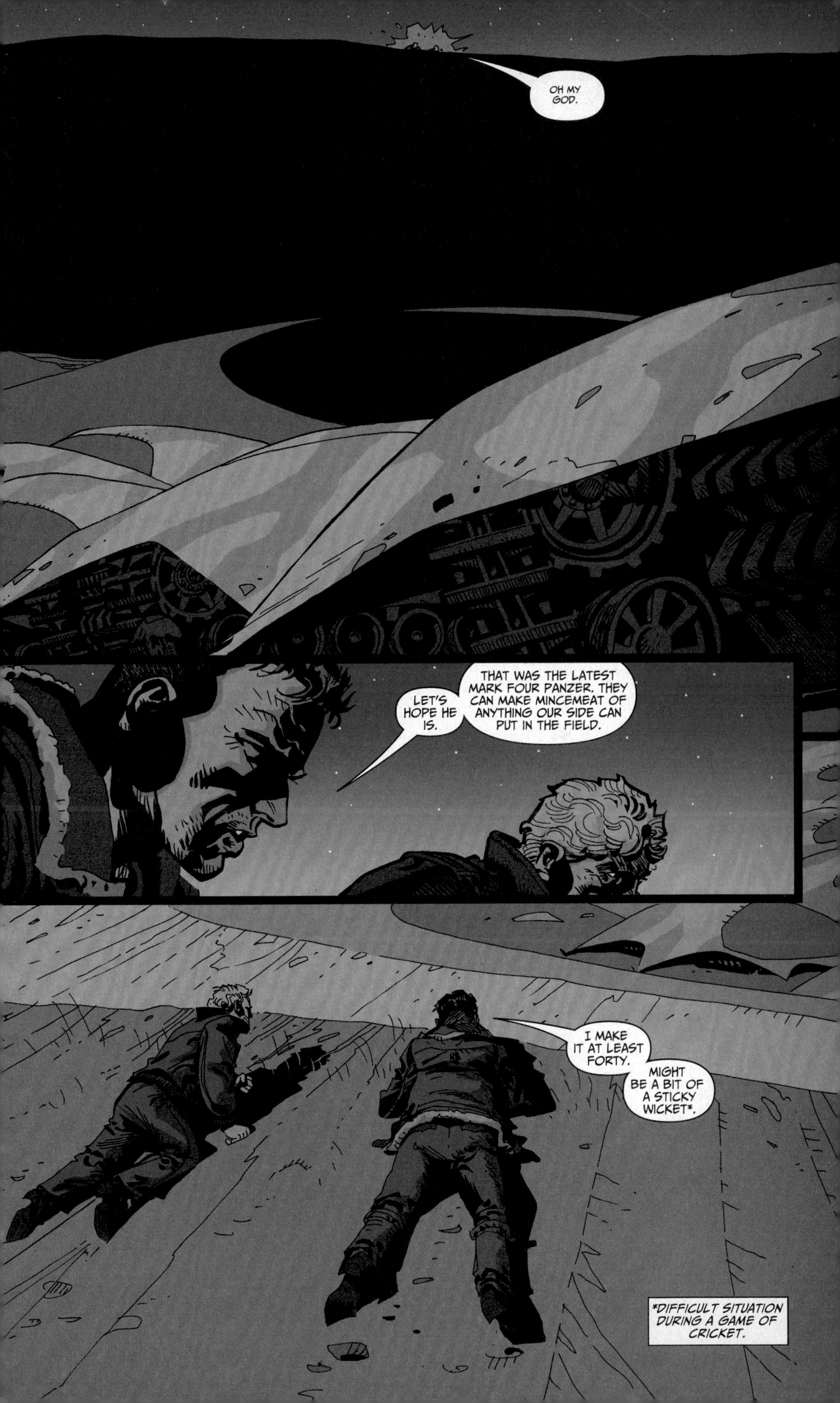
OH MY GOD.
LET'S HOPE HE IS.
THAT WAS THE LATEST MARK FOUR PANZER. THEY CAN MAKE MINCEMEAT OF ANYTHING OUR SIDE CAN PUT IN THE FIELD.
I MAKE IT AT LEAST FORTY.
MIGHT BE A BIT OF A STICKY WICKET*.
*DIFFICULT SITUATION DURING A GAME OF CRICKET.

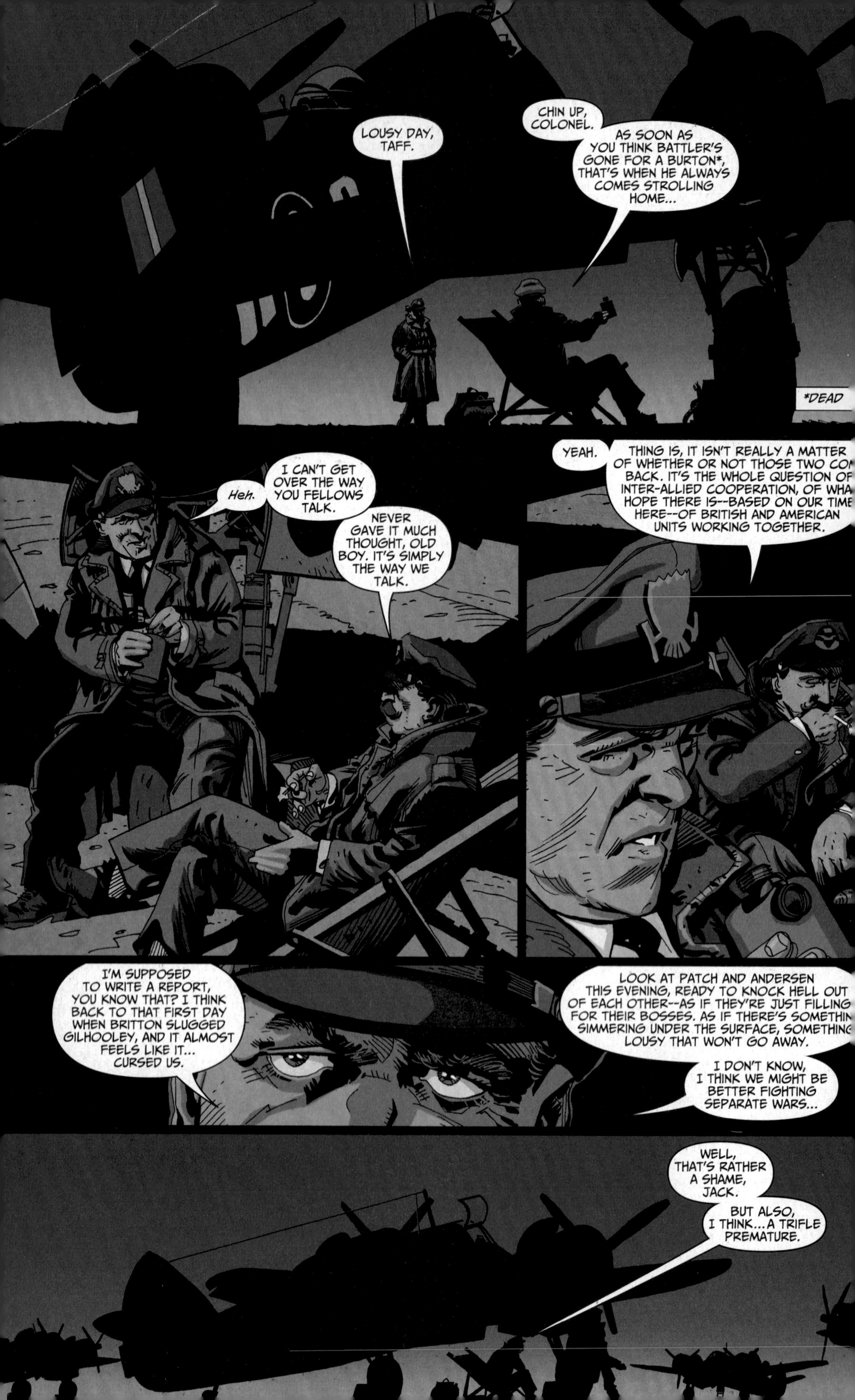
LOUSY DAY, TAFF.
CHIN UP, COLONEL.
AS SOON AS YOU THINK BATTLER'S GONE FOR A BURTON*, THAT'S WHEN HE ALWAYS COMES STROLLING HOME...
*DEAD
Heh.
I CAN'T GET OVER THE WAY YOU FELLOWS TALK.
NEVER GAVE IT MUCH THOUGHT, OLD BOY. IT'S SIMPLY THE WAY WE TALK.
YEAH.
THING IS, IT ISN'T REALLY A MATTER OF WHETHER OR NOT THOSE TWO CO BACK. IT'S THE WHOLE QUESTION OF INTER-ALLIED COOPERATION, OF WHA HOPE THERE IS--BASED ON OUR TIME HERE--OF BRITISH AND AMERICAN UNITS WORKING TOGETHER.
I'M SUPPOSED TO WRITE A REPORT, YOU KNOW THAT? I THINK BACK TO THAT FIRST DAY WHEN BRITTON SLUGGED GILHOOLEY, AND IT ALMOST FEELS LIKE IT... CURSED US.
LOOK AT PATCH AND ANDERSEN THIS EVENING, READY TO KNOCK HELL OUT OF EACH OTHER--AS IF THEY'RE JUST FILLING FOR THEIR BOSSES. AS IF THERE'S SOMETHIN SIMMERING UNDER THE SURFACE, SOMETHING LOUSY THAT WON'T GO AWAY.
I DON'T KNOW, I THINK WE MIGHT BE BETTER FIGHTING SEPARATE WARS...
WELL, THAT'S RATHER A SHAME, JACK.
BUT ALSO, I THINK... A TRIFLE PREMATURE.

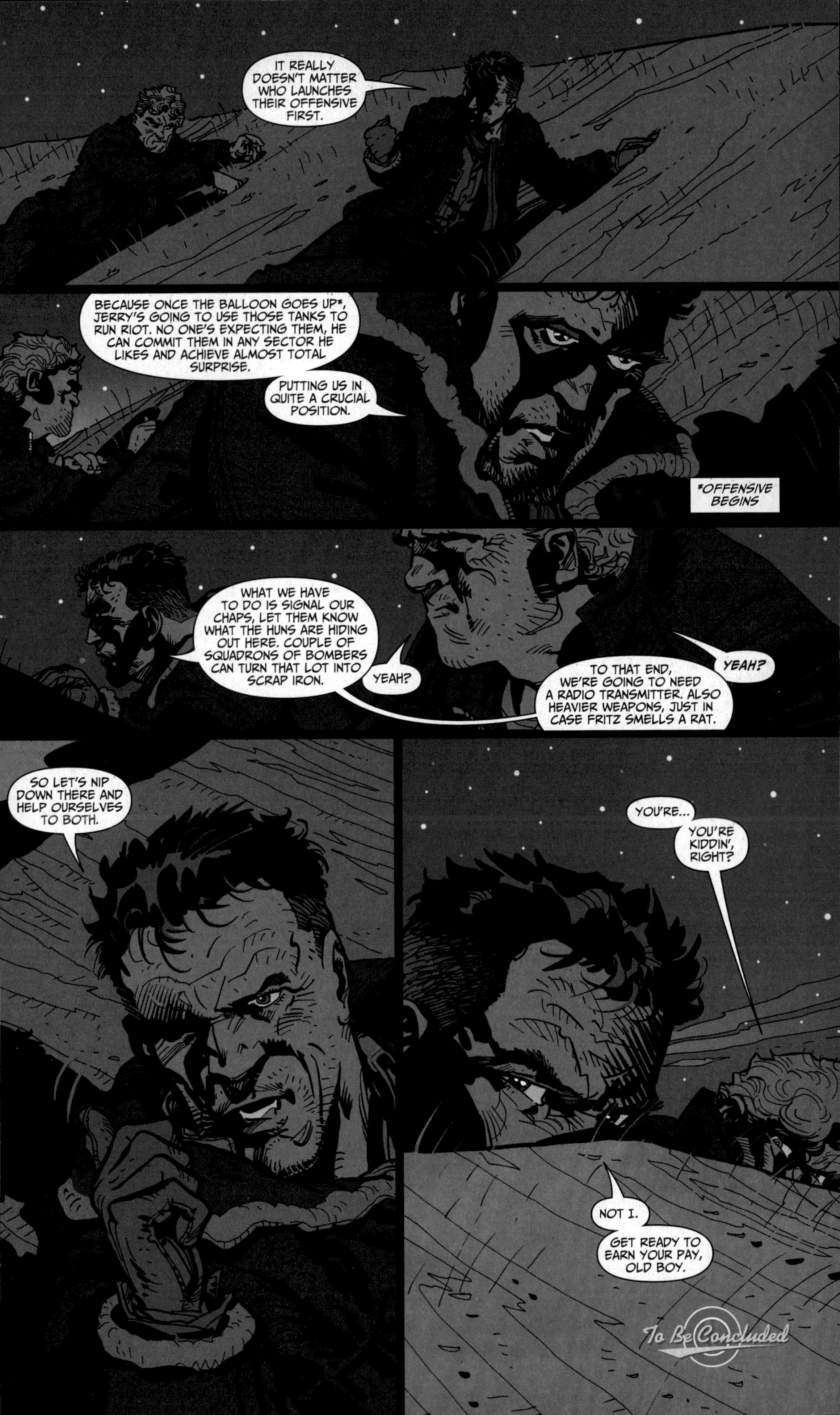
IT REALLY DOESN'T MATTER WHO LAUNCHES THEIR OFFENSIVE FIRST.
BECAUSE ONCE THE BALLOON GOES UP*, JERRY'S GOING TO USE THOSE TANKS TO RUN RIOT. NO ONE'S EXPECTING THEM, HE CAN COMMIT THEM IN ANY SECTOR HE LIKES AND ACHIEVE ALMOST TOTAL SURPRISE.
PUTTING US IN QUITE A CRUCIAL POSITION.
*OFFENSIVE BEGINS
WHAT WE HAVE TO DO IS SIGNAL OUR CHAPS, LET THEM KNOW WHAT THE HUNS ARE HIDING OUT HERE. COUPLE OF SQUADRONS OF BOMBERS CAN TURN THAT LOT INTO SCRAP IRON.
YEAH?
TO THAT END, WE'RE GOING TO NEED A RADIO TRANSMITTER. ALSO HEAVIER WEAPONS, JUST IN CASE FRITZ SMELLS A RAT.
YEAH?
SO LET'S NIP DOWN THERE AND HELP OURSELVES TO BOTH.
YOU'RE...
YOU'RE KIDDIN', RIGHT?
NOT I.
GET READY TO EARN YOUR PAY, OLD BOY.
To Be Concluded

CHAPTER 5

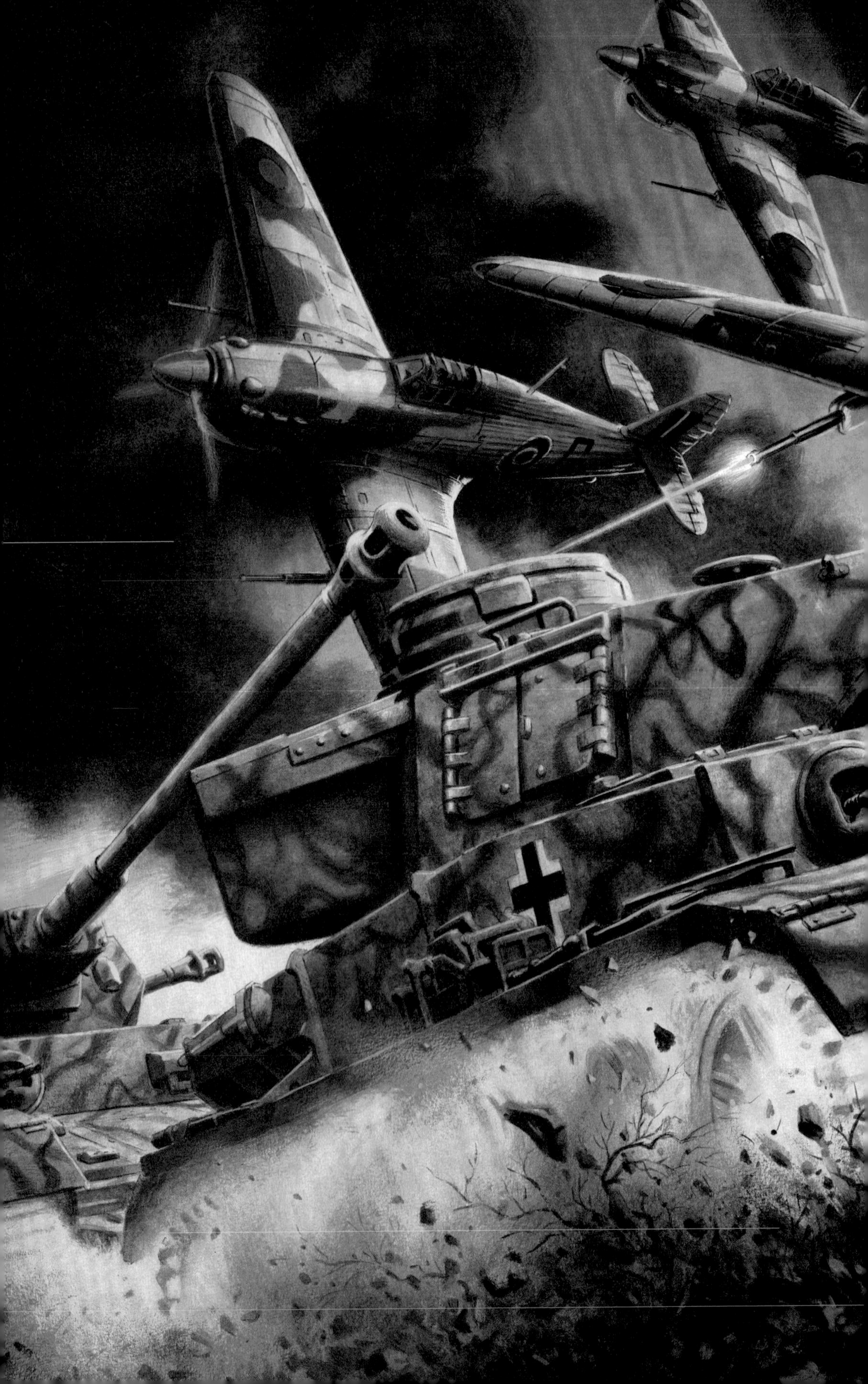

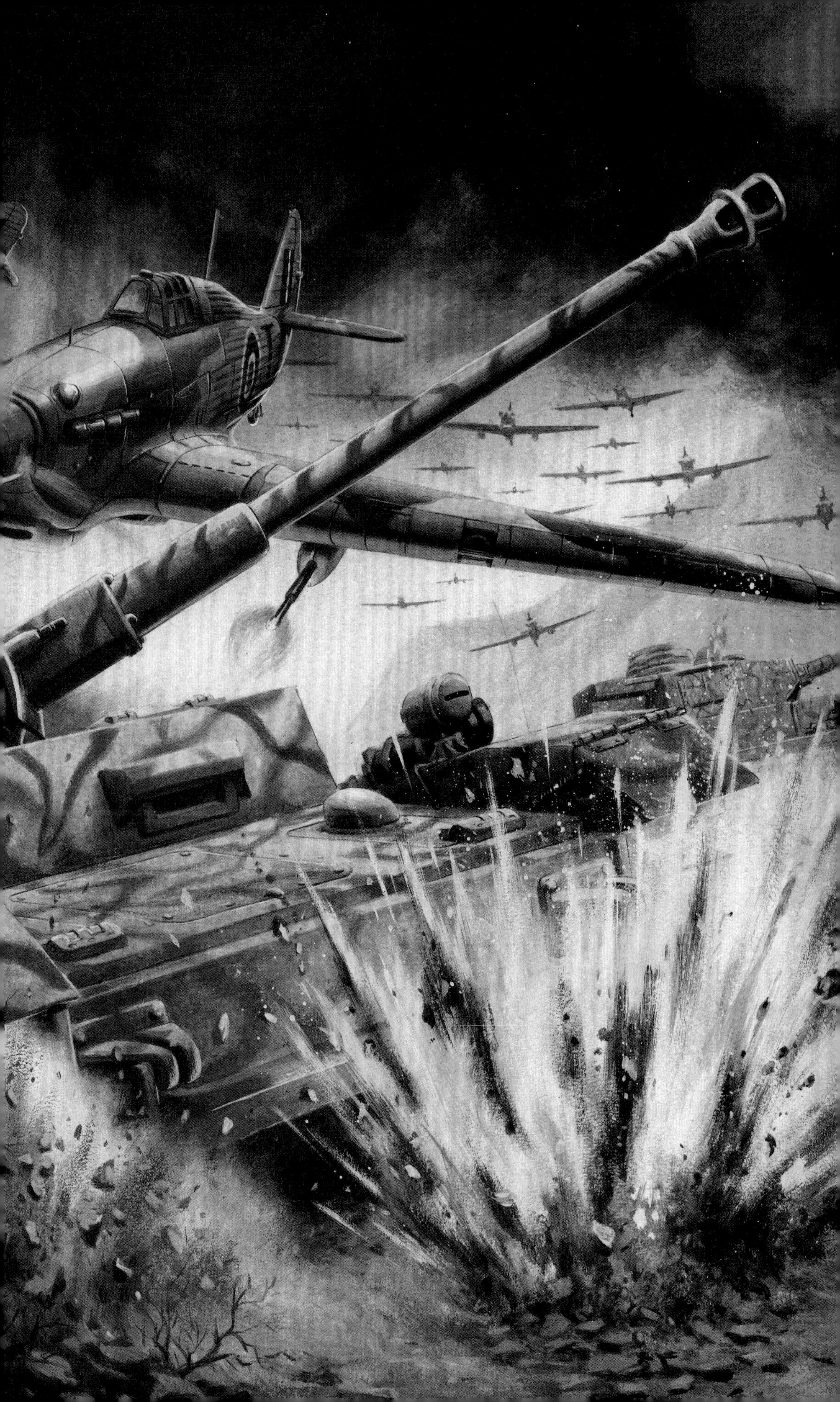

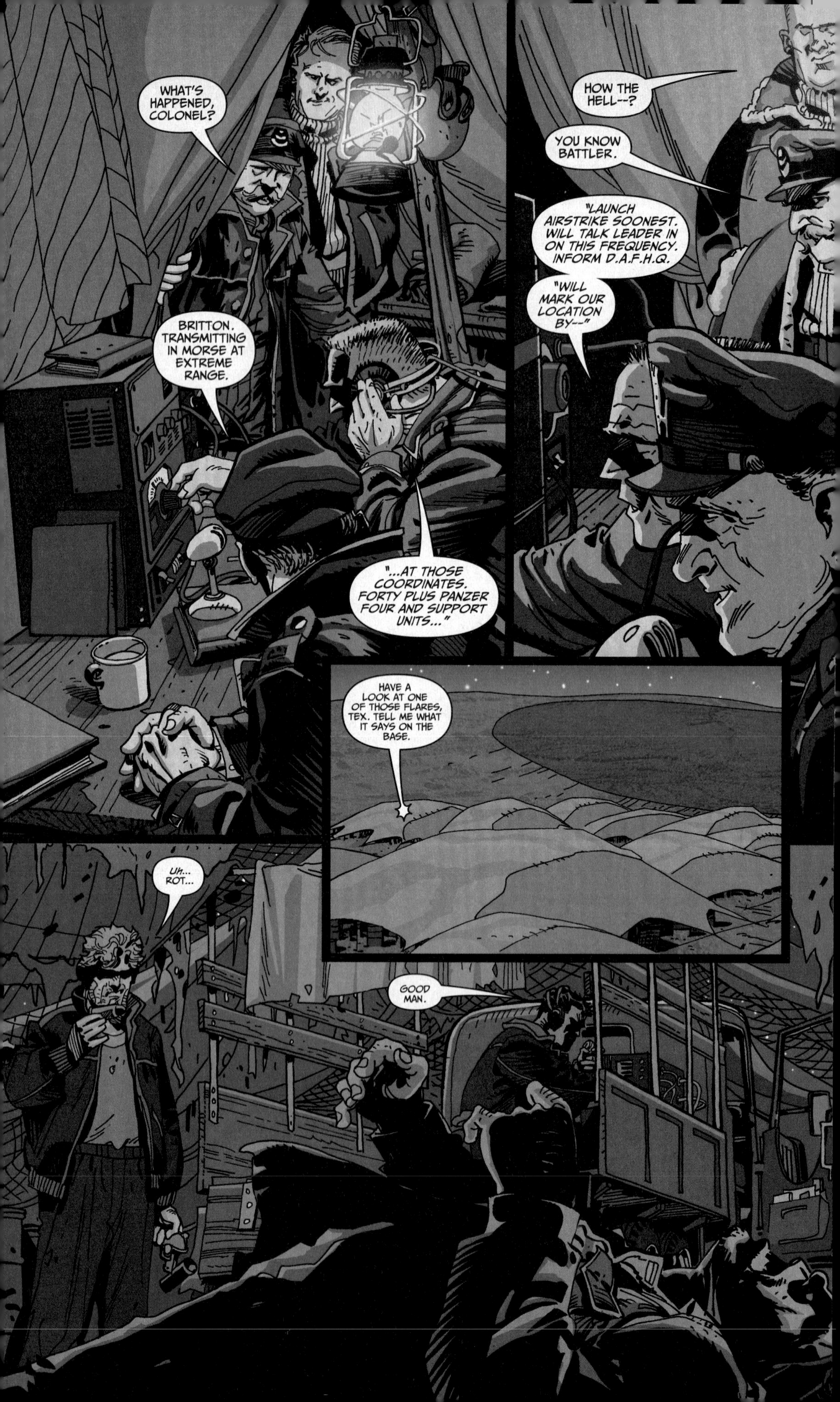
WHAT'S HAPPENED, COLONEL?
BRITTON. TRANSMITTING IN MORSE AT EXTREME RANGE.
"...AT THOSE COORDINATES. FORTY PLUS PANZER FOUR AND SUPPORT UNITS..."
HOW THE HELL--?
YOU KNOW BATTLER.
"LAUNCH AIRSTRIKE SOONEST. WILL TALK LEADER IN ON THIS FREQUENCY. INFORM D.A.F.H.Q.
"WILL MARK OUR LOCATION BY--"
HAVE A LOOK AT ONE OF THOSE FLARES, TEX. TELL ME WHAT IT SAYS ON THE BASE.
Uh... ROT...
GOOD MAN.

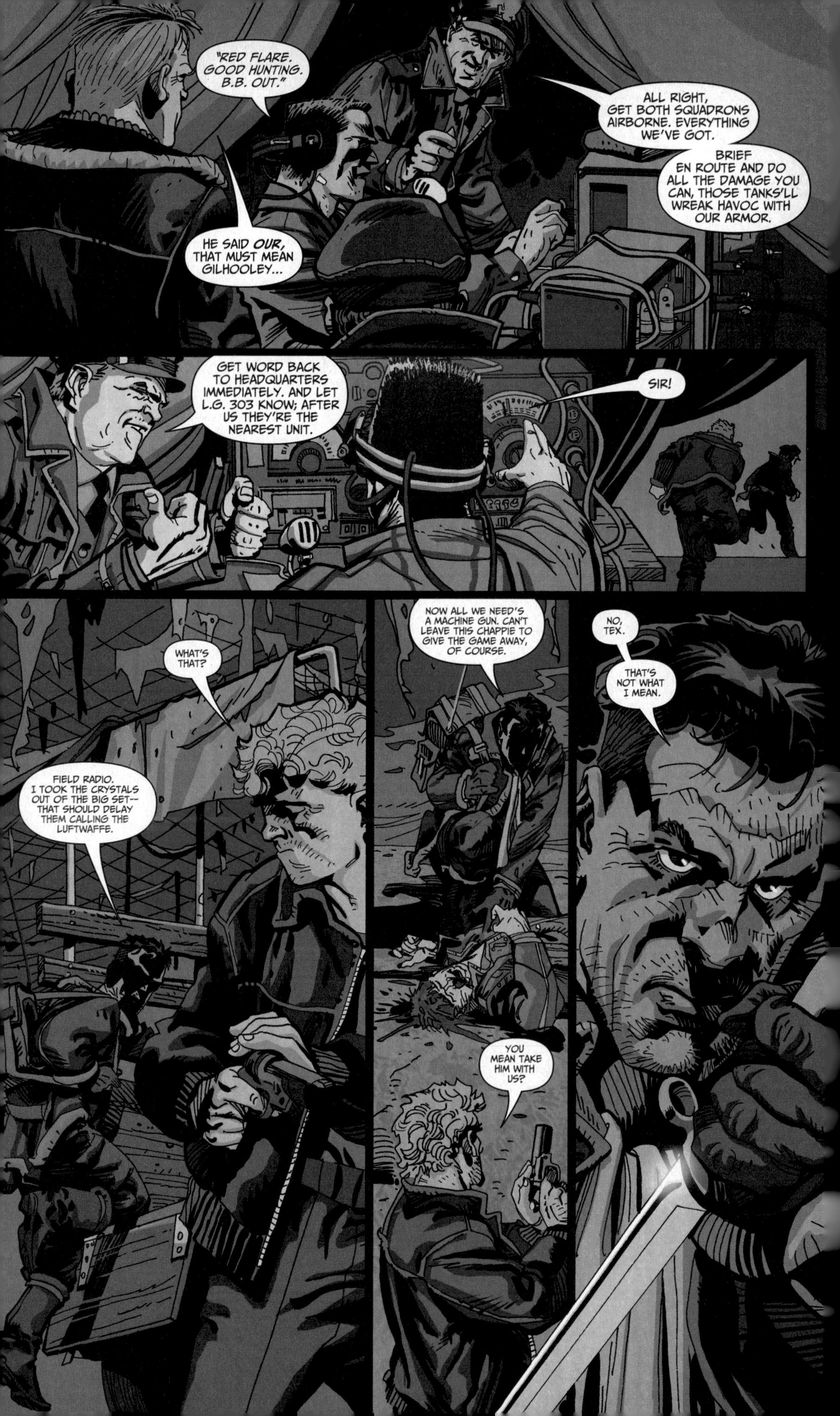
"RED FLARE. GOOD HUNTING. B.B. OUT."
ALL RIGHT, GET BOTH SQUADRONS AIRBORNE. EVERYTHING WE'VE GOT.
BRIEF EN ROUTE AND DO ALL THE DAMAGE YOU CAN, THOSE TANKS'LL WREAK HAVOC WITH OUR ARMOR.
HE SAID OUR, THAT MUST MEAN GILHOOLEY...
GET WORD BACK TO HEADQUARTERS IMMEDIATELY. AND LET L.G. 303 KNOW; AFTER US THEY'RE THE NEAREST UNIT.
SIR!
WHAT'S THAT?
FIELD RADIO. I TOOK THE CRYSTALS OUT OF THE BIG SET-- THAT SHOULD DELAY THEM CALLING THE LUFTWAFFE.
NOW ALL WE NEED'S A MACHINE GUN. CAN'T LEAVE THIS CHAPPIE TO GIVE THE GAME AWAY, OF COURSE.
YOU MEAN TAKE HIM WITH US?
NO, TEX.
THAT'S NOT WHAT I MEAN.

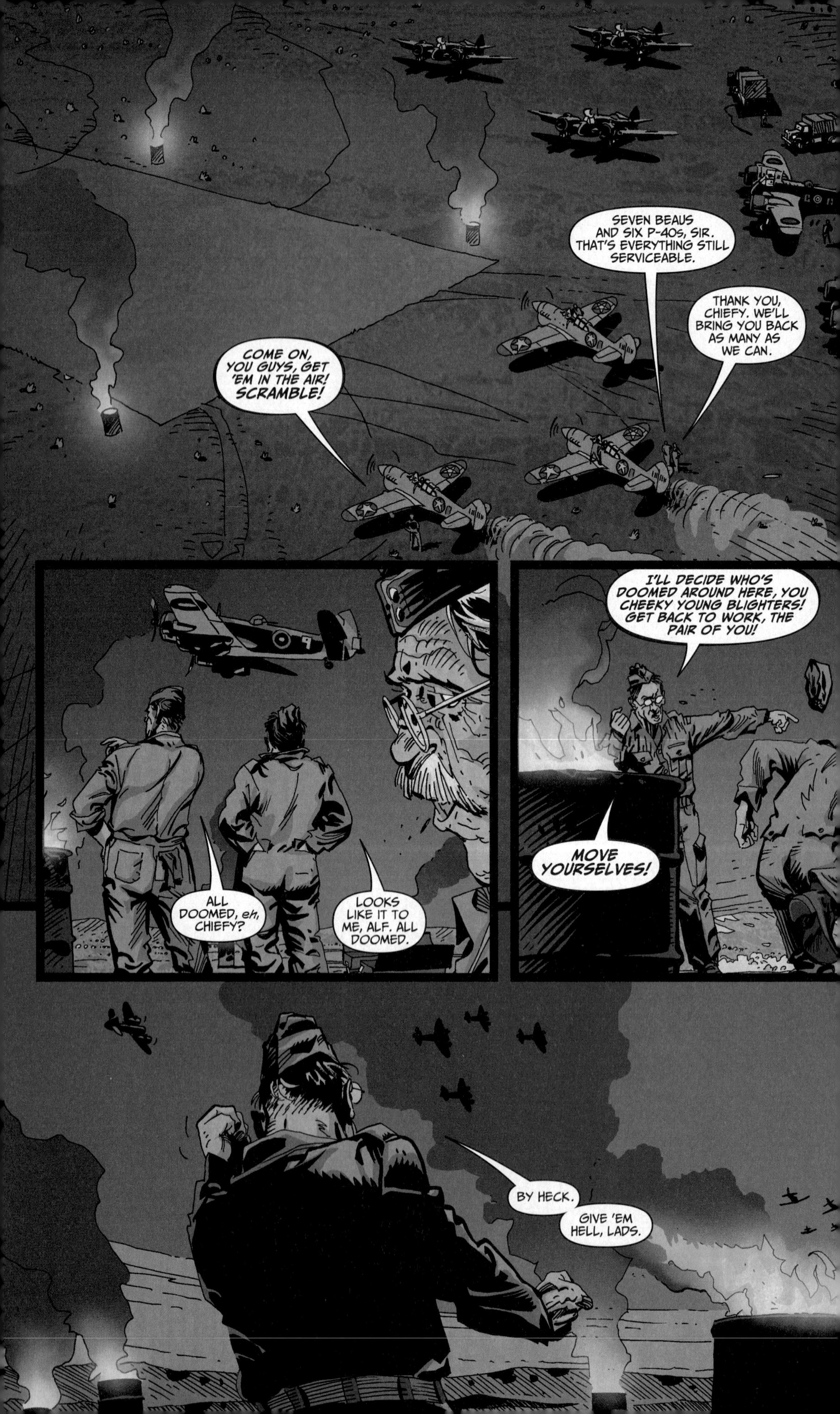
SEVEN BEAUS AND SIX P-40s, SIR. THAT'S EVERYTHING STILL SERVICEABLE.
THANK YOU, CHIEFY. WE'LL BRING YOU BACK AS MANY AS WE CAN.
COME ON, YOU GUYS, GET 'EM IN THE AIR! SCRAMBLE!
ALL DOOMED, eh, CHIEFY?
LOOKS LIKE IT TO ME, ALF. ALL DOOMED.
I'LL DECIDE WHO'S DOOMED AROUND HERE, YOU CHEEKY YOUNG BLIGHTERS! GET BACK TO WORK, THE PAIR OF YOU!
MOVE YOURSELVES!
BY HECK.
GIVE 'EM HELL, LADS.

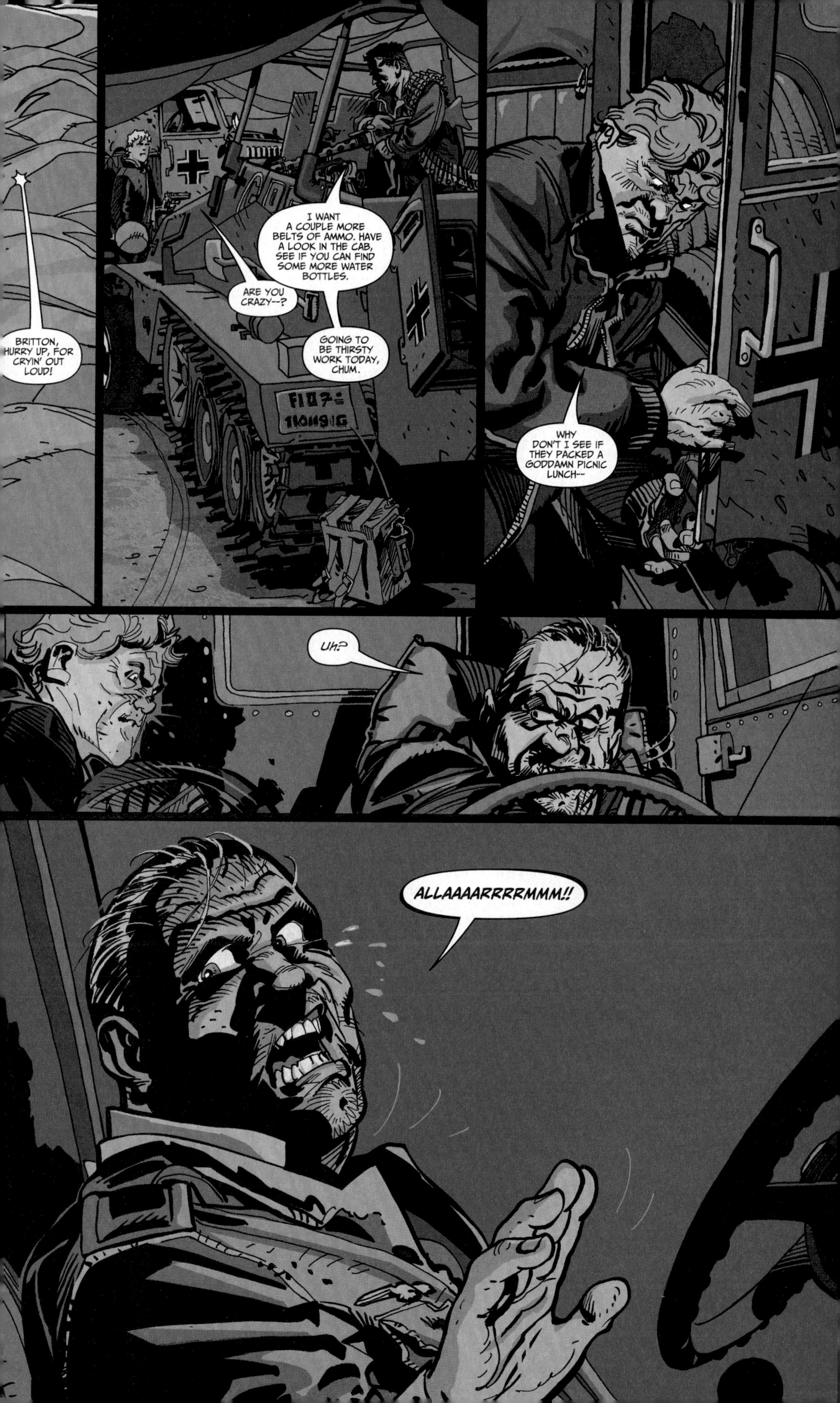
BRITTON, HURRY UP, FOR CRYIN' OUT LOUD!
I WANT A COUPLE MORE BELTS OF AMMO. HAVE A LOOK IN THE CAB, SEE IF YOU CAN FIND SOME MORE WATER BOTTLES.
ARE YOU CRAZY--?
GOING TO BE THIRSTY WORK TODAY, CHUM.
WHY DON'T I SEE IF THEY PACKED A GODDAMN PICNIC LUNCH--
Uh?
ALLAAAARRRRMMM!!

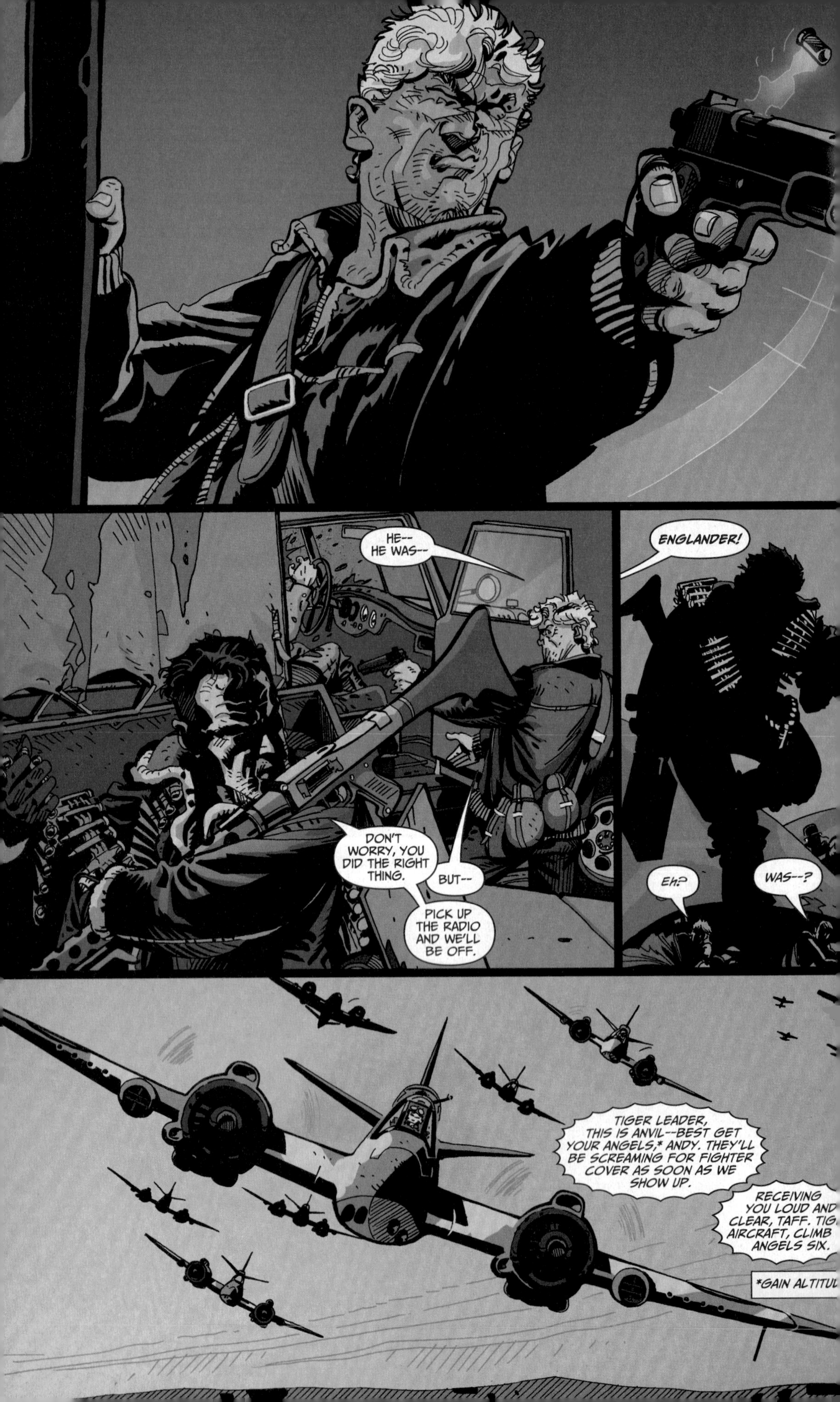
HE--
HE WAS--
ENGLANDER!
DON'T WORRY, YOU DID THE RIGHT THING.
BUT--
PICK UP THE RADIO AND WE'LL BE OFF.
Eh?
WAS--?
TIGER LEADER, THIS IS ANVIL--BEST GET YOUR ANGELS,* ANDY. THEY'LL BE SCREAMING FOR FIGHTER COVER AS SOON AS WE SHOW UP.
RECEIVING YOU LOUD AND CLEAR, TAFF. TIG AIRCRAFT, CLIMB ANGELS SIX.
*GAIN ALTITU

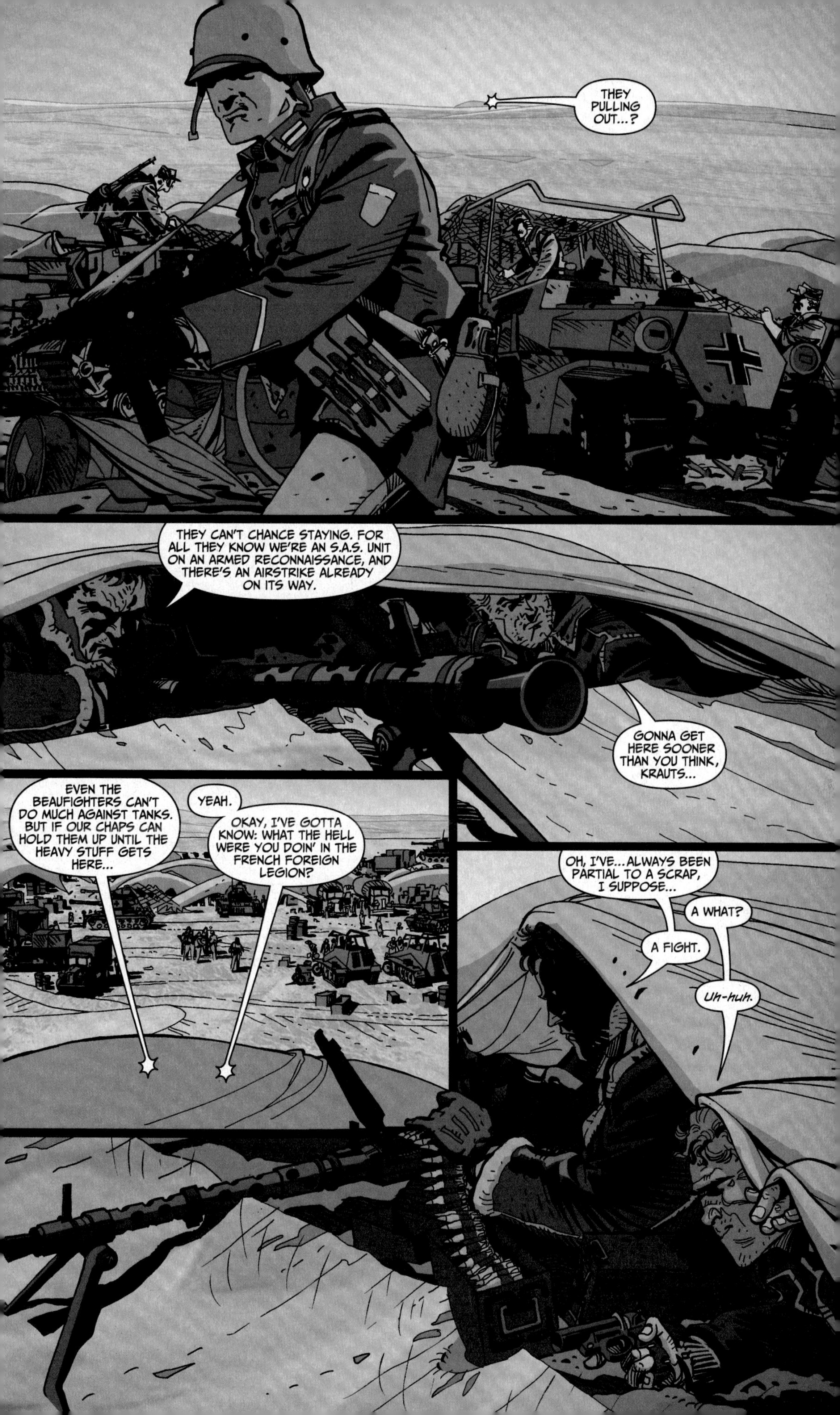
THEY PULLING OUT...?
THEY CAN'T CHANCE STAYING. FOR ALL THEY KNOW WE'RE AN S.A.S. UNIT ON AN ARMED RECONNAISSANCE, AND THERE'S AN AIRSTRIKE ALREADY ON ITS WAY.
GONNA GET HERE SOONER THAN YOU THINK, KRAUTS...
EVEN THE BEAUFIGHTERS CAN'T DO MUCH AGAINST TANKS. BUT IF OUR CHAPS CAN HOLD THEM UP UNTIL THE HEAVY STUFF GETS HERE...
YEAH.
OKAY, I'VE GOTTA KNOW: WHAT THE HELL WERE YOU DOIN' IN THE FRENCH FOREIGN LEGION?
OH, I'VE...ALWAYS BEEN PARTIAL TO A SCRAP, I SUPPOSE...
A WHAT?
A FIGHT.
Uh-huh.

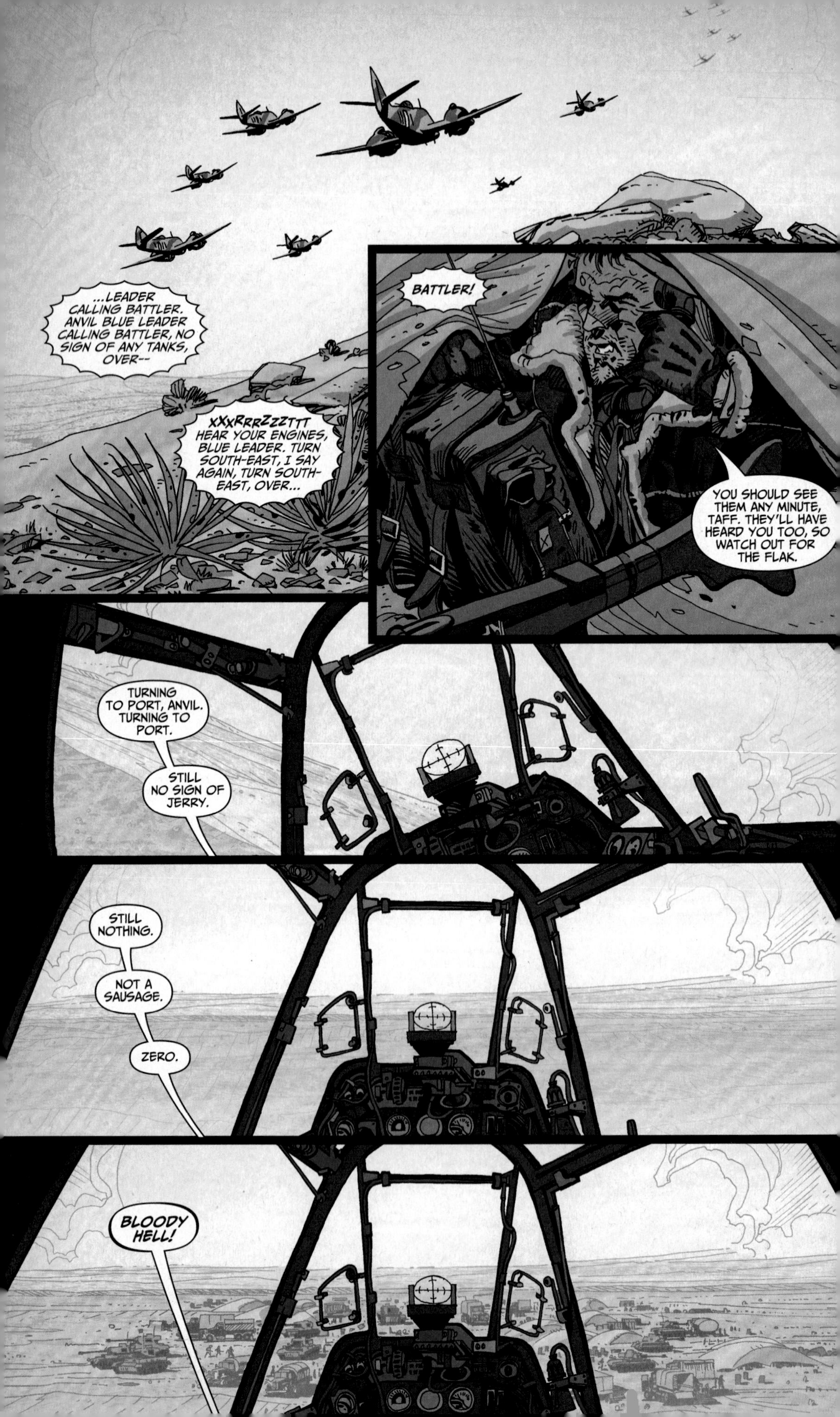
...LEADER CALLING BATTLER. ANVIL BLUE LEADER CALLING BATTLER, NO SIGN OF ANY TANKS, OVER--
XXXRRRZZZTTT HEAR YOUR ENGINES, BLUE LEADER. TURN SOUTH-EAST, I SAY AGAIN, TURN SOUTH-EAST, OVER...
BATTLER!
YOU SHOULD SEE THEM ANY MINUTE, TAFF. THEY'LL HAVE HEARD YOU TOO, SO WATCH OUT FOR THE FLAK.
TURNING TO PORT, ANVIL. TURNING TO PORT.
STILL NO SIGN OF JERRY.
STILL NOTHING.
NOT A SAUSAGE.
ZERO.
BLOODY HELL!

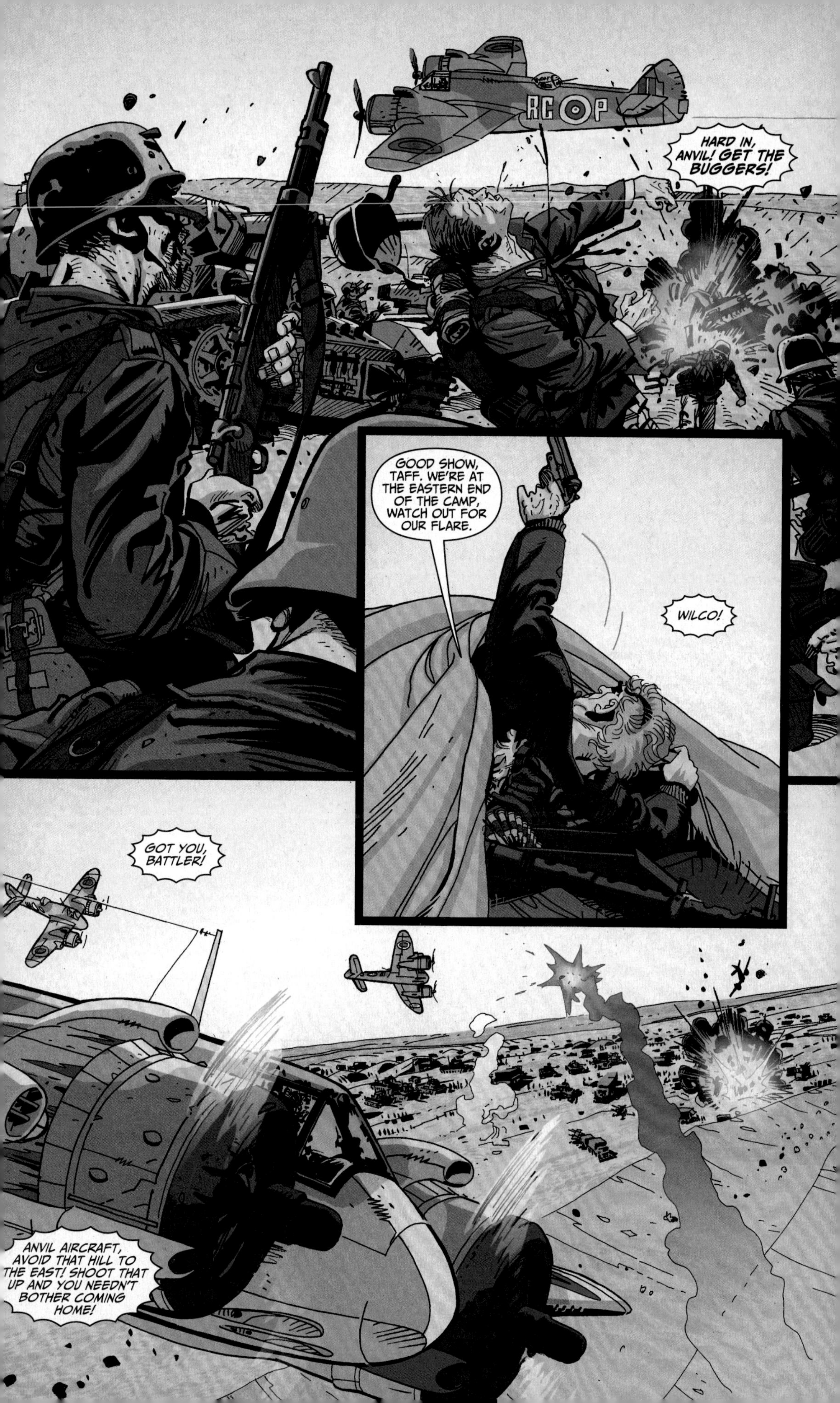

RC P
HARD IN, ANVIL! GET THE BUGGERS!
GOOD SHOW, TAFF. WE'RE AT THE EASTERN END OF THE CAMP, WATCH OUT FOR OUR FLARE.
WILCO!
GOT YOU, BATTLER!
ANVIL AIRCRAFT, AVOID THAT HILL TO THE EAST! SHOOT THAT UP AND YOU NEEDN'T BOTHER COMING HOME!

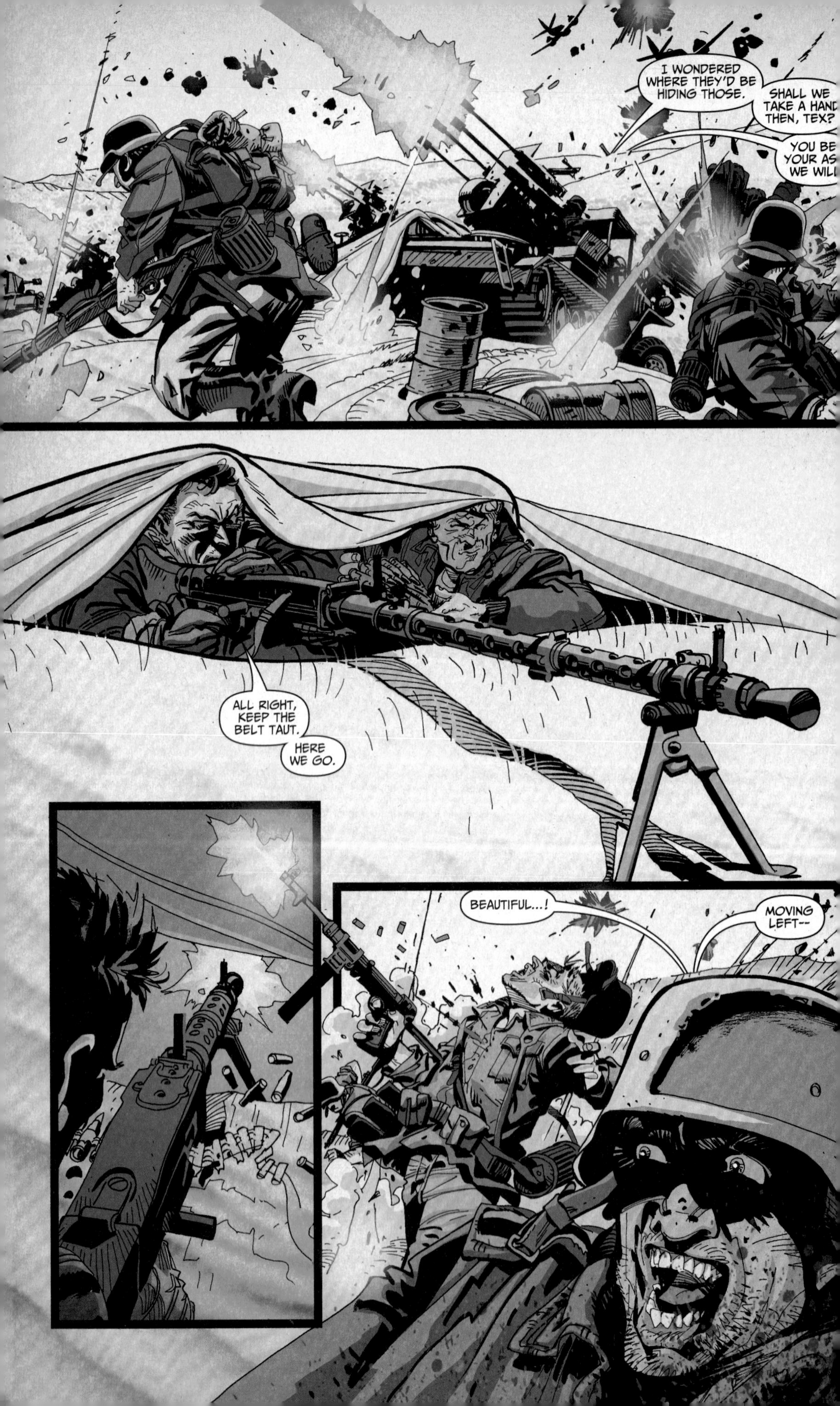
I WONDERED WHERE THEY'D BE HIDING THOSE.
SHALL WE TAKE A HAND THEN, TEX?
YOU BE YOUR AS WE WILL
ALL RIGHT, KEEP THE BELT TAUT.
HERE WE GO.
BEAUTIFUL...!
MOVING LEFT--

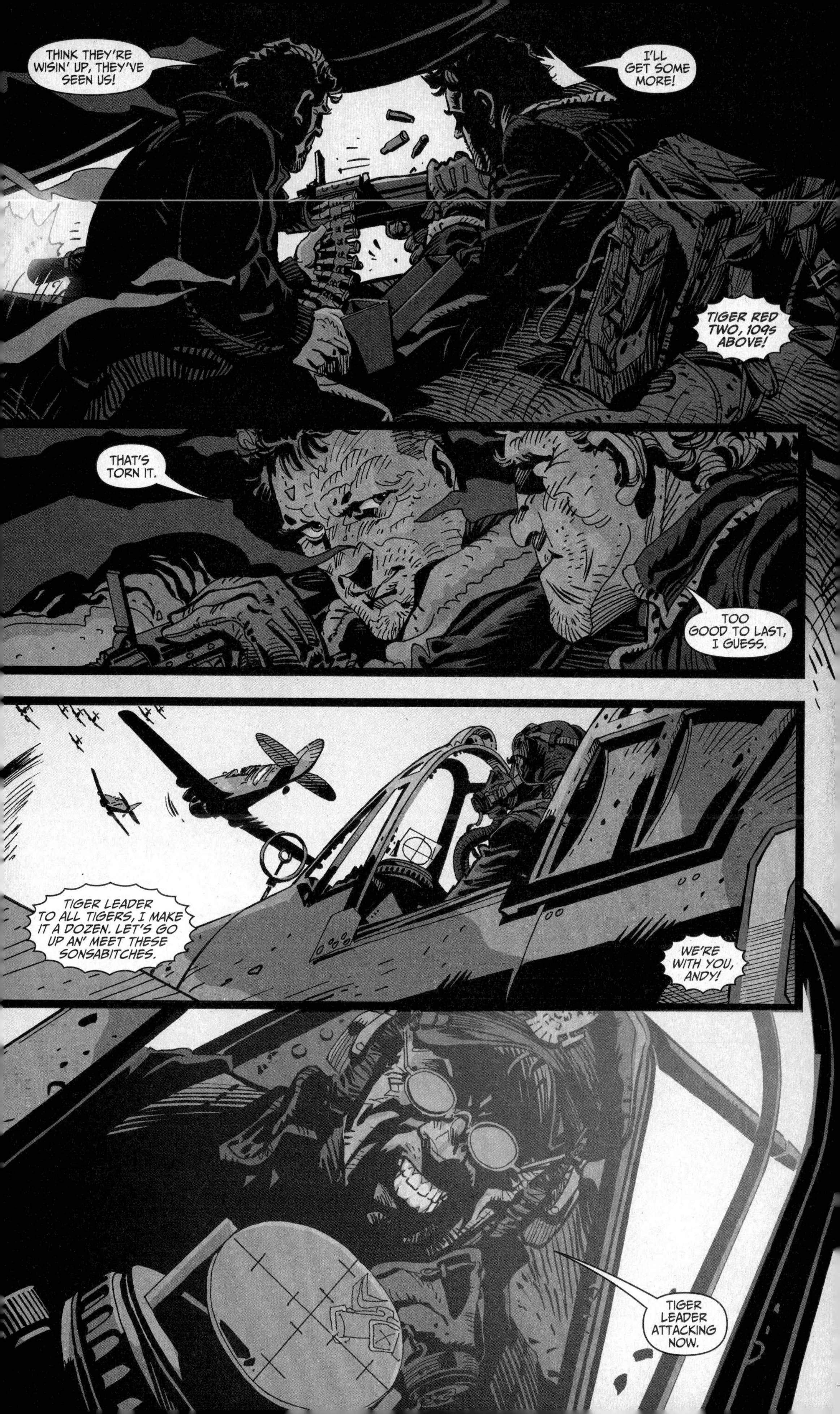
THINK THEY'RE WISIN' UP, THEY'VE SEEN US!
I'LL GET SOME MORE!
TIGER RED TWO, 109s ABOVE!
THAT'S TORN IT.
TOO GOOD TO LAST, I GUESS.
TIGER LEADER TO ALL TIGERS, I MAKE IT A DOZEN. LET'S GO UP AN' MEET THESE SONSABITCHES.
WE'RE WITH YOU, ANDY!
TIGER LEADER ATTACKING NOW.

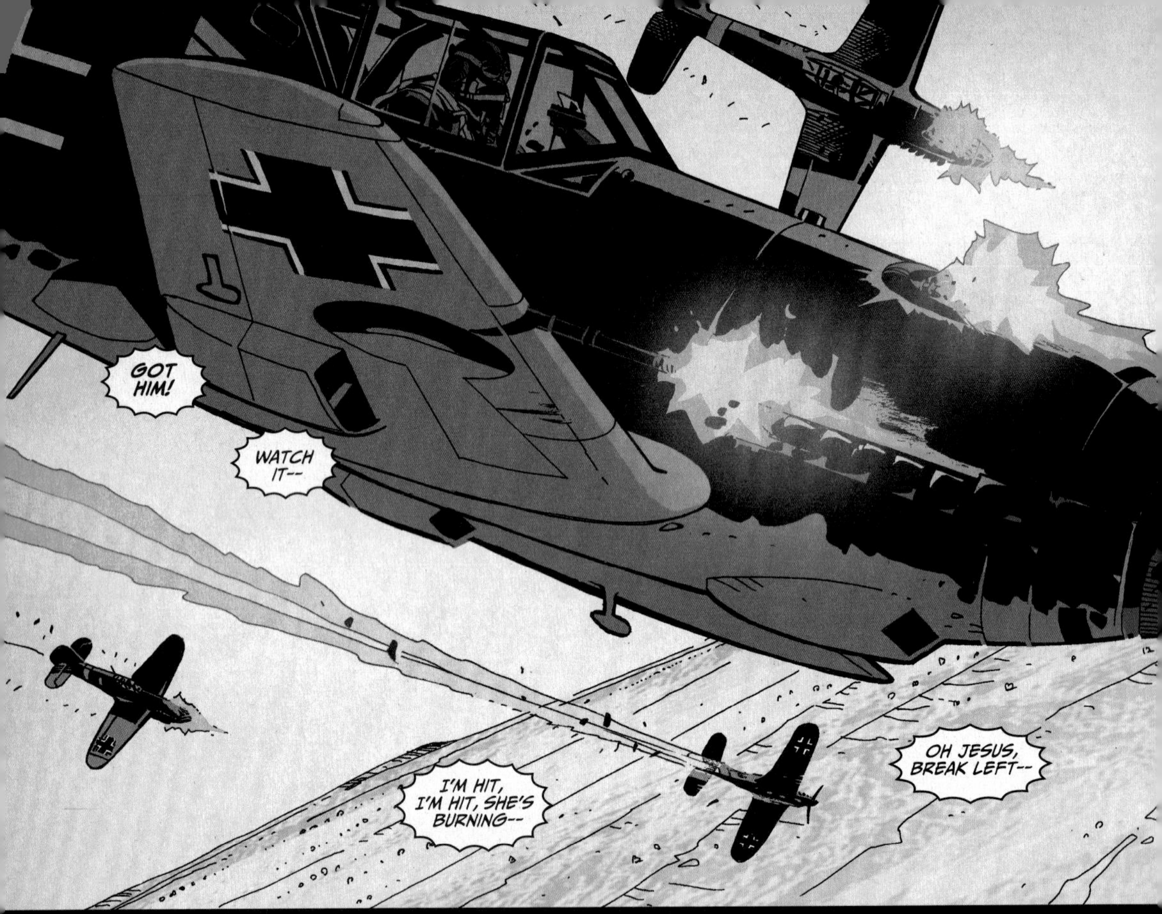
GOT HIM!
WATCH IT--
I'M HIT, I'M HIT, SHE'S BURNING--
OH JESUS, BREAK LEFT--

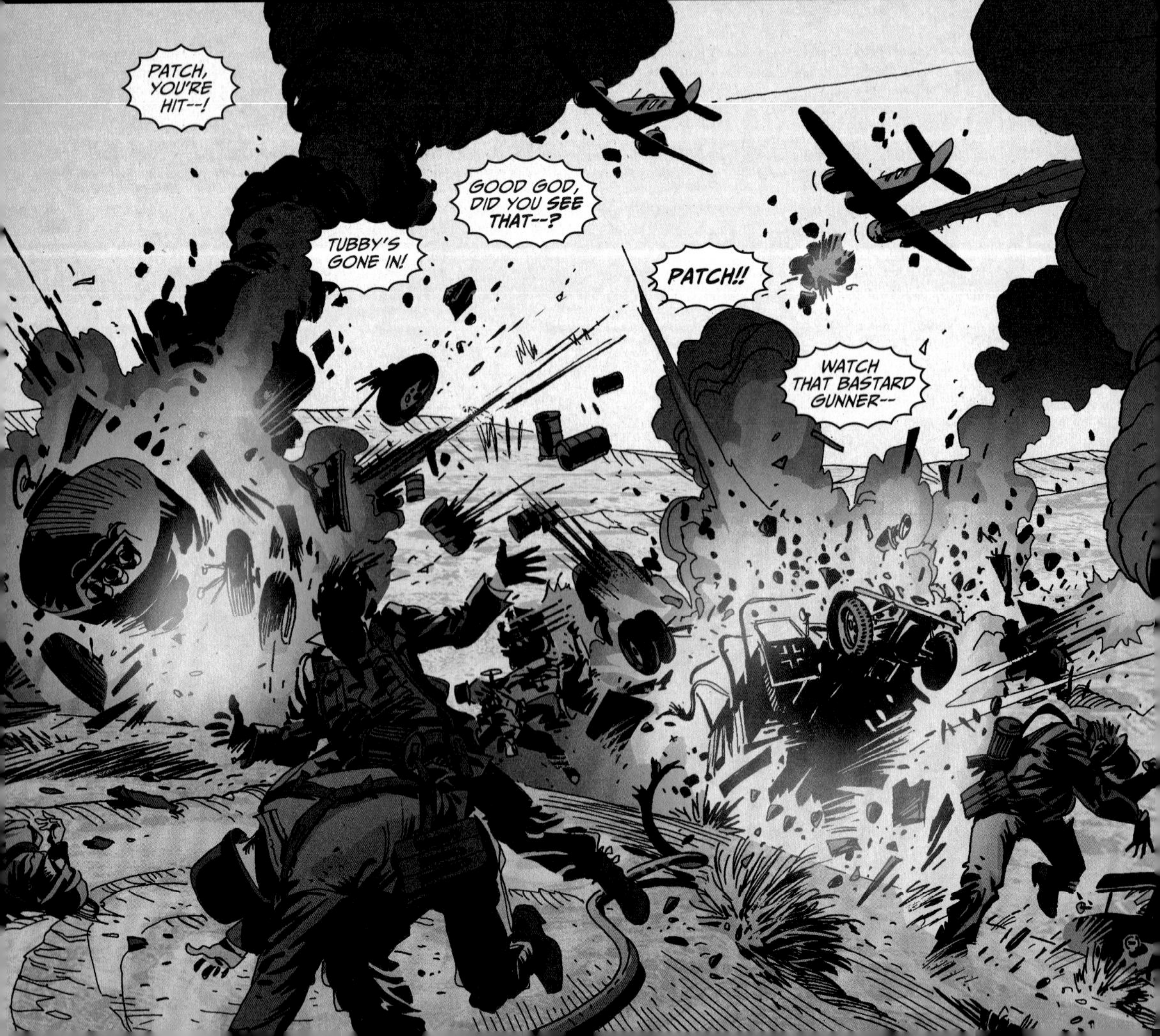
PATCH, YOU'RE HIT--!
GOOD GOD, DID YOU SEE THAT--?
TUBBY'S GONE IN!
PATCH!!
WATCH THAT BASTARD GUNNER--

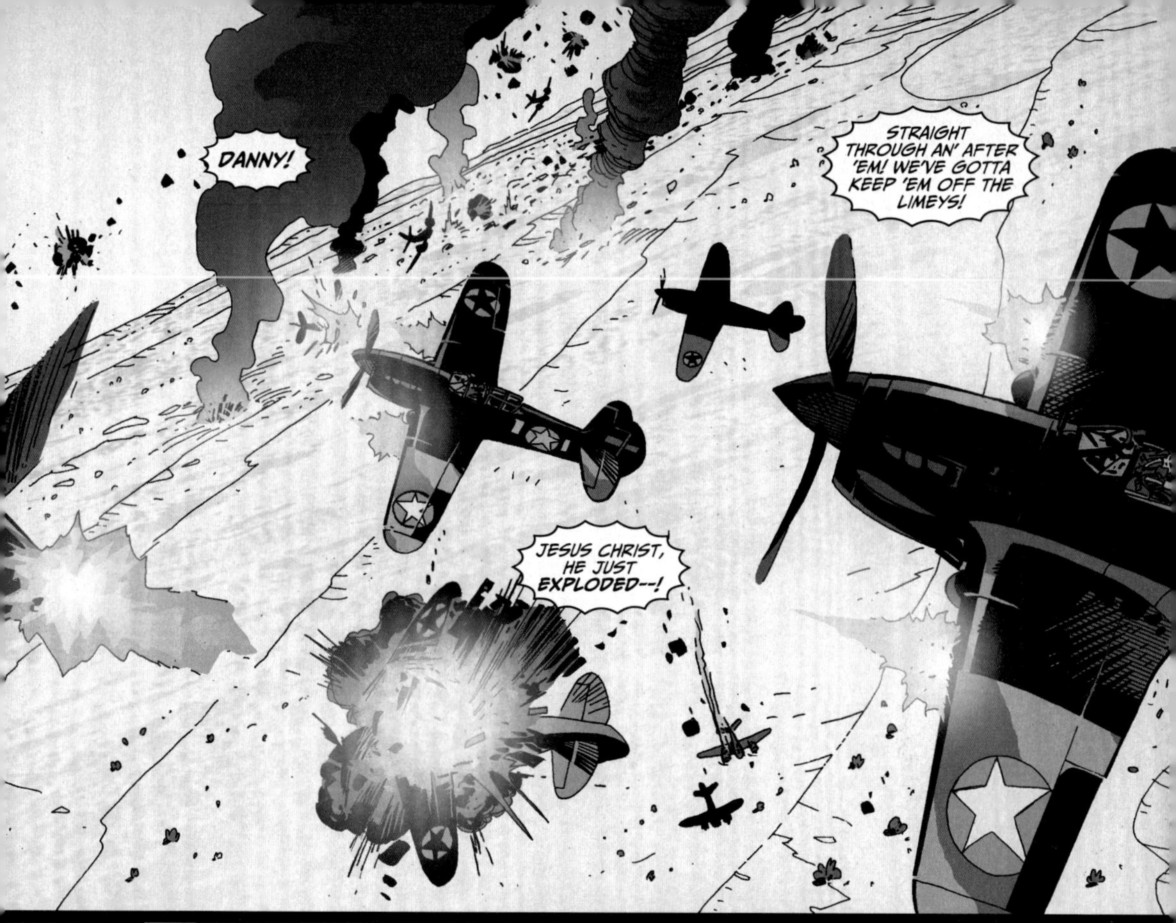

DANNY!
STRAIGHT THROUGH AN' AFTER 'EM! WE'VE GOTTA KEEP 'EM OFF THE LIMEYS!
JESUS CHRIST, HE JUST EXPLODED--!

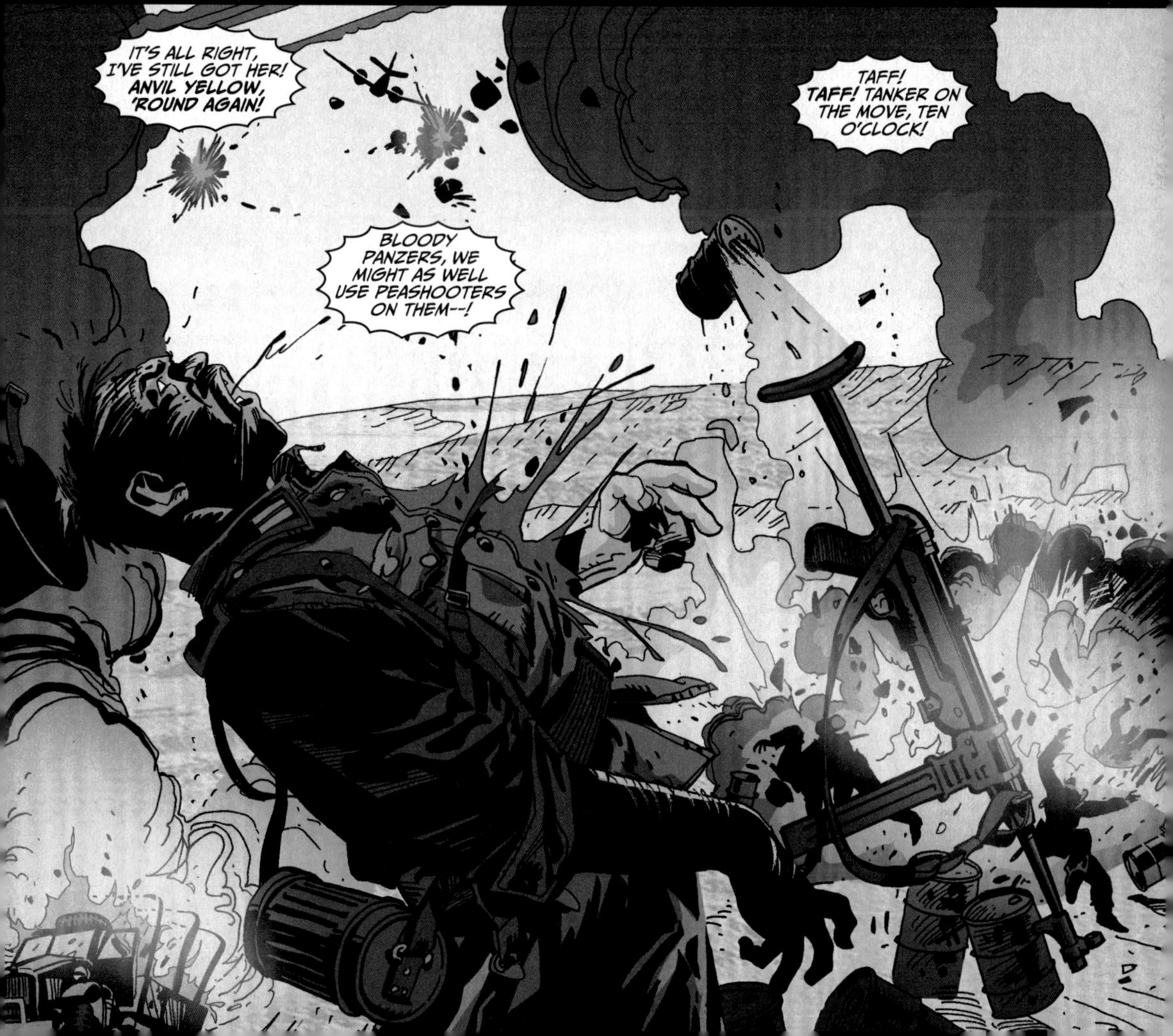

IT'S ALL RIGHT, I'VE STILL GOT HER! ANVIL YELLOW, 'ROUND AGAIN!
TAFF! TAFF! TANKER ON THE MOVE, TEN O'CLOCK!
BLOODY PANZERS, WE MIGHT AS WELL USE PEASHOOTERS ON THEM--!

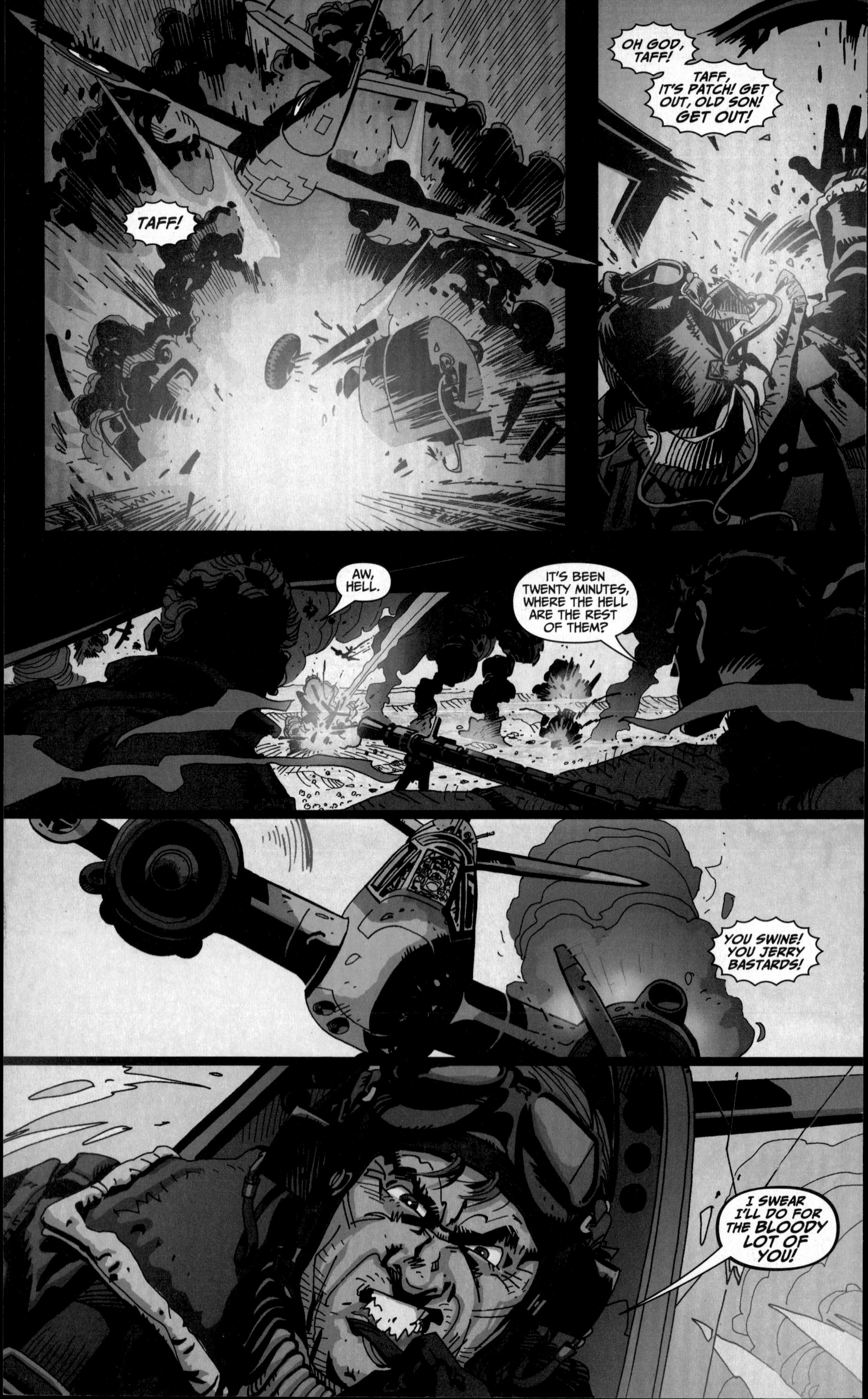
TAFF!
OH GOD, TAFF!
TAFF, IT'S PATCH! GET OUT, OLD SON! GET OUT!
AW, HELL.
IT'S BEEN TWENTY MINUTES, WHERE THE HELL ARE THE REST OF THEM?
YOU SWINE! YOU JERRY BASTARDS!
I SWEAR I'LL DO FOR THE BLOODY LOT OF YOU!

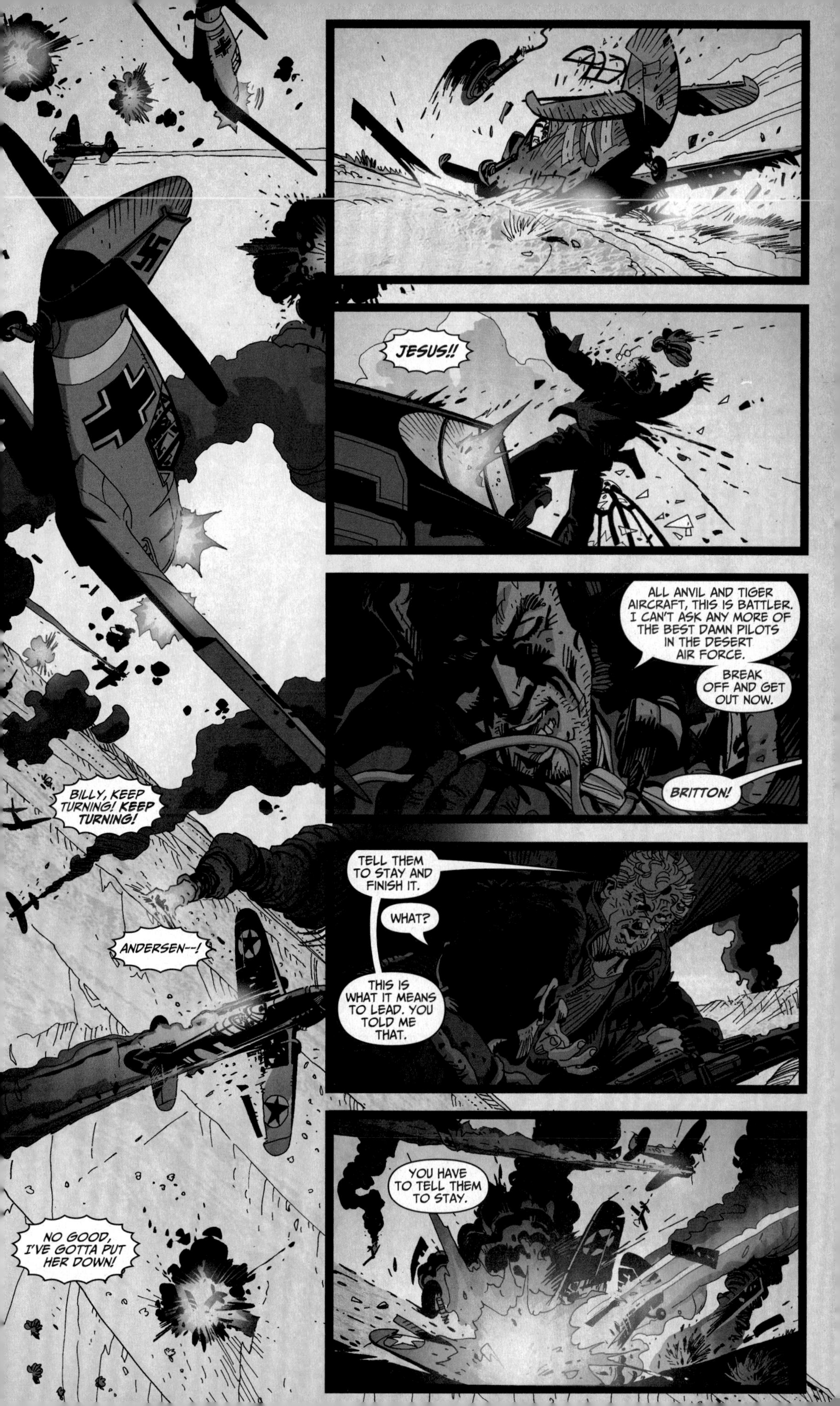
JESUS!!
ALL ANVIL AND TIGER AIRCRAFT, THIS IS BATTLER. I CAN'T ASK ANY MORE OF THE BEST DAMN PILOTS IN THE DESERT AIR FORCE.
BREAK OFF AND GET OUT NOW.
BRITTON!
BILLY, KEEP TURNING! KEEP TURNING!
TELL THEM TO STAY AND FINISH IT.
WHAT?
THIS IS WHAT IT MEANS TO LEAD. YOU TOLD ME THAT.
ANDERSEN--!
YOU HAVE TO TELL THEM TO STAY.
NO GOOD, I'VE GOTTA PUT HER DOWN!

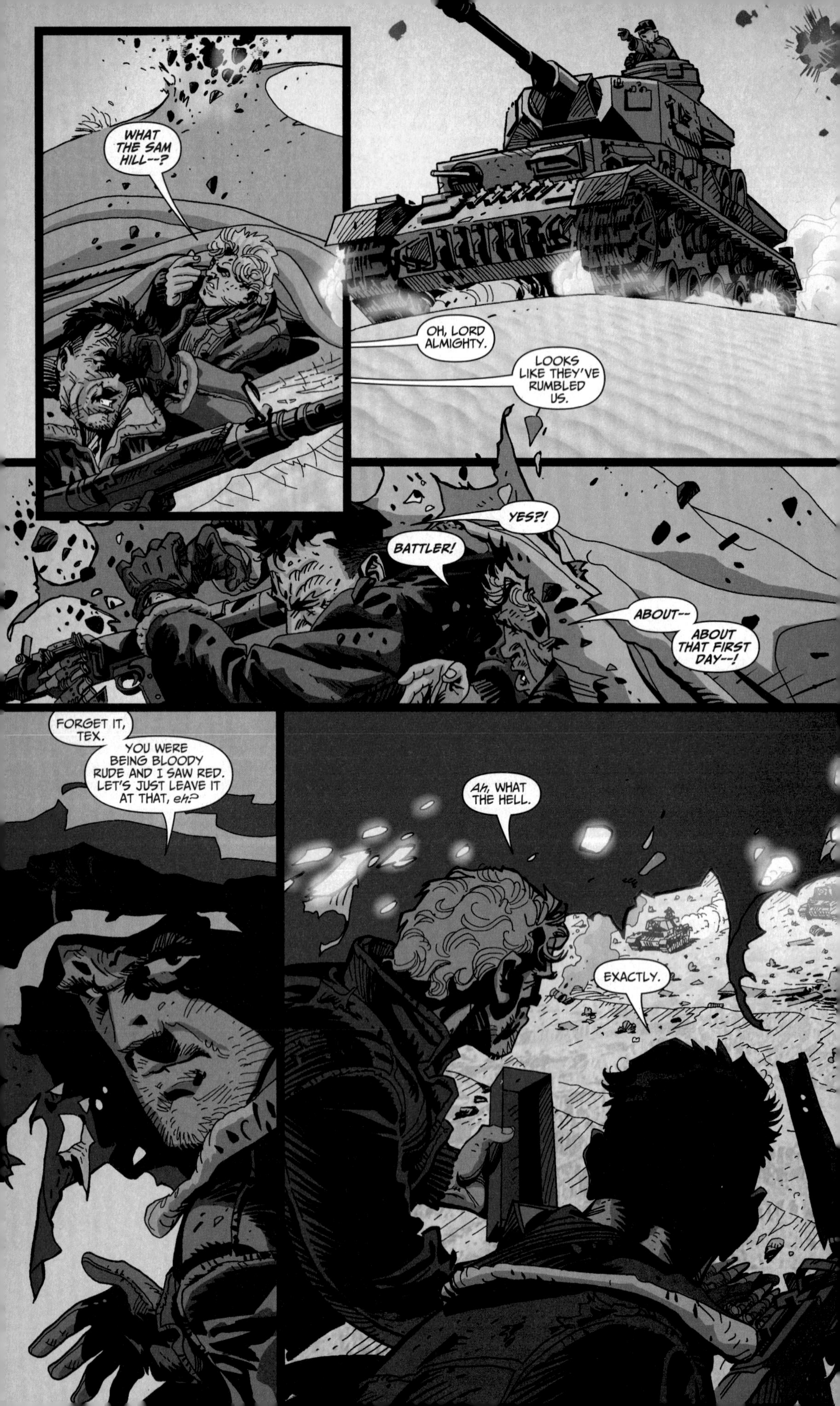
WHAT THE SAM HILL--?
OH, LORD ALMIGHTY.
LOOKS LIKE THEY'VE RUMBLED US.
YES?!
BATTLER!
ABOUT--
ABOUT THAT FIRST DAY--!
FORGET IT, TEX.
YOU WERE BEING BLOODY RUDE AND I SAW RED. LET'S JUST LEAVE IT AT THAT, *eh?*
Ah, WHAT THE HELL.
EXACTLY.

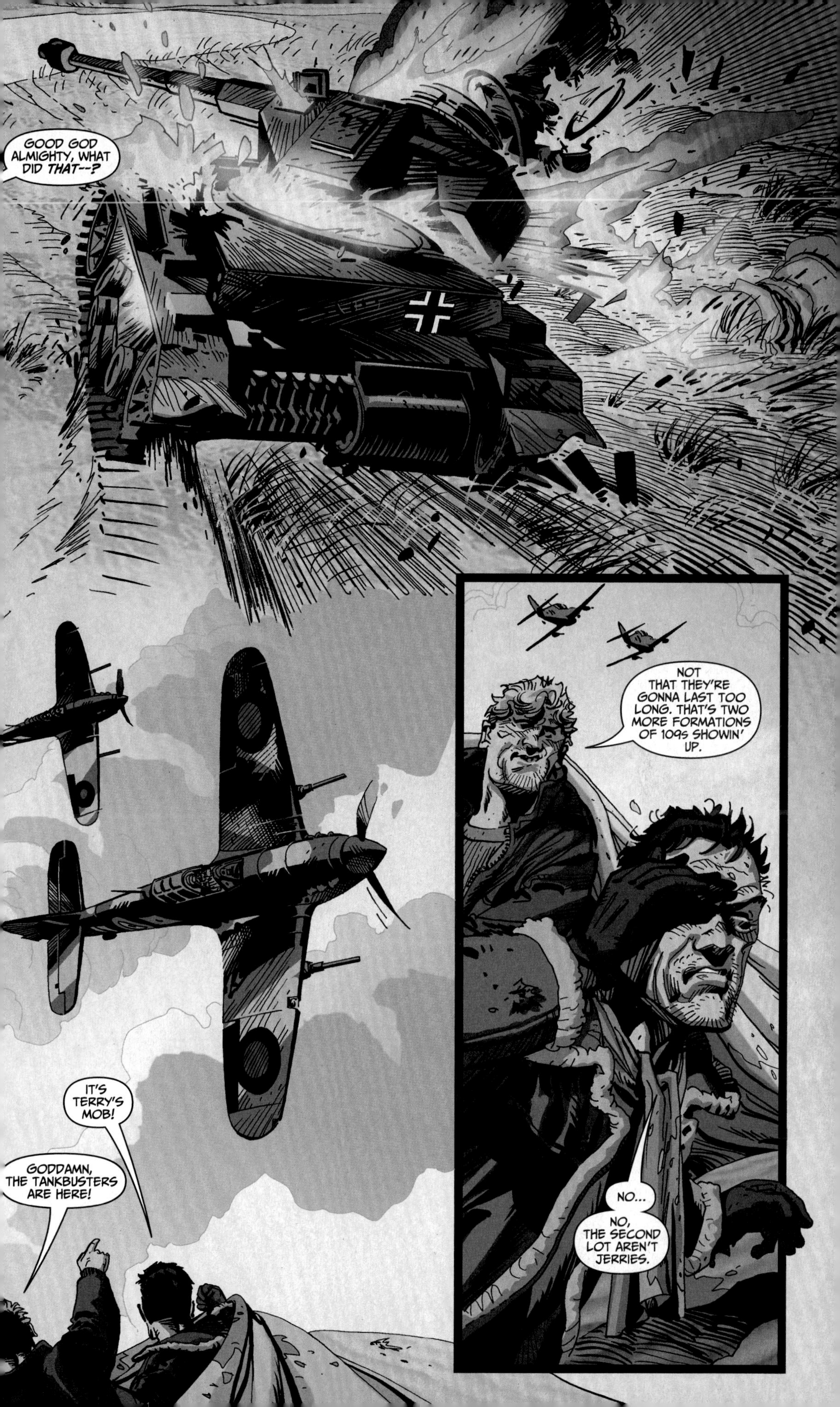
GOOD GOD ALMIGHTY, WHAT DID THAT--?
IT'S TERRY'S MOB!
GODDAMN, THE TANKBUSTERS ARE HERE!
NOT THAT THEY'RE GONNA LAST TOO LONG. THAT'S TWO MORE FORMATIONS OF 109s SHOWIN' UP.
NO...
NO, THE SECOND LOT AREN'T JERRIES.

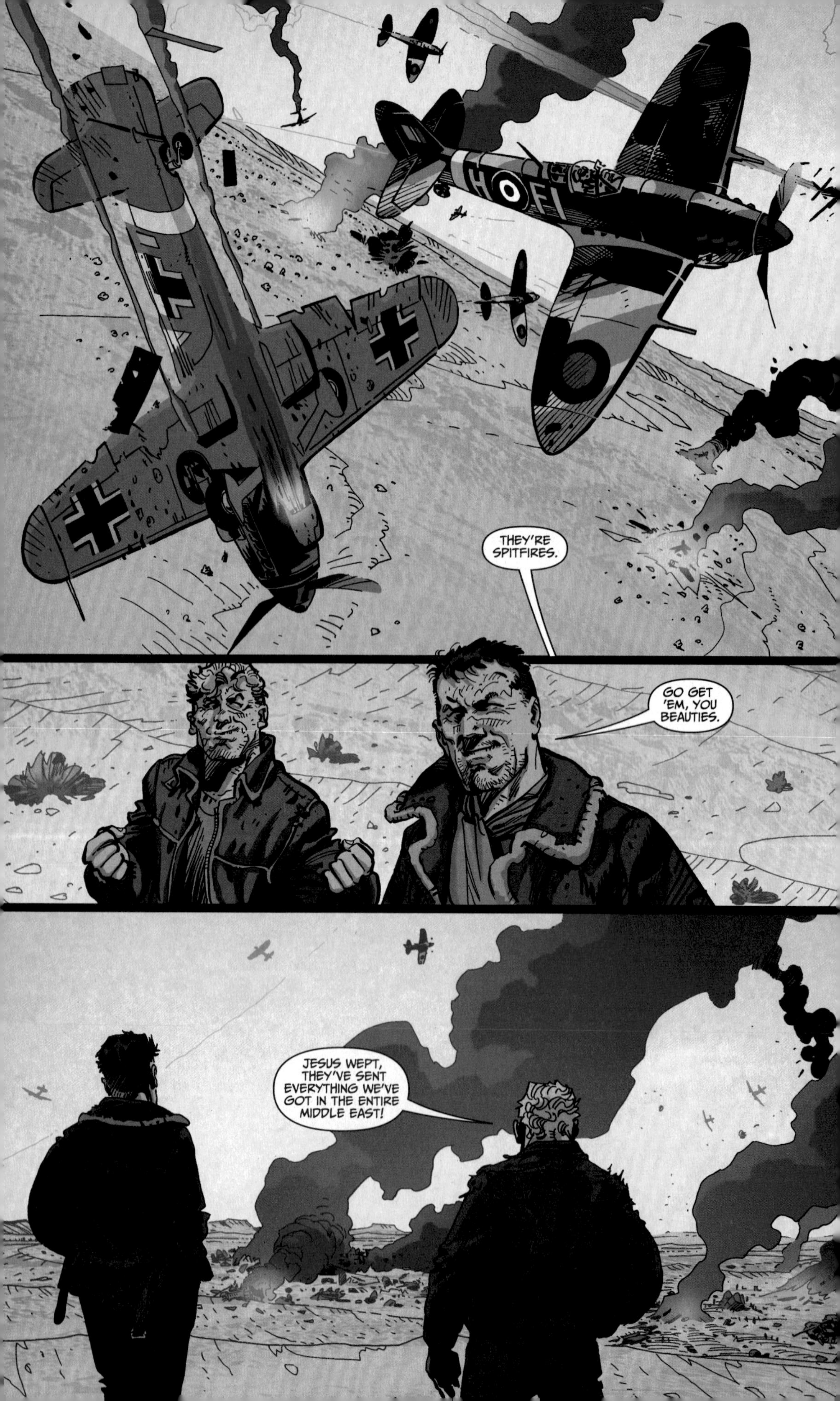
THEY'RE SPITFIRES.
GO GET 'EM, YOU BEAUTIES.
JESUS WEPT, THEY'VE SENT EVERYTHING WE'VE GOT IN THE ENTIRE MIDDLE EAST!

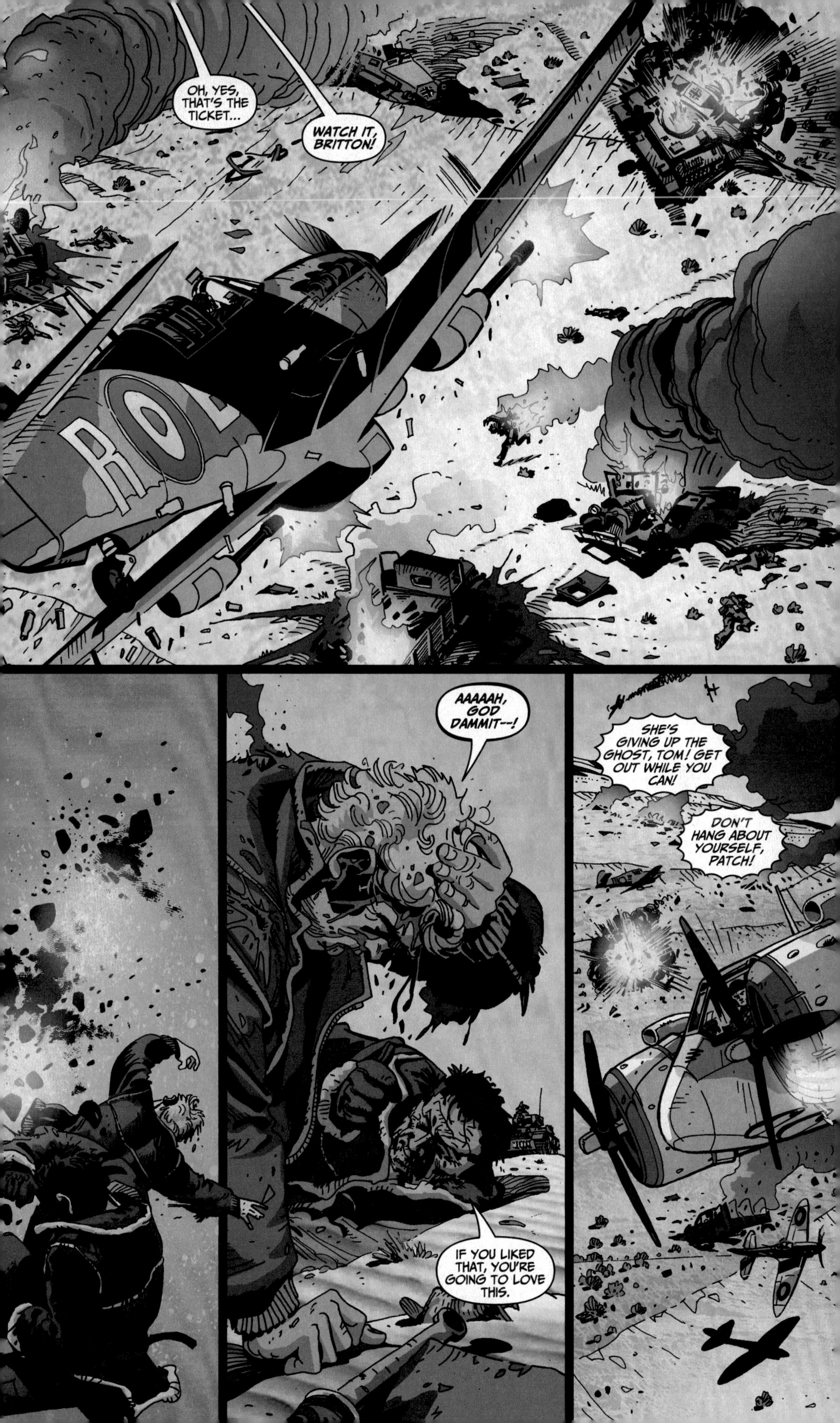
OH, YES, THAT'S THE TICKET...
WATCH IT, BRITTON!
AAAAAH, GOD DAMMIT--!
IF YOU LIKED THAT, YOU'RE GOING TO LOVE THIS.
SHE'S GIVING UP THE GHOST, TOM! GET OUT WHILE YOU CAN!
DON'T HANG ABOUT YOURSELF, PATCH!

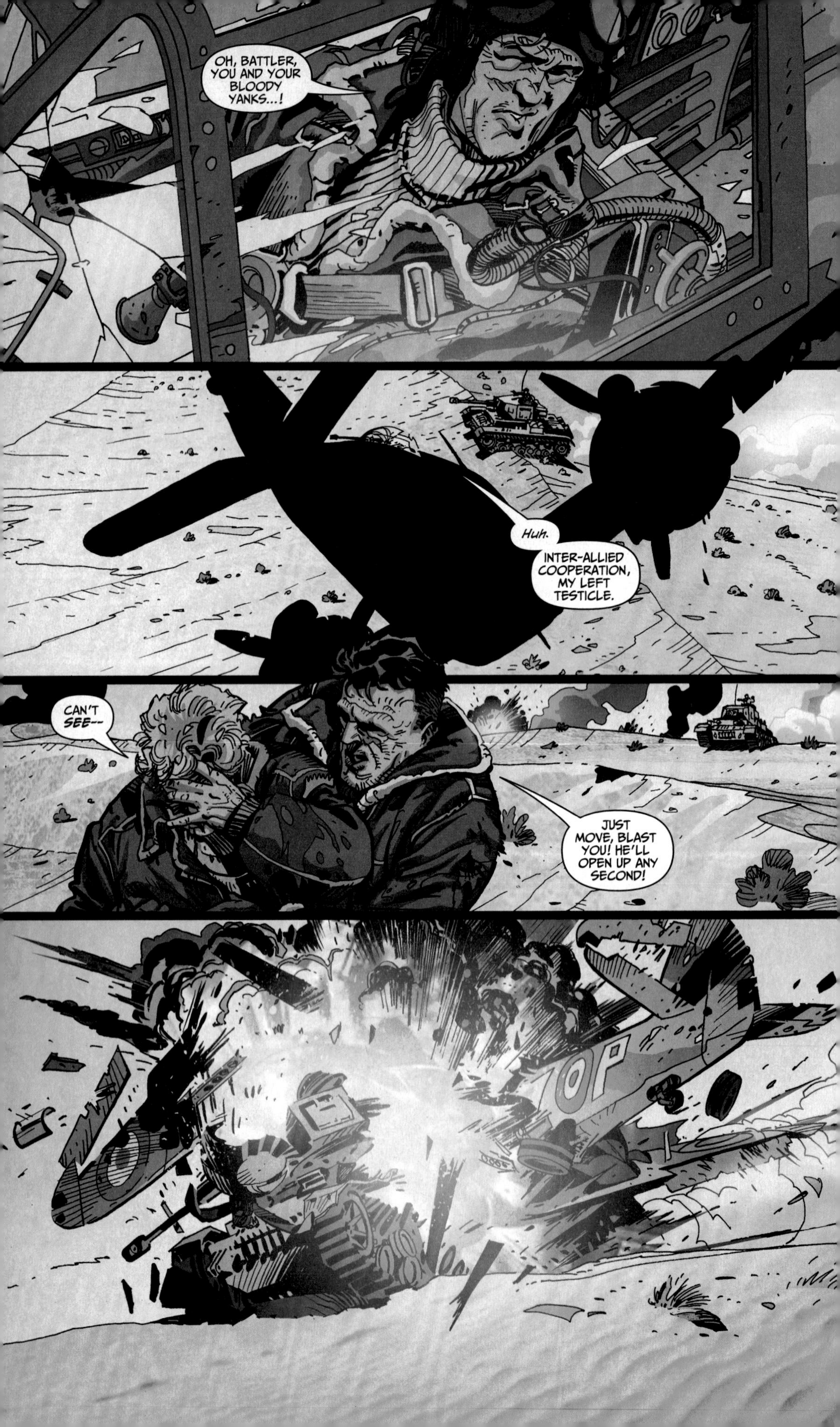
OH, BATTLER, YOU AND YOUR BLOODY YANKS...!
Huh.
INTER-ALLIED COOPERATION, MY LEFT TESTICLE.
CAN'T SEE--
JUST MOVE, BLAST YOU! HE'LL OPEN UP ANY SECOND!

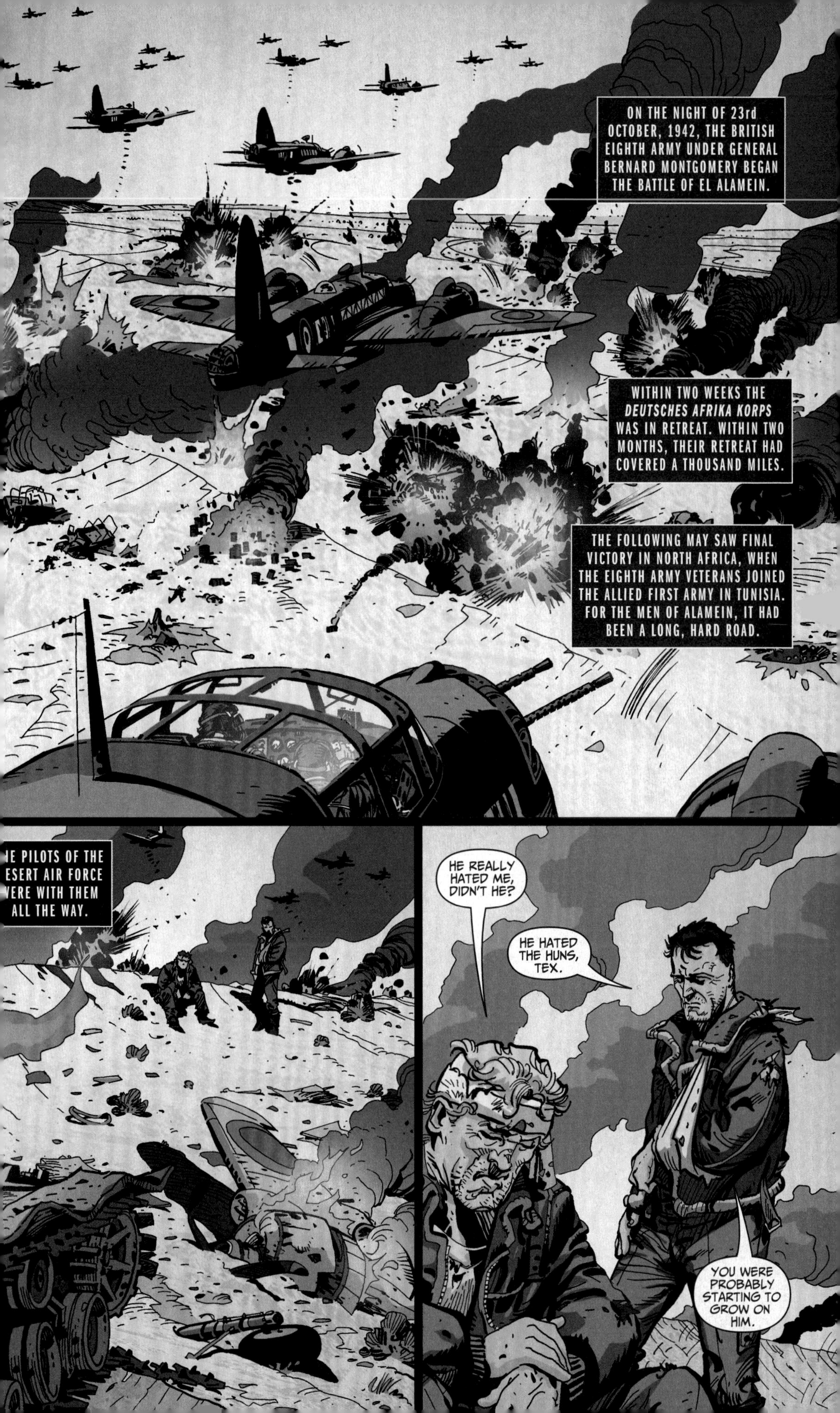

ON THE NIGHT OF 23rd OCTOBER, 1942, THE BRITISH EIGHTH ARMY UNDER GENERAL BERNARD MONTGOMERY BEGAN THE BATTLE OF EL ALAMEIN.
WITHIN TWO WEEKS THE *DEUTSCHES AFRIKA KORPS* WAS IN RETREAT. WITHIN TWO MONTHS, THEIR RETREAT HAD COVERED A THOUSAND MILES.
THE FOLLOWING MAY SAW FINAL VICTORY IN NORTH AFRICA, WHEN THE EIGHTH ARMY VETERANS JOINED THE ALLIED FIRST ARMY IN TUNISIA. FOR THE MEN OF ALAMEIN, IT HAD BEEN A LONG, HARD ROAD.
E PILOTS OF THE ESERT AIR FORCE VERE WITH THEM ALL THE WAY.
HE REALLY HATED ME, DIDN'T HE?
HE HATED THE HUNS, TEX.
YOU WERE PROBABLY STARTING TO GROW ON HIM.

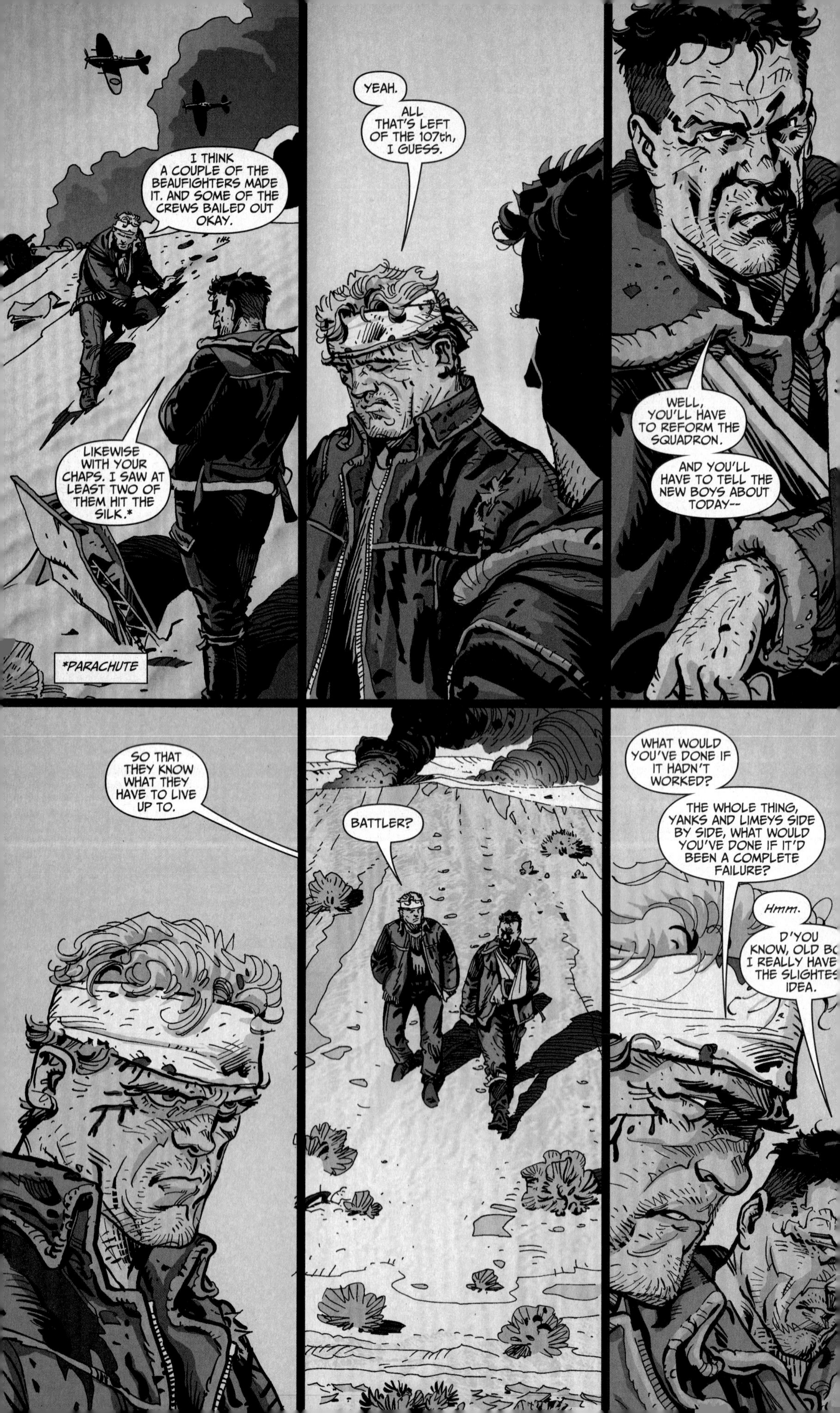
I THINK A COUPLE OF THE BEAUFIGHTERS MADE IT. AND SOME OF THE CREWS BAILED OUT OKAY.
LIKEWISE WITH YOUR CHAPS. I SAW AT LEAST TWO OF THEM HIT THE SILK.*
*PARACHUTE
YEAH.
ALL THAT'S LEFT OF THE 107th, I GUESS.
WELL, YOU'LL HAVE TO REFORM THE SQUADRON.
AND YOU'LL HAVE TO TELL THE NEW BOYS ABOUT TODAY--
SO THAT THEY KNOW WHAT THEY HAVE TO LIVE UP TO.
BATTLER?
WHAT WOULD YOU'VE DONE IF IT HADN'T WORKED?
THE WHOLE THING, YANKS AND LIMEYS SIDE BY SIDE, WHAT WOULD YOU'VE DONE IF IT'D BEEN A COMPLETE FAILURE?
Hmm.
D'YOU KNOW, OLD BO I REALLY HAVE THE SLIGHTES IDEA.

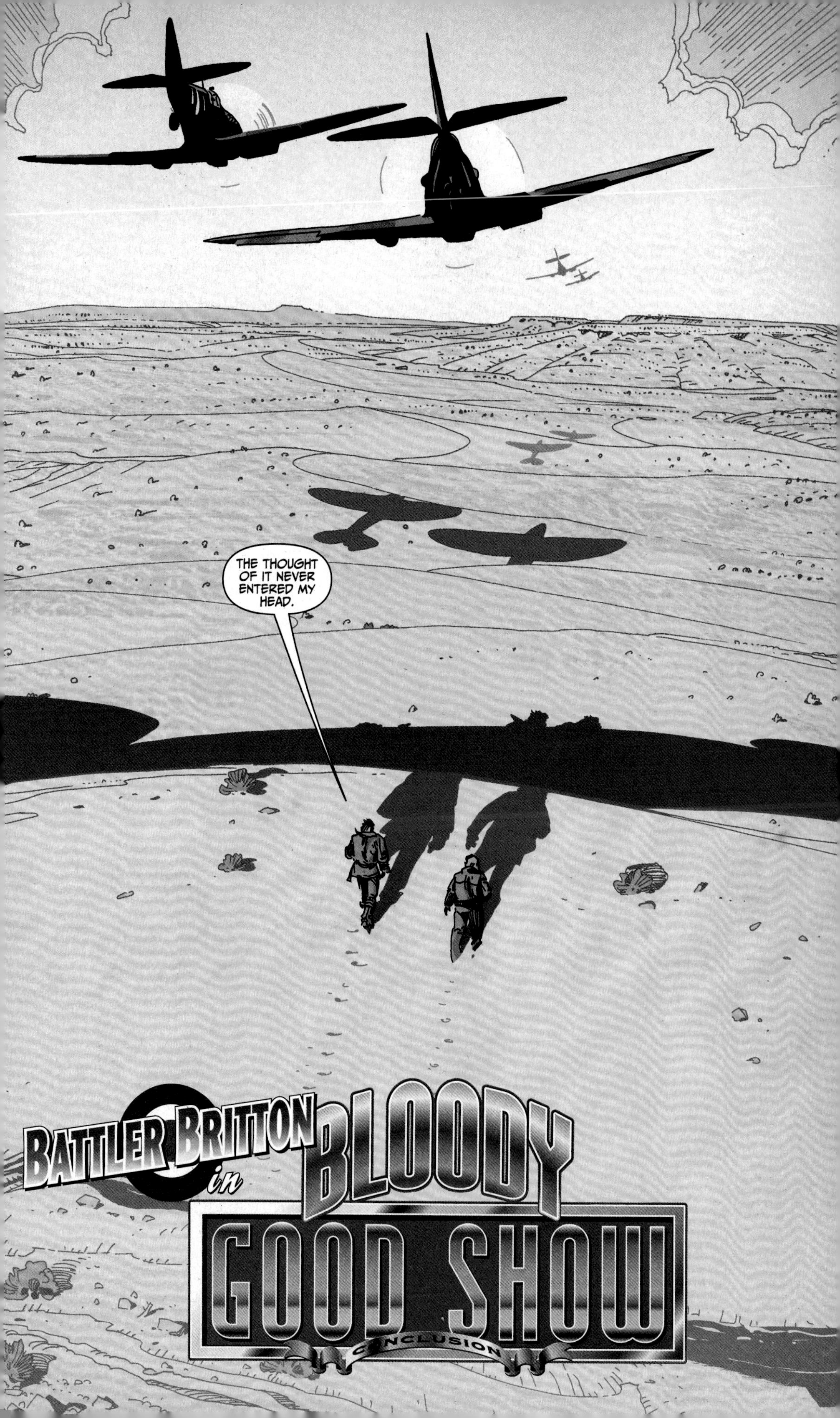
THE THOUGHT OF IT NEVER ENTERED MY HEAD.
BATTLER BRITTON in
BLOODY GOOD SHOW
CONCLUSION

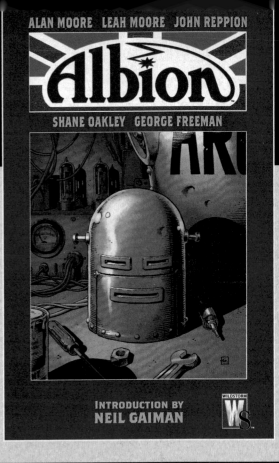